REA

ALLEN COUNTY PUBLIC LIBRARY
3 1833 02550 2888

D1603275

PRICELESS SPIRIT

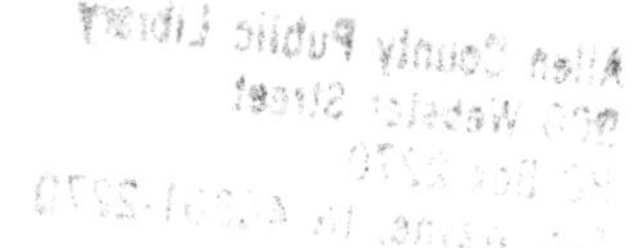

PRICELESS SPIRIT

A History of the Sisters of the Holy Cross, 1841–1893

by

SISTER M. GEORGIA COSTIN, C.S.C.

UNIVERSITY OF NOTRE DAME PRESS
Notre Dame London

Manufactured in the United States of America

Library of Congress Cataloging-in-Publication Data

Costin, M. Georgia, 1923–
Priceless spirit : a history of the Sisters of the Holy Cross. 1841–1893 / by M. Georgia Costin.
p. cm.
Includes bibliographical references and index.
ISBN 0–268–03804–X
1. Sisters of the Holy Cross—History—19th century.
2. Monasticism and religious orders for women—Indiana—History—19th century. I. Title.
BX4496.C67 1994
271′.97—dc20 93–23642
CIP

∞*The paper used in this publication meets the minimum requirements of the American National Standard for Information Sciences—Permanence of Paper for Printed Library Materials, ANSI Z39.48-1984.*

The spirit of faith . . . reveals to the eyes and to the heart of a religious the adorable Will of God, and makes every line of her Rules a source of contentment and merit; it is that holy spirit of faith which transforms the exercises, the duties and labors of a religious life, into so many manifestations of the love of the Divine Spouse to His chosen one; it is that priceless spirit of faith which ennobles every act of an humble and devoted Sister. . . . The spirit of faith sustains her in the hour of fatigue, of trial, of affliction, of sickness; for in the light of faith, the tribulations of this life bear no comparison, in her estimation, with the degree of glory awaiting her in eternity.

Reverend Edward F. Sorin, C.S.C.
Preface to the Rule of 1872

CONTENTS

PREFACE

The Sisters of the Holy Cross became an autonomous congregation, separate from the Marianites of Holy Cross, in 1869. For the next seventy-two years there was very little communication between the two groups.

As the centenary approached in 1941, all of Holy Cross took a renewed interest in the foundation of the community. Opening steps were taken for the canonization of the Reverend Basil Anthony Moreau, founder. The brothers Catta were engaged to write his biography, for which they did extensive and laudable research. But their finished product presents a rather one-sided view. The Cattas were determined to show Father Moreau not only as a very holy priest, which he surely was, but as a capable administrator, which perhaps he was not. Chief among those who earned the Cattas' disapproval by sometimes disagreeing with the founder was the Reverend Edward Sorin, founder of the Holy Cross mission in America, whom, as Father James Connelly has remarked, "no one has accused of being a saint" (*Fruits of the Tree* I: 106–7).

Canonizable Sorin may not have been, but with all his faults (an overenthusiasm for wielding authority more or less includes all of them) he appears to have been, in a closer look at the records concerning him, a spiritual and devoted man, utterly consecrated to his task in Indiana and determined to make it succeed for the glory of God—and perhaps to some degree for the glory of Edward Sorin. His affection for the Sisters was real and deep, its expression not limited to perfunctory statements on special occasions. His spirituality was uncontaminated by Jansenism and shows a joy not altogether reserved for the next life.

The young Sisters of the centenary era (of whom the writer was one) were offered a third-generation view of the early members of the community. The view of Father Sorin, as passed on by those who had not known him personally, withheld a total admiration in favor of a reluctant admission that he knew how to accomplish things. The generation just ahead of us had no regard for him as a spiritual leader. It is ironic to remember that we were required to memorize the several pages of the spiritually poetic "Preface" to our Rule, under the impression that Father Moreau had written it. Our superiors and teachers, without access to early community documents, believed that. They were wrong; not Father Moreau but Father Sorin wrote the "Preface" they so revered.

The only persons who did not seem to share this view were the very old Sisters, some of them still at Notre Dame in those days, Sisters who had been young when Sorin was old. They still referred to Sorin as "Father Superior," and spoke of him with great admiration, love, and reverence. Even a postulant could wonder why the legend differed so much from these living memories.

In the course of years and the workings of obedience, this curious postulant was eventually given access to much material which had been withheld from the centenary writers and the time to work through it, another benefit the centenary writers never enjoyed. The picture of Sorin provided by those documents and the Sisters who worked with him differs a great deal from the official account circulating fifty years ago and lingering ever since. Though it would be impossible to capture with complete accuracy such complex characters as Father Sorin, Mother Angela, Mother Ascension, and others, even if one had known them personally in life, it may be hoped that something is contributed here to render a truer picture of them to their own spiritual descendants. For these descendants in Holy Cross deserve a clear picture of their religious forebears, and these forebears deserve the just respect and affection that they really earned, whatever we determine the degree of it to be.

For the opportunity to learn new things about our congregational history and to pass on what I have learned, I must first thank Sister M. Francis Bernard (O'Connor), C.S.C., superior general of the Sisters of the Holy Cross during the preparation for and celebration of our sesquicentennial. A historian herself, Sister felt that the whole story of our separation from the French motherhouse had never been told, and commissioned me to find it and tell it. In this I received endless assistance from two other splendid historians, Sister M. Campion (Kuhn), C.S.C., chief archivist at Saint Mary's, Notre Dame, and the Reverend James T. Connelly, C.S.C., archivist at the Province Archives of the Holy Cross priests of the Indiana Province. Sister Campion read the manuscript as it developed, and Father Connelly read it when it had been more or less completed, and it would never have seen finished form without the help of both of them. Hours of searching were often shortened by the organized mind and photographic memory of Sister M. Alma Louise (Fitch), C.S.C., who knows where everything is. I am also grateful for the continued support of Sister Catherine O'Brien, current president of the Sisters of the Holy Cross, and the members of her council.

Michel Marcy of the Modern Language Department of Saint Mary's College gave countless hours to checking my translations, reconstructing them when necessary, and helping me to read faded documents nearly 150 years old. The Reverend Jacques Grisé of the General Archives of Holy Cross in Rome supplied documents on request and helpful commentary when he found it necessary. Mr. Robert Hahl of the Cushwa-Leighton Library at Saint Mary's College took care of the esoteric data, such as the speed of sailing ships and cardinals' first names. I am also grateful for the encouragement of the members of the Holy Cross History Conference, who heard much of this material at different times, and for the help of Gloria Long and other members of Holy Cross Shared Services who showed me what to do with a word processor.

1

These Fortunate Shores, 1841–42

On August 15, 1840, five obscure priests of the diocese of Le Mans, France, made religious vows. Three of them remained fairly obscure. The other two profoundly affected the history of the Catholic Church from then on: one by founding a religious congregation of priests and Brothers and later one of Sisters, which eventually developed into three communities; the other by founding a great Catholic university in the American Middle West.

Basil Anthony Moreau and Edward Sorin both had the charism and the graces which God gives to those destined to begin great works for him. Both had been brought up in pious French families. Moreau was the son of a peasant farmer and wine merchant, Sorin the son of landed gentry or prosperous bourgeoisie. Sorin probably had the better educational opportunities. Moreau was fifteen years older and had been a seminary professor and the equivalent of a religious superior on the day they both made their first — and final — profession.

Father Moreau had gathered about himself a group of priests, some of them seminary professors like himself, to serve as "Auxiliary Priests," assisting the overworked parish priests with missions, retreats, confessions, and Sunday liturgies. Gradually these men began to form a semi-religious life-style for themselves, and eventually the possibility of vows had come up. Father Moreau had deepened his own natural piety in retreats at the Sulpician Solitude at Issy, but he never made a conventional novitiate. He nevertheless obtained permission to make religious vows, which he did on the date mentioned above. The Most Reverend Jean-Baptiste Bouvier, bishop of Le Mans, who had given the permission, received the vows. Later that day the four other priests made vows into the hands of Father Moreau. There had been no formal religious training for any of them, but they now constituted a religious community. Because the suburb where their house was located was known as Holy Cross, they called themselves the Congregation of Holy Cross.

Many excellent works have covered the foundation and early days of Holy Cross. Our purpose here takes us on another track.

As a seminarian, Edward Sorin had been briefly inflamed with missionary zeal on hearing an American bishop speak of his work in the wilderness. But either he put it aside or it died down of itself for the time being. Later, however, the successor of that same bishop came to Le Mans, and Father Moreau agreed to send a group of missionaries to America. There was never any question as to who would lead them.

In 1835, Father Moreau had taken over the direction of the Brothers of St. Joseph from the aged Father Jacques-François Dujarié. The addition of the Auxiliary Priests to this group formed the Congregation of Holy Cross. Within a short time Father Moreau also formed a group of women domestic workers into "pious girls" connected with the community. In 1841 four of these made a short novitiate with the Good Shepherd nuns, received a habit of sorts on August 4, 1841, and became the Sister Marianites of Holy Cross. The pattern of the community was complete.

The call for missionaries heard in Le Mans had come from the vast pioneer diocese of Vincennes, Indiana. It was here accordingly that the first group of missionaries turned their faces. Father Sorin and six Brothers left Le Mans on August 5, the day after the first four Sisters had received the habit. The oldest of the group was Brother Vincent, who would have a long and edifying career in America as teacher, superior, novice master, and administrator. Brother Joachim was a tailor who had to double as cook, but the hardships of mission life proved too much for him and on April 13, 1844, he became the first religious of Holy Cross to die in America. Brother Lawrence was a farmer of "unusual business acumen" whose name, because of his invaluable assistance at Saint Mary's, appears in the Sisters' records far more often than the names of most Sisters. Brother Marie, later called Francis Xavier, was a carpenter who outlived all the rest of the group. Brother Anselm was a young teacher, still a novice, who drowned in Madison, Indiana, in 1845. Brother Gatien was in his middle teens, good at mathematics and a genius at languages, but he did not remain in the community.

This group arrived in New York in September 1841. Following a water route through the Great Lakes and then a long trip on foot and and by wagon through forests, they reached Vincennes the morning of Sunday October 10, having started walking at 5:30 A.M., and staggered into the rude little cathedral in time for the bishop's nine o'clock Mass.

Vincennes, however, was not to be a permanent field of endeavor, in spite of Father Sorin's arrival panegyric comparing it to the heavenly Jerusalem. At first the Holy Cross men were given a choice of two rural sites for their headquarters, and they chose St. Peter's, a farm about thirty miles from the see city. This was intended by the bishop to become a center both for more missionaries arriving from France and for local vocations which would flock to join Holy Cross.

Celestin de la Hailandière, second bishop of Vincennes, seems to have had a vision remarkably similar to Father Moreau's. There would be one congregation with three branches, priests, Brothers, and Sisters. These would come originally from France, but would eventually sever their ties with the mother country and become a diocesan community under the authority of the bishop of Vincennes.

The bishop did not, however, at first make clear the whole scope of the plan. There was no precise contract between the motherhouse and the diocese stipulating the responsibilities of each. Father Sorin understood that he and the Brothers remained under the authority of Father Moreau. While never quite denying this, Bishop de la Hailandière never quite agreed to it either. After many discussions with Father Sorin and much correspondence with Father Moreau, the bishop offered two plans. In the first, the Holy Cross men would become entirely dependent on the diocese, which would issue their assignments and provide their upkeep; they could not be changed out of the diocese by Father Moreau or future superiors in Le Mans. In the second, Le Mans would continue to hold authority, and any support the bishop gave would be considered "charitable assistance," to be refunded in full if the motherhouse ever moved the missionaries out of the diocese.

The bishop seems to have had the idea that the third entity in his plans would be the Sisters of Providence. These had been founded in Ruillé-sur-Loire, in the Le Mans diocese, by the same Father Dujarié who had founded the Brothers of St. Joseph, later the Holy Cross Brothers. So these Sisters already had as much historical connection with the men of Holy Cross as had the newly formed Sister Marianites. If the bishop did indeed plan for the Sisters of Providence to join the Holy Cross men as a congregation limited to the diocese of Vincennes, it would explain his later adamant opposition to the Marianites' setting up an American novitiate.

Father Sorin and the Brothers set to work energetically at St. Peter's, and within months had the beginnings of a "college," actually a boarding school for boys at which they would be taught at whatever educational level they found themselves. But the Eudist priests had already opened such a school in Vincennes, and the bishop was nervous about having two schools so close together. In the end, he offered Father Sorin another site. One biography reconstructs the episode:

> "We need colleges, and many of them, and without delay! But so close to Vincennes is not exactly the best place at present. Wait a minute," he added incautiously, "about a hundred leagues north of here, in a region said to have a fine future, even though it is less populated right now than the southern part of the state, I hold the rights to a large property left by my predecessor, and specifically set aside for an orphanage or something of that sort. I would have no hesitation in letting you have it to work out the plans which I don't think are quite right for St. Peter's."[1]

Holy Cross had adopted from the start the principle of collegiality which has now become standard practice in religious communities. When Father Moreau was writing the Rules and Constitutions for the Brothers, he asked them to come to retreat bearing "a little summary of all the suggestions you have been able to gather from conversations with your pastors . . . and to add to these your own observations."[2]

Sorin now put the same principle to work. He informed the Brothers that the bishop had offered them a different location, and presented the advantages and disadvantages as he saw them. He gave the Brothers five days for prayer and reflection and then put the matter to a vote. The decision to move was unanimous.

It was then late August 1842. They did not make the move until November. There is no record of the reason for this delay, but Father Sorin's only biographer to date suggests that they did not want to bring their possessions by oxcart at a time when the roads would be muddy from the fall rains. The group may have waited for the first frosts and then regretted it, as the winter of 1842–43 came on unusually fast and was unusually severe.

They arrived at the present site of Notre Dame on November 26, 1842. There had already been a heavy snowfall. Instead of dwelling on the inconvenience of this, Father Sorin saw it as a double metaphor. He wrote to Father Moreau:

> Some hours later, we were at Notre Dame du Lac, where I am now, from where I am at this moment writing to you. Everything was frozen, but everything seemed beautiful; especially the lake, with its thick carpet of sparkling white snow, naturally reminded us of the spotless purity which ought to distinguish the new inhabitants of these fortunate shores.[3]

There was one small building on the lakeshore, a log cabin a story and a half high. It had been used as a chapel and temporary lodging by previous missionaries to the Indians. Father Sorin and the Brothers moved into it, sleeping and eating on the ground level, and using the little loft as a chapel. They had one cot, which the Brothers insisted on Father Sorin's using, while they themselves slept on the ground in spite of the icy weather. For furniture, they managed with what they had been able to bring by oxcart, plus what could be spared as loans from some of the settlers in South Bend. However, they soon began to make preparations for another contingent which would be coming from Vincennes, for the original six Brothers from France had already doubled their number while in Vincennes. A priest of the Vincennes diocese had also asked for admission to Holy Cross, and he was serving as superior of the Brothers left behind. (He decided, however, not to accompany them north.)

The first need seemed to be for a suitable place of worship, which would accommodate the little community and the Catholics of the surrounding area, both Potawatomi Indians and settlers. The Brothers went to work on some of the abundant trees around the lake, cutting them and hauling them to a spot chosen for a church forty-six by twenty feet. On an appointed day men from the area came for a church-raising but offered no further help either manual or financial. The church was ready for use by the feast of St. Joseph, March 19, at a cost of a thousand francs from the community's limited resources.

A second story had been run through the length of the building to serve as living quarters for the Sisters who Father Sorin hoped would soon be coming. It took something from the area allotted for the lower level. "We shall say nothing of the height of the first story," remarks Father Sorin wryly, and then he says it. "It was not necessary to be very tall in order to touch the rafters with your head."[4] But it provided a place for the co-workers whose apostolate he already envisioned as more extensive than it could be in France. Father Sorin and the Brothers had hardly settled at Notre Dame when Father Sorin wrote to Father Moreau:

> Once the Sisters arrive — and their presence is ardently desired — they must be prepared not only to look after the laundry and the infirmary, but also to conduct a school, perhaps even a boarding school. Who knows but that God has waiting for them here, as at St. Peter's, some good and pious novices?[5]

2

An Association of Pious Persons, 1840–42

The Brothers of St. Joseph were primarily teachers, and in Le Mans under the direction of Father Moreau they had been able to extend their apostolate. They soon had a growing boarding school requiring considerable domestic help. The Brothers could manage the cooking, but Father Moreau preferred to hire women for the clothesroom and the laundry. Above all, he needed women to care for the sick and sometimes frightened little fellows in the infirmary, women whose devotion did not depend on what they were paid.

Hired girls came and went, and eventually a very small core settled down to the quasi-religious life. They rose at five o'clock and made their way to the Brothers' chapel for morning prayer, meditation, and Mass. Their residence changed three times in two years, and for most of that time they lived some distance from the school. On winter mornings this meant a long, cold walk in the dark, over rutted paths slippery with snow and ice, without breakfast or even a hot drink. There is no record of it, but it may be trusted that the Brothers provided them with some breakfast after Mass.

Then they went to their work. They made their "particular examen" at noon and had spiritual reading together after work, one reading aloud while the others sewed, mended, or knitted. It is not clear whether they performed this exercise at the school or back at their house.

The walk back often meant enduring the insults and ridicule of people they met in the streets, especially while they were wearing a uniform given them in 1840. This consisted of a light blue dress, dark blue apron, white neckerchief, "a fluted cap turned down over the face,"[1] and a rosary hanging from a leather belt. They seem to have tried this for a short time but refused to continue wearing it because of the taunts it brought upon them. Who designed it or even who made it is not recorded.

After about a year of this life, Father Moreau began taking the most promising of these women to Mother Mary of St. Dositheus, superior of the Good Shepherd convent in Le Mans, for further training in the religious life. There were three of them there when he brought them Léocadie Gascoin.

The Gascoins were a family of comfortable rural middle class who worked on their own estate in Bas-Maine. As a little girl Léocadie attended the parish school at Monteney, conducted by the Sisters of Evron. When she was fifteen her father sent her to a small private boarding school in Laval conducted by the Misses Lachambre, Catholic spinsters who encouraged her natural piety and provided moral teachings and a finishing-school knowledge of the classics. She was well educated for her time and class when at age nineteen she returned to take over the management of her father's estate.

An encounter with one of the "Auxiliary Priests" led her to Father Moreau and Holy Cross. The young women under Father Moreau's direction had been praying for someone with the talent and background to become their superior. Léocadie was younger than any of them (she was twenty-three by then), but on the advice of Mother Dositheus did not reveal this fact.

The Good Shepherd nuns made the habits for the first four Sister Marianites of Holy Cross on the occasion of the first reception, August 4, 1841. Léocadie Gascoin received the name Sister Mary of the Seven Dolors. The name Sister Mary of Calvary was given to Marie Robineau, who would be in America within two years. The other two were Sister Mary of Holy Cross (Léonie Chopin) and Sister Mary of the Compassion (Renée Bouteiller).

> The habit . . . consisted of a dark black serge dress, a round cape, a cincture of sky-blue wool, a white bandeau, a fluted cap hanging down around the face, and over it a flat cap with strings tying under the chin. On the right side hung the rosary of Our Lady of the Seven Dolors with large beads. They wore a black veil over their heads, and finally over their heart, the emblem of the Mother of Sorrows, who had been taken as patroness and model: a silver heart pierced with seven swords and worn on a sky-blue cord.[2]

Father Sorin and the first six missionary Brothers bound for the United States may have attended this first reception of the Marianite habit. They left for America the next day, August 5, 1841. It was about a year later that Bishop de la Hailandière suggested that they go to his property in the north. The letter Father Sorin wrote describing the new property under its dazzling white carpet of snow could not have reached Le Mans until well after Christmas 1842. The group at Le Mans rallied at once to the call for more missionaries. Father Sorin requested another priest, two more Brothers, and three Sisters. There was only one Brother who could be spared, but otherwise Father Moreau went beyond the request; he sent two priests and a seminarian, and four Sisters.

Bishop Bouvier of Le Mans was not offering enthusiastic support to the idea of religious women of Holy Cross. He had taken Father Dujarié's Sisters of Providence under his personal protection. The Sisters of Evron were also doing well. Bishop Bouvier saw no need for another community of religious women in his diocese, and he would not consent to give Father Moreau's Sisters any canonical sanction. Therefore the vows they made in his diocese could be private ones only.

Subject to that understanding, Sister Mary of Calvary and Sister Mary of the Heart of Jesus (Savary) made a private "profession" in the chapel of Our Lady of Holy Cross at Le Mans on May 26, 1843, the Sunday after Ascension Thursday. Sister Mary of Nazareth (Chauvin) and Sister Mary of Bethlehem (Desneaux) each made a private vow of perpetual obedience to Father Moreau.

In his own handwriting, Father Moreau recorded these vows on the first page of a ledger which he gave to these four Sisters for the purpose of keeping their council minutes. He also personally recorded the next event.

> The next day, the 29th, the Sisters named below received the following obediences for Notre Dame du Lac in America, namely:
>
> Sister Mary of the Heart of Jesus was named assistant and mistress of the school as needed;
>
> Mary of Calvary, first councillor, chief linen-keeper and admonitress to the assistant;
>
> Mary of Nazareth, second councillor and infirmarian, or teacher with the assistant, whom she will accompany if the assistant has a school;
>
> and Mary of Bethlehem, in charge of the cows and dairy.

It was further noted that the council would consist of the first three Sisters, "to the exclusion of Mary of Bethlehem." This suggests that Sister Bethlehem was illiterate, not inexperienced. Sister Heart of Jesus was the person in charge, and she was exactly nineteen years and two months on May 28, 1843. (She was named "assistant" because Father Sorin would be the ecclesiastical superior.) Sister Nazareth was twenty-one years, two months, and eighteen days; Sister Calvary was five days short of her twenty-fifth birthday. Sister Bethlehem was forty-five.

These four Sisters had spent the previous three weeks at the house of the Good Shepherd, part of the time in retreat, part of the time being further instructed by Mother Dositheus in the spirit and practice of the religious life.

Father Moreau had been working since March in order to be able to give them the first draft of a constitution, which it was hoped they could submit to the bishop of Vincennes.

> The first Constitution defined the "Community of the Sisters of Holy Cross" as an association of pious persons, subjected by the ordinary vows to a common life, under the direction of a Holy Cross priest, under the patronage and supervision of the Bishop of Le Mans, and under the authority of the Holy See.[3]

The chief purpose of the community was "to provide the priests, the Brothers, and the boarding students of Sainte-Croix with all services" — housework and mending mainly. This limitation was imposed by the bishop of Le Mans. In "foreign lands," however, they were free to pursue the apostolates of teaching and nursing, "but only in houses directed by Holy Cross priests." The Sisters in America soon had to give this "directed by" a most liberal interpretation, as the Sisters quickly outnumbered the priests and spread to many places where the Holy Cross priests could not provide day-to-day supervision.

Father Moreau wanted his Association of Holy Cross to be a reflection of the Holy Family, which in turn he saw as a reflection of the Holy Trinity. The Brothers of Holy Cross, called Josephites, were to be, like St. Joseph himself, an image of God the Father; the priests, called the Salvatorists, were to make Christ present in the world by their eucharistic and sacramental ministrations and in their own lives; and the Sisters, called Marianites, were, like Mary, to give life in whatever form it was needed and to whoever needed it.

Sisters Calvary and Heart of Jesus were the first Marianites to make vows. Although she had not made any vows herself, Mother

Seven Dolors received their vows, which spoke of obedience to the "future superioress."[4] She then bestowed black veils and silver hearts on the newly professed. The other two leaving for America presumably also wore the black veil, but not the heart; the matter of the heart came up in council minutes early in their sojourn in Indiana.

The departing missionaries made the journey from Le Mans to Le Havre, their port of embarkation, by carriage, taking three days. There were eight of them: Father Francis Cointet, who would serve as their superior en route; Father Théophile Marivault; Francis Gouesse, a seminarian; Brother Eloy; and the four Sisters. Father Moreau went along to see them off. When he found that the steerage space allotted to the Sisters did not offer enough privacy, Father Moreau obtained hammer and nails and put up some boards himself. Then he decided to stay on the ship with them until it put in at Brest, just to make sure everything was all right.

On June 3, 1843, Father Moreau gave his missionaries a final blessing and the ship pulled away from the shores of France. Summer weather had not yet settled on the Atlantic, and it was not an easy crossing. In one long and terrible storm they all feared for their lives. Father Cointet wrote Father Moreau an account of it.

> Toward the middle of the night we awoke with a start. A storm had broken out. Shortly afterwards, Sister Mary of Nazareth came into our room, trembling and half dead with fright. She wants to go to Confession before dying, said she; if she can arrive in America, never will she return to France. These are the first words which terror forced from her; but she was not, any more than we were, at the end of life's sufferings.[5]

Father Cointet admitted that he himself was too sick to be of any help to anyone, but Father Marivault went about the ship, hearing confessions in various languages through interpreters and baptizing at least three children. Sister Calvary was the least affected by the storm and assisted at the baptisms. Before they got off the ship, however, her health had failed more seriously than that of anyone else in the party.

The shaken travelers debarked in New York July 11, and were received at the home of the Samuel Byerly family. Mr. Byerly was a convert of two years' standing who made it a point to be gracious to missionaries coming and going through the port of New York. Father Sorin and the Brothers had stayed with him on their arrival. He must have had an enormous house, for when the Holy Cross group arrived he was already entertaining a party of Jesuits who had suffered fire and shipwreck on their way to America. The Cattas (official biographers of Father Basil Moreau and Mother Mary of the Seven Dolors; see Preface) say that the Sisters were taken in by a religious community;[6] even so it would have been a large number for the Byerlys to house.

Father Cointet's reaction to his new country paralleled that of many immigrants:

> I had always imagined America much backward in civilization. But if it were necessary to judge it by New York, I should have been greatly mistaken. At the sight of these beautiful edifices, of this luxury, of diversity of remarkable objects, I could not recover from my surprise. One sees houses here, which, especially because of their interiors, would pass for as many chateaux in France.[7]

In the awe and admiration, there is a note of disappointment, followed at once by an attempt at self-consolation: "But at Notre Dame du Lac, one does not find, I think, so much magnificence."

The party stayed twelve days in New York, resting and recuperating.

Since this is probably the last time this story will be written, some attempts must be made to gather up a few incidents about which differing accounts have been given. The reader is invited to draw whatever conclusion seems most likely. The first of these little community mysteries concerns the Brother who went to France.

Community tradition is that Father Sorin found the party long overdue, and that he knew some Sisters had been assigned to Indiana but was not sure whether any men were coming with them. Thinking the Sisters might need an escort, he sent a "Brother John, an Englishman by birth,"[8] all the way back to France for them. The parties crossed each other on the ocean, going in opposite directions. Sister Mary of Providence (Daget), however, had belatedly received permission to come to America, and Brother John brought her back, along with a large bell which Father Moreau wished to send.

The Cattas' version is that the Brother's name was James and that he had been sent to meet the travelers in New York, with money for their land-and-water passage to Indiana.

> This Brother James, a young American who had entered the novitiate at Notre Dame du Lac, and who was as yet little accustomed to religious discipline, had been seized with a sudden desire to see Europe and had simply taken a boat for France![9]

There are only three Brothers named James or Jacques in the *Matricule generale* who lived within the possible years for this, and none of them was ever in America.

The mystery grows more confusing by a reference in Father Cointet's letter from New York.

> Another advantage which this delay procures for us is that we shall go to South Bend in the company of Brother John's brother and sister. The latter speaks French very well, and she will establish her residence with her husband in the vicinity of the city of South Bend, near Notre Dame du Lac.
>
> We had the sorrow to leave Le Mans without being accompanied by Brother John, whom they had made us hope for and who is now sailing toward Sainte-Croix, and here we are, happy enough to end our voyage in the company of the family of this same Brother. His approaching arrival at Ste. Croix dispenses me from giving you many details concerning Notre Dame du Lac.[10]

If "they had made us hope for" Brother John in Le Mans, they surely knew he was coming, and he was not some young madcap who was "seized with a sudden desire to see Europe."

Once they had recovered strength and energy, the party pushed on. "We traveled on a canal . . . in a vessel pulled by horses that walked on a path alongside the canal."[11] In Buffalo they saw "a magnificent cascade," but it was not Niagara Falls, which they denied themselves the pleasure of seeing, "because we were not rich enough."[12] They crossed Lake Erie by boat and arrived wearily in Detroit. The men received hospitality at the house of Bishop Peter Paul Le Fevre, and the Sisters were taken in by a devout French family, the Riopelles.

Sister Calvary was quite unable to go any farther, but Father Cointet felt that he and the others should move on after a brief rest. The night before their planned departure, however, he himself fell off a balcony at the bishop's residence and painfully injured his back. Brother Eloy felt he would have to remain to care for Father Cointet. So it was a party of three Sisters and a seminarian, under the temporary superiorship of Father Marivault, who struck southwest for Notre Dame, probably by oxcart.

Sister Calvary felt able to go on before Father Cointet was fully recovered. Father Cointet decided that Brother Eloy should go too and serve as her escort. He left something to be desired in the role.

> The only means of transportation available was a heavy farm wagon drawn by two oxen — this mode of travel was much too cumbersome for our good Brother who preferred to go on foot. After walking a few miles, he would await the clumsy vehicle, remount, and drop off again when his patience grew thin. Finally he kept going and was soon out of sight; Sister Mary of Calvary shouted after him, but he was blissfully out of earshot, as well as out of view. What was she to do, alone and penniless in a strange land? Providence came to her help in the shape of a gentleman who fortunately understood French. He hired someone to take her to the next town; but she probably did not mention her lack of funds for we read in the chronicle that she thought of selling her silver heart in order to purchase food. Again Providence came to the rescue. As she was getting down from the wagon hired by the first good Samaritan, a second approached and addressed her in French. This time, Sister made known her need. The stranger took her to a nearby hotel, ordered a substantial meal, and paid for a carriage to take her to Notre Dame du Lac.
>
> As Sister Mary of Calvary neared her destination, she saw a Brother, not the ungallant Eloy, running toward her. "Hurry," he cried, "we are all waiting for you. I'll get some hay for your bed." This proved to be another providential meeting, for the road was almost closed by a jungle growth of vegetation, and the good Brother was obliged to cut his way through with his hatchet.[13]

Sister Calvary found her Sisters living in a log cabin or log house which was also being used as a chapel. Some confusion exists because the sentence about the second story for the Sisters running the length of the building (see chapter 1) is followed two pages later in Father Sorin's *Notre Dame Chronicles* by the statement that "the Sisters had to themselves the ground floor below the chapel where they spent nearly two years." This may have been at a later time. The account continues, "Except for the fact that there was only one window and that in consequence of the close atmosphere there was a large stock of fleas and bed bugs, they were, as they say in America, pretty comfortable." More windows to open might have aired out the fleas, but would have been a generous invitation to lake-breeding mosquitoes. It seems only reasonable, however, that the building would have been arranged so that religious, parishioners from the village of South Bend, and occasional Potawatomis coming to Mass would not have to pass through the Sisters' sleeping quarters.

The Sisters had few personal possessions, so they were quickly settled. Their chief work was the care of the clothing, linen, and bedding. In a letter back to the motherhouse, they commented that the Brothers' clothing no longer offered any firm places on which to sew the patches.[14] Sister Bethlehem turned her attention to cows and poultry, and Sister Heart of Jesus, with Father Sorin as tutor, continued the lessons in English which she had started in Le Mans.

Father Moreau had declared them a council, and so, on September 11, 1843, the Sisters held their first council meeting. It says something of their sense of the future that the first decree they made was that the postulants were not to go out unaccompanied. At the time they had no postulants nor any immediate prospects of any, nor any opportunity to go very far from their own doorway. At the same meeting and in the same spirit, Sister Calvary was named assistant in the novitiate. They also took the occasion to reorganize the clothesroom. Father Sorin, as superior and presider at the meeting, solemnly signed these rather charming minutes.

Two weeks later they held another meeting and decreed the first of a long series of changes in the Holy Cross habit. They tried to change "the headdress of the lay Sisters." This indicates a certain lack of clarity on their own status; they were not organized into choir and lay religious, but apparently they had had experience back in France of communities that were. We have theorized that Sister Bethlehem may have been illiterate, and they may have considered that her exclusion from the council disqualified her as a choir religious and made her a lay Sister. At any rate, many other changes had to be made in the headdress in the next few years, and this one does not seem to have been important.

In November the mysterious Brother John arrived back from France with Sister Providence and a large bell which Father Moreau wanted the Sisters to have. Sister Providence took her place as a clotheskeeper and soon after began serving as infirmarian to the boys of all ages (from eight up) who were beginning to arrive at the "college." She does not, however, seem to have contributed anything to the peace of the house. There are frequent records in the council minutes of complaints against her, especially for taking and keeping for herself articles which belonged to the entire group.

By the time they celebrated their first Christmas in America, the Sisters had three postulants, the Misses Elizabeth Daily, Mary Sweeney, and Mary Dougherty. All were Americans of Irish descent. It is unlikely that any of them spoke French (though Miss Daily seems to have learned it well; when she died in Le Mans, she was holding the office of first assistant to the superior general of the Marianites), so there was a new urgency for the French Sisters to continue to try to learn English. The postulants shared all the Sisters' duties and gave all the necessary indications of having true Holy Cross vocations. They could not remain postulants forever; the novitiate must be established. Sister Heart of Jesus was prepared to fulfill her obedience as mistress of novices. Father Sorin sent the good news to Bishop de la Hailandière.

Unfortunately, the bishop did not find this good news at all. He refused to give permission for the novitiate. He had the Sisters of Providence in Terre Haute and they would be quite sufficient for the needs of the diocese. No novitiate for the Sisters at Notre Dame.

South Bend is located six miles south of the Indiana-Michigan state line. On the other side of the line lay the diocese of Detroit, where the Holy Cross travelers had already been most kindly received. Father Sorin wrote to Bishop Le Fevre, asking permission to establish the Sisters' novitiate in the village of Bertrand, just over the state line. "Persuaded that God wills these Sisters in Bertrand," the bishop replied, "I do not hesitate to give my consent. . . . May heaven bless your generous efforts, and may God give success to this foundation."[15]

When Bishop de la Hailandière heard about this, he protested indignantly. Apparently it was not a matter of merely having enough Sisters for his own diocese. He did not want the Sisters of the Holy Cross to have a novitiate anywhere. Especially if they set up a novitiate outside the diocese of Vincennes, he would never be able to realize his dream of a diocesan congregation made up of the Holy Cross men and the Sisters of Providence. He was so vehement that Bishop Le Fevre wrote that he would have to withdraw the permission for the Sisters to live in his diocese. Father Sorin went to Detroit to plead the case personally. Providentially, Bishop John Baptist Purcell of Cincinnati was also in Detroit. He added his powers of persuasion to Father Sorin's and the permission was restored. (Bishop Purcell would be heard from again in the history of Holy Cross.)

Like the preceding one, the winter of 1843–44 was very severe. The Sisters and postulants were still in the unheated cabin. Sister Calvary became gravely ill and was pronounced dying. Father Sorin administered the last sacraments, but prayed and urged the Sisters to pray for her recovery. He made a vow that if she recovered, he would build a chapel on the island in the middle of the lake. Sister Calvary did recover, and the chapel was begun the following spring, with Sister Calvary laying the first stone.

This episode highlights three of Father Sorin's qualities observable throughout his life. First, there was his care and concern for the Sisters. True, they had to share his risks and hardships at the beginning, but that was what they had come for. But Sister Calvary was clearly more in his estimation than just another pair of hands. This is the beginning of a considerable body of evidence that Father Sorin cared deeply and personally about the Sisters who worked with him, and that, being human, he cared for some more than others.

Secondly, his spirit of faith is evident in refusing to take the word of whoever said Sister Calvary was dying. It appears from other episodes that the level of medical care in the South Bend area at the time was not very high. Sister Calvary's state of *in extremis* may have been the opinion of the other Sisters or of an Indian medicine woman. In case the medical opinion was correct, Father Sorin provided the anointing; but he had no hesitation in offering God terms that he felt God wouldn't refuse — and he was right.

Thirdly, there was a religious spirit in Father Sorin that helped him keep certain priorities not always clear to everyone else. What did the Brothers who had to chop down the trees for the new chapel think of the whole idea? Notre Dame needed many buildings; a chapel was one thing they already had. Furthermore, this would not be a chapel of easy access, able to take care of their growing group. It had to be approached by boat, and was certainly not convenient for community exercises. It was the fulfillment of a promise, but it was also a sort of free gift to Our Lady of the Lake. Father Sorin could have promised something more practical, but he knew that women sometimes like a gift that is merely delightful, rather than practical, and he offered such a gift to his Lady. The proof that he certainly found his way into her favor now stands on the three square miles occupied by the University of Notre Dame.

With the permission for the novitiate cleared up, Father Sorin purchased a house from Joseph Bertrand, founder of the town of Bertrand, Michigan. In early summer Sister Heart of Jesus moved there, to be ready to receive her novices. Sister Calvary, fully recovered, was named directress in her place at Notre Dame. The postulants decided to make a last pilgrimage to the chapel on the island.

> On the return trip the skiff capsized. Father Gouesse, an excellent swimmer, brought them safely to shore, but . . . this delayed them considerably, and it was almost evening before they set out for Bertrand, accompanied by Sister Mary of Calvary, who, despite the lateness of the hour, insisted on returning at once to Notre Dame. The driver, either through lack of skill or because of the darkness, drove the wagon into a deep [ditch]. He had to walk more than a mile in search of help, and it was over an hour before he returned with an emergency squad which finally succeeded in releasing the sunken wagon. Sister Mary of Calvary probably recalled an almost similar circumstance when she was stranded on her way to Notre Dame du Lac.[16]

This time again she got safely home. And after their unplanned swim and the six-mile buckboard ride, the postulants must have slept well their first night in Bertrand.

3

Wild Roses and Sweetbriar, 1843–47

The house in Bertrand had three rooms on the ground floor, used as a parlor, classroom, and a combination kitchen-refectory, and two rooms upstairs used as dormitory and community room. Religious exercises were made either in the upstairs room or in St. Joseph's Church, Bertrand, of which Father Cointet had become pastor. Fifty years later, Mother Compassion, who was a novice there, remembered wild roses and sweetbriar around the front door, and a scroll on the second floor reading, "God sees me." Later a statue of Our Lady of Consolation was sent from France, and now, gilded, it stands in the chapel of Our Lady of Loretto at Saint Mary's.

There is a community story linking this statue to Mother Compassion (Gleeson). Sister Eleanore (Brosnahan) in *On the King's Highway* says that Margaret Gleeson, as "a young girl," saw the box as part of the cargo of a ship which had left Le Havre, stopped at Queenstown, Ireland, to pick up passengers, including Margaret and her parents on their emigration from Ireland, and continued to New York; that the box was addressed to Notre Dame, Indiana, and that Margaret told her parents that those were the Sisters she was going to join. Later the box was thrown overboard to lighten the ship in a storm at sea. It floated down the St. Lawrence River and beached itself at St. Joseph, Michigan, to be rescued and placed on the pier on the same day that eighteen-year-old Margaret arrived at St. Joseph by lake steamer from Chicago preparatory to taking the stage for Bertrand. The address on the box still being readable, the coachman was taking it to the Sisters at Bertrand. Sister Eleanore claims that Mother Compassion used to tell this story to the novices in recreation.

This is another community myth. The Gleesons came to America in 1841, the year the Sisters were founded in France and two years before any Sisters came to America. The account in *On the King's Highway* has Margaret actually sitting on the box on the pier and speculating about its contents. Mother Compassion's own account of her journey says, "About noon we arrived at St. Joseph, Michigan, and had dinner at a Catholic home. I do not remember the name. At about 2 P.M. we took the stage for Niles and Bertrand. We arrived at Bertrand about 8 P.M." There is no mention of any box. It may also be noted that there was no "Notre Dame, Indiana" until Congress granted the request for a post office on January 6, 1851. Letters and packages for the community came addressed to South Bend or to St. Joseph County.

The habit of Holy Cross was given for the first time in the New World at St. Joseph's Church in Bertrand on September 8, 1844. Miss Sweeney became Sister Mary of Holy Cross, Miss Dougherty, Sister Mary of Mount Carmel, and Miss Daily, Sister Mary of the Nativity. The state of Michigan has since erected a historical marker to note the occasion and the place. A fourth postulant, Miss Bridget Coffee, received the habit in December and the name Sister Mary of St. Basil. It should be noted that their receiving the habit does not mean that any two of them were dressed alike. There was an attempt at uniformity in the headdress, which was still undergoing various changes; otherwise "habits" were made out of whatever material happened to be available.

The novices shared the laundry work of the Sisters at Notre Dame, and Father Sorin provided the subsistence for both groups, each of which was entirely without money. Some of the laundry was brought by horse and wagon to Bertrand; the council notes suggest that this was mostly dormitory, refectory, and kitchen laundry. The rest — chapel, infirmary, and personal washing, plus the overflow from the Bertrand consignment — was done in the lakeside washhouse of the Sisters at Notre Dame, who were also engaged in sewing, cooking, and sacristy and infirmary duties. When the water had to be boiled, the novices at Bertrand walked to a neighbor's property, borrowed a boiler, used it and returned it. Laundry was rinsed in the St. Joseph River, "a process," says Mother Eleanore, "perhaps no harder on the Sisters' backs than carrying pails of water up the steps would have been."[1] When no wagon was available to bring the laundry to Bertrand, a messenger would be sent and the Sisters would walk the six miles to Notre Dame, do the washing with the Sisters there, and walk back. This was not the favored method, however, "because," says Mother Elizabeth, "the clear, clean water supplied by the river . . .

was . . . far better for washing purposes than the stagnant, muddy lake water at Notre Dame."[2]

Mother Elizabeth continues:

> The regular supplies of meat, bread, and a few other things were brought from Notre Dame for a long time in open wagons; the flies enjoyed the fresh meat, unless, as the road was cut through the forest, a low-hanging bough gave a general sweep [note: and knocked the food into the dirt, apparently]. The bread *frozen in winter,* or *dried* so hard by the sun in summer, that even an anchorite might envy; if it had not been for the kindness of Mr. and Mrs. Claffey . . . they would have suffered much more, as the loaves sent from there were given to the children.[3]

On at least one occasion no food wagon came, and Sister Mary of St. Basil took a schoolgirl with her and walked to Notre Dame to get some bread. When Father Cointet heard of this, he gave the Sisters five dollars against future emergencies. In that time and place, five dollars would have been a princely sum and must have represented about a month's collections at St. Joseph's Church.

The children who got the good bread from Claffeys' were among those who began to collect around the Sisters from the first. Sister Heart of Jesus was requested by the people of Bertrand and encouraged by Father Sorin to begin instruction, religious and otherwise, of the local children almost as soon as she arrived in Bertrand. Within a few weeks three or four orphan girls had somehow found their way to the wild roses and sweetbriar, and that number was destined to increase. Sister Emerentiana (Nowlan), the first serious community archivist, picks up the remark from the Notre Dame *Chronicles* that "either because they were younger, or for the lack of discipline, these little children did not in general give as much satisfaction as the orphan boys at the lake."[4]

In late October 1844 three new recruits arrived from France, after a crossing every bit as rough as the first one. Sisters Mary of the Five Wounds (Paillet), Mary of the Circumcision (Chanson), and Mary of the Crucifixion (Argot) joined the group at Notre Dame, and Sister Five Wounds became the superior. In December she and Sister Bethlehem made final profession at Notre Dame, but before this happy occasion another "first" had to be recorded. Sister Mary of Nazareth, she who had been seasick enough to die on the way over, found herself unable to go on in these straightened circumstances and left the community sometime between May and November 1844. An unconfirmed report says that she stuck to her resolution never to embark on the seas again and married a farmer in the South Bend area.

Another apostolate which developed almost immediately was that of visiting the sick. Sister Emerentiana again quotes the Notre Dame *Chronicles*, which record this fact, and which then go on to make a trenchant comment on Bertrand:

> From the very first in Bertrand there were always some Sisters specially charged to visit the sick in the village and neighborhood whenever they were called upon. By this means, the Sisters on many occasions became the instruments of the conversion of many infidels [unbaptized] who otherwise would have died in their unbelief. However it must be confessed that if the necessity of looking to the novitiate and of obtaining for it some good for the college had not been so urgent, it would be hard to understand this first year at Bertrand, which was and will be for a long time to come, nothing more than a dead town.[5]

By the spring of 1845 there were eleven Sisters on the American mission, six at Notre Dame and five at Bertrand. But there was plenty of work for more. Sister Five Wounds was dispatched to France to beg (literally) for money and to seek out more subjects. But Father Moreau did not permit the begging, reprimanded the Sister for coming to France without his permission, and kept her in France for fifteen months, thus weakening rather than strengthening the American mission. The Sisters in America started making novenas for subjects, and at the close of one of these, on May 7, 1845, Margaret Gleeson and Mary Long arrived from Chicago. Mary Long did not persevere, but Margaret Gleeson became Sister (later Mother) Compassion, and fifty years later wrote an invaluable memoir from which much community history (and a little bit of myth) descends. Mary McIntyre and Mary Coffee, the latter a sister of the newly received Sister Basil, also arrived and became Sisters Conception and John Evangelist.

On his first arrival at Notre Dame, Father Sorin had found a band of Indians, whose ancestors had been converted by Jesuits two generations before, awaiting the ministrations of a "blackrobe," and for some time Father Sorin had tried to get permission to devote his life entirely to that apostolate. He and the other priests of Holy Cross juggled the mission to the Indians along with the work at Notre Dame and neighboring parishes — "neighboring" including anything within a sixty-mile radius.

In the spring of 1845 the Sisters got their first chance to assist in the Indian mission. Sisters Crucifixion and Holy Cross went to the village of Pokagon, now Silver Creek, Michigan, to teach religion and English to the Potawatomis. (The Indians' English must have been worth hearing; Sister Holy Cross came from County Tyrone and Sister Crucifixion had just arrived from France.) It was the first mission away from Notre Dame–Bertrand, and the beginning of an apostolate which continued for eight years. There were also Indians within walking distance of Notre Dame, as we learn from Sister Calvary, who seemed to attract adventure.

> I went to visit an Indian girl who had long been ill. Unacquainted with the forest road, I had asked a little girl to accompany me. Suddenly, my guide made me a sign to be careful. Just ahead, coiled about a tree trunk, was an enormous snake, the tail of which lay across my path. The little Indian maid gleefully jumped over it, but I was almost petrified with fear, and carefully picked my way. . . . The glaring eyes of the reptile froze me with terror.[6]

Sister Calvary seems to have enjoyed making the most of any experience. Her monster sounds like a python or a boa constrictor, neither of which has ever inhabited Indiana. If the little girl jumped over the snake, she probably knew it was harmless.

Daily life in the novitiate at Bertrand was not for the weak. Everyone rose at five every day, Sundays included, winter and summer. Morning meditation was at five-thirty, followed by half an hour for the study of catechism. After breakfast they went to their work until time for particular examen just before dinner. The noon meal was followed by a walk, unless it was the growing season (April-October), in which case they weeded the vegetable garden for recreation. Then more work until five o'clock, when they had "protract," a French custom of reporting to the mistress of novices, in public, all their actions good and bad during the day. Then followed the visit to the Blessed Sacrament (in St. Joseph's Church for the first three years), supper, another short recreation during which mending was attended to, and night prayer, always ending with the *Stabat Mater* sung standing. Mass was an unusual privilege and did not figure in the daily schedule.

The winter of 1845–46 was another severe one, and the novices simply could not keep warm enough in Bertrand to stay healthy. Father Sorin had quarters arranged for them at Notre Dame and moved them all down. Most of the other Sisters remained with the children.

Three postulants received the habit in February 1846. None of these persevered, but the ceremony is noteworthy for the change it records in the attitude toward the Sisters. The *Catholic Miscellany* for that week noted that many Protestants attended, and

> there was neither contempt nor ridicule on the occasion — very different from a former one fifteen months previous. . . . It was then all sympathy for the young ladies, who were looked upon as dupes of priestcraft and superstition.[7]

In 1846, according to Mother Compassion,

> Father Sorin went to France. . . . Before leaving he . . . exhorted all to be faithful to duty. He said that when a superior leaves, the devil comes and tries to take his place. Father always in season and out of season preached devotion to the Blessed Mother; he tried to inspire all with love for her by his words and his example.[8]

While Father Sorin was gone, a small blacksmith shop in Bertrand was moved to the convent property and attached to the ground floor as an extra room. The orphans slept here "in narrow wooden beds like shelves."[9] It was also used as a parlor and office, and later Father Sorin used it for interviews with the Sisters, "he inside, they outside on the porch."[10] (One hopes some other arrangement was made in cold weather.)

By this time the Sisters at Notre Dame were able to move out of the log chapel loft and into "the brick house which until then had served as a temporary college building,"[11] probably the building known today as Old College. They had the privilege of having the Blessed Sacrament reserved long before the Sisters in Bertrand. Mother Compassion remembered "one occasion in winter when the road was very slippery, and Reverend Father Superior had to take off his boots and walk in his stockings to come to say Mass for the Sisters."[12]

While Father Sorin was in France in 1846, Sister Mary of the Heart of Jesus experienced some kind of problem with her health. Apparently the local doctor, if there was one, could not help. Father Stephen Badin, the first priest ordained in the United States (1793) and the original owner of the Notre Dame property, was at Notre Dame and was going to Detroit. He suggested that she come along and consult a doctor there. Accompanied by Sister Assumption (Riopelle), a member of the Detroit family with whom the first four Sisters had stayed on their way to their mission in Indiana, Sister Heart of Jesus made the trip. It is not recorded whether she was helped by a Detroit physician or not, but the trip had other repercussions.

Meanwhile, a look at some of the council decisions during these months will give a picture of life both at Bertrand and at Notre Dame. In February, a Madame Reneau, apparently a sort of lodger-servant with the Sisters, was asked to be more help to Sister Bethlehem, "so that she can be present for prayers and community exercises."[13] The council decided that "a shirt will be made for Father Badin from the white cotton material"[14] (America's first priest was very much a part of the local scene at the time); "asked for twelve pillow cases. . . . Father [Granger] said it was an expense which could be put off till later. . . . for tablecloths. Refused."[15] For table napkins, "Father Granger said two or three would be enough for each person."[16] On April 20 they were specifically forbidden to take anything from the clothesroom "without the permission of Father Sorin," even though he was in Europe at the time. They were also forbidden to give away any food, "except in extraordinary cases." This suggests that their generosity had encouraged begging by the Indians, or perhaps by some of those Bertrand "infidels."

When they asked for lightweight underskirts to replace their woolen ones in summer, the request was refused because such things were not mentioned in the Constitutions, and Father Granger suggested that they write to Sainte-Croix and ask that the provision be included in the next edition of the Rules. When Sister Mary of Bethlehem asked for "a Brother or a boy" to help her get the cows out into the field in the morning and bring them back in the evening, Father Granger again refused and told her to "follow the custom of the country."[17]

Father Granger also kept all the new postulants at Notre

Dame during this time. Sisters Compassion and Conception had come to Notre Dame to learn the process of bookbinding, and they were appointed to teach the postulants their community prayers.

Father Sorin arrived back at Notre Dame August 22, 1846. He brought with him the long-missing superior, Sister Five Wounds, along with Sisters Cenacle, Dositheus, Ascension, Joseph, and Infant Jesus, plus three postulants; also one priest (Father Baroux), two seminarians, three Brothers, and a Brother postulant. The Sisters were distributed between Notre Dame and Bertrand and began peacefully to prepare for retreat and professions.

Then one day, apparently before the retreat, Father Sorin summoned all the Sisters to appear in the chapel at Notre Dame. He had learned of Sister Heart of Jesus' journey to Detroit to consult a doctor and was monumentally displeased. Mother Compassion was there:

> [W]hen we were all assembled . . . Father Superior present . . . Mother Superior brought Sister Mary [of the Heart of Jesus] into the chapel dressed in secular dress. She knelt on the floor, made her accusation, and asked pardon of us all. Reverend Father Superior said she deserved to be sent away, but as she begged to be kept, they would excuse her. The novices present, who loved her, cried aloud to see her dressed like a Lady.[18]

At the conclusion of the retreat, September 10, Sisters Cenacle, Holy Cross, Nativity, and Mount Carmel made profession. Sister Cenacle became superior at Notre Dame, and Sister Five Wounds took over as mistress of novices. Sister Heart of Jesus, in disgrace, was sent to Pokagon until her transfer to Canada could be arranged. After some years in Canada[19] she went to New Orleans, from where, "sad to say," says Mother Compassion, "she left the community."[20]

The *Marianite Annals* give us an idea of what the newcomers had to adjust to.

> One day during the noon recess, while the Sisters were having lunch, they heard loud piercing cries of joy. On investigation they found that the children were running after three huge bears with all the happy excitement of French children chasing butterflies.[21]

During the winter of 1846–47 a log chapel, which Father Badin had built some years before on the Bertrand road, was moved to the convent and attached to the house the same way the blacksmith shop had been. The Sisters now had a chapel, but still did not have permission to reserve the Blessed Sacrament.

Sister Cenacle moved to Bertrand in 1847 and an immediate improvement was seen, both in the religious spirit and in the condition of the school. "Good order and discipline were established in the . . . House, which had suffered much during the absence of superiors in France."[22] Sisters Basil and Circumcision made their professions on March 25, and all went well through the spring. Then an unexpected disaster is recorded in the council minutes for June 3. "Sister Mary of Calvary, after the grave fault which she has just committed, may not enter the establishment of the Sisters at Notre Dame du Lac, nor the house at Bertrand."

Apparently Sister Calvary's spirit of adventure had taken her a step too far. There is no record of the nature of the "grave fault," nor of where she went immediately after being barred from both Holy Cross convents. There was, however, by this time, an alternative to the local and Indian missions.

When Father Sorin and the Brothers had first arrived in Vincennes in 1842, a firm friendship had sprung up between Father Sorin and a diocesan priest named Father Julien Delaune. Like the Holy Cross missionaries, Father Delaune had come from France at the behest of the bishop of Vincennes. He was pastor of St. Peter's but unselfishly assisted the Holy Cross personnel in taking over the area. He then served as pastor in Madison, Indiana, and Father Sorin sent Brother Anselm to teach the boys of his parish. This good work came to an end when Brother Anselm drowned while swimming in the Ohio River, July 12, 1845.

Apparently at the recommendation of Father Delaune, Bishop Guy Ignatius Chabrat, coadjutor bishop of Bardstown, Kentucky, wrote in late 1845 to ask Father Sorin if Holy Cross could take over St. Mary's College at Lebanon, Kentucky, near Louisville. The Jesuits had founded the college but were going to abandon it in order to concentrate on the founding of St. John's College (later Fordham University) in New York City. Father Sorin agreed to try to staff St. Mary's, subject to approval, which he was optimistic about getting from Father Moreau and the council at Le Mans.

Perhaps this optimism communicated itself too well to Father Delaune and the authorities in Bardstown. They went ahead with plans for continuing the Kentucky college much too fast for the taste of their correspondents in Le Mans. The complicated details are all laid out elsewhere.[23] At any rate, it was necessary to send Sisters for some minimal housekeeping and organizational duties.

Father Sorin had hoped that a few faculty members would be sent at once from Le Mans, but only one priest could be spared. This was Father Augustin Saunier, who happened to be at Notre Dame when Sister Calvary incurred Sorin's displeasure. Father Saunier offered to take her to Lebanon, where Sister Mary of the Five Wounds, who had spent less than a year as mistress of novices in Bertrand, Sister Mary of the Nativity, and Sister Mary of the Crucifixion had already gone. A letter from Sister Five Wounds to Father Sorin describes Sister Calvary's arrival. "Having come without shoes, and after the miseries she suffered on the way, finding herself in the kitchen again,"[24] she was given a pair of blue slippers.

Now there was only one of the original four still left in Indiana: Sister Mary of Bethlehem, still tending her cows.

There was much sickness in Indiana that summer of 1847, and on August 1 Sister Mary of Mount Carmel became the first Sister Marianite of Holy Cross to die anywhere in the world. She was three weeks short of her forty-second birthday and just eleven months professed. She had spent her brief religious life doing the laundry at Notre Dame and, as she worked in the washhouse, giving out the rosary for her assistants to answer. It was said that she had such great faith "that when at work she always took care to face in the direction of the tabernacle."[25]

But the blows of losing Sister Calvary and Sister Mount Carmel were nothing compared to the next disaster fate had in store. Bishop Le Fevre of Detroit came to Bertrand on Sunday November 6, 1847, to confirm a group of children and adults (probably including some Indians) whom Father Cointet and the Sisters had instructed. Afterwards in the convent the Sisters all knelt while Mother Cenacle asked permission to have the Blessed Sacrament reserved in their chapel. The bishop granted their petition and great was the rejoicing that evening.

There was no Mass on Monday morning, Father Cointet either having resumed his missionary efforts or gone partway with the bishop. Sister Presentation went over to tidy up the church and returned at noon saying there were a number of articles she could not find.

Sister Assumption said, "I will go with you after dinner and find them." They returned to the church and Sister Assumption put her hand on the tabernacle door, which fell down as soon as she touched it.[26]

The robbers had entered by one of the windows, which they had reached by means of a board; then they unscrewed the hinges of the door of the tabernacle, after rifling which, they carried off the chalice which was in a box near the altar.[27]

Besides the chalice, the thief had taken the ciborium, silver cruets, altar cover, boys' cassocks, and altar wine. The Sisters fled back to the convent to report. Mother Cenacle immediately

called the Sisters and pupils together, and all went in tears to make reparation, while the workman was sent to Notre Dame for Father Superior.

After some time in silence, Mother Cenacle in a trembling voice intoned the *Parce Domine*, in which all joined who could sing. This was repeated several times, after which the beads were recited until the arrival of Father Sorin.[28]

Father Sorin describes his experience.

About one o'clock in the afternoon, a messenger came to me in great haste. Something dreadful had happened at Bertrand! I immediately started; and when I arrived at the Sisters' house, I found only one present. I inquired of her where the others were; and with eyes filled with tears, she silently pointed to the church. I went there, and when I entered that sacred edifice, which but yesterday contained so many happy souls, I beheld the Sisters weeping and praying. Their little girls, many of whom had made their First Communion the day before, were also in tears, and a number of Catholics in the village. All eyes were fixed on the tabernacle, the door of which, hanging open, told plainly of the terrible crime that a sacrilegious hand had committed.[29]

Mother Compassion remembered that

[Father Sorin] examined the tabernacle and found a few sacred hosts in the corporal. After some delay, Father Sorin brought [these] to the Sisters' chapel. It was raining. The procession formed; Sister Compassion held the lantern and Sister Gonzaga held the

> umbrella over Father; all the others followed. The Blessed Sacrament was placed in our little tabernacle, and from that time on we had our Blessed Lord with us.[30]

It is probably hard for today's religious, with a slightly different sacramental outlook, to grasp what an utter tragedy this was (far worse than a death), not only for the Sisters in Bertrand, but for the whole community. For the next several months the priests at Notre Dame made a pilgrimage every Wednesday, on foot, to St. Joseph's Church, calling at the convent in silence for the key, making a holy hour, returning the key, and walking back to Notre Dame, still in silence. Father Moreau, when he heard about it, ordered acts of reparation throughout the congregation, so that the sacrilege in Bertrand was atoned for by Holy Cross religious in France, Canada, Kentucky, and Algeria. Fifty years later Mother Compassion wrote that she was "sure those present would never forget that *Parce Domine*."[31]

The ciborium and chalice were eventually found under a bed in a Bertrand hotel. Nothing else was recovered, though the thief himself was apprehended after he became drunk enough one night to boast about his depredations.

4
As Edifying as Carthusians, 1847–49

Christmas of 1847 was probably subdued in the aftermath of the sacrilege, but by January the Sisters had pulled themselves together and were dealing with the practicalities. The stewardess applied herself to the budget for the coming year and calculated that personal maintenance, including food, was costing six-and-a-half cents per day per person, and that their maintenance that year, pupils and all, would come to $1,115.

But the winter was hard, with the usual sicknesses. Mother Cenacle's health failed, and in February, accompanied by Sister Assumption (who had also been the companion on the medical excursion to Detroit), she went to Fort Wayne to see a doctor. She remained there all through March, and Sister Assumption sent back reassuring messages.

In April Father Sorin made the long journey to the see city of Vincennes. Bishop de la Hailandière, whose pleas had brought Holy Cross to Indiana, had not been an easy man to deal with. Holy Cross had fared better than most of the clergy and religious in the diocese, simply by virtue of being so far away. Finally, with many of the secular clergy having left the diocese, the administrative and financial matters in a snarl, and remonstrations coming from his brother bishops in every mail, Bishop de la Hailandière had resigned; and Rome, on the advice of the Sixth Provincial Council of Baltimore, had accepted the resignation and appointed the Most Reverend John Stephen Bazin, auxiliary bishop of Mobile, Alabama, as the third bishop of Vincennes. Bishop Bazin had been installed in the Vincennes cathedral on October 24, 1847, but with the winter setting in, it had not been possible for Father Sorin to make a trip south to pay his respects. An early meeting was urgent, as Bishop Bazin had named Father Sorin vicar general for the northern part of the diocese.

Father Sorin arrived, however, to find the bishop gravely ill, though still conducting business from his sickbed. Father Sorin did not linger in Vincennes. Holy Week was coming on, and he wanted to be back at Notre Dame by Easter.

He returned (by carriage or horseback?) by way of Fort Wayne, planning to escort Mother Cenacle and Sister Assumption back to Bertrand. Arriving at St. Augustine's convent, where the Sisters of Providence were providing hospitality, he was stunned to find that Sister Assumption's assurances had been falsely based. Mother Cenacle was dying.

Father Sorin did not spend that Easter at Notre Dame. The records say he arrived in Fort Wayne on April 20 or 21, which would have been Holy Thursday or Good Friday, and stayed four days to be a source of consolation to Mother Cenacle. He then hurried back to Bertrand to urge the Sisters to pray and (in spite of the Easter alleluias) to do penance for the recovery of their superior. God had other plans, however. Mother Cenacle died April 28. We do not know whether the news of her death reached Notre Dame and Bertrand before or after the news that Bishop Bazin had died on Easter Sunday, April 23, after an episcopate of six months.

Father Sorin was staggered by Mother Cenacle's death. He let Father Cointet preach the eulogy at the Requiem Mass celebrated for her at Notre Dame (her body could not be returned for several months, till the cold weather came back). Giving in, strangely for him, to Victorian sentimentality, he had a black-draped crucifix kept at her place in the chapel and in the refectory until a new superior arrived from Canada almost a year later. He wrote that

> Her short life in religion was a long series of acts of all the virtues; her long malady placed in a strong light her great courage and her lively faith; and of her death it was said that if the angels were to die, they would surely die such a death as hers. May she obtain for me that my last moments be like those that closed her angelic career.[1]

The following August, at the close of the Sisters' retreat, he gave each of them a memento of Mother Cenacle. Meanwhile, Sister Assumption, the bilingual American from Detroit, was appointed acting superior, and life for the living went on. Sister Assumption was the first American to serve as a Marianite superior.

The problem of a permanent superior was a serious one. At first Father Sorin tried to borrow one. The saintly Mother Theodore Guerin, American foundress of the Sisters of Providence, was making an official Visitation[2] in Madison, Indiana, when Mother Cenacle died. In his acquaintance with her during his year at St. Peter's, Father Sorin had recognized in her a spirit as indomitable as his own, and a deep attachment to the religious life. Mother Theodore was one of those rare religious for whom the old cliché would hardly be an exaggeration, that if all the rule books were destroyed, they could be rewritten from observing her life.

Hearing of Mother Cenacle's death, Mother Theodore

> acceded to Father Sorin's invitation to visit Notre Dame and especially Bertrand to offer her condolences to the afflicted Sisters who had so recently lost their estimable superior. She remained a week and noted with pleasure and surprise the growth of the Communities and the extensive improvements made by Father Sorin.[3]

Mother Theodore was also pleased to encounter her old friend Brother Vincent, whom she had known when his community and hers were newly founded at Ruillé by Father Dujarié; also "one of the Sisters who had belonged to Father Dujarié's household at Ruillé,"[4] and who can only have been Sister Bethlehem.

The Providence chronicle, "Important Events," records:

> Father Sorin gave Mother a pretty statue of the Blessed Virgin and the works of St. Teresa. But he wished to receive in exchange a most precious gift. . . . He earnestly begged Mother Theodore to remain some time at South Bend. Seeing his request was useless, he entreated her to give him one of her Sisters to form his little band to the religious life. Later on he renewed his request by letter, but it was not possible for us to comply.[5]

The Sisters were temporarily looking out for their own formation, under what guidance Father Sorin could give them with a large number of other matters demanding his attention. With Sister Assumption, the council was composed of Sister Circumcision and Sister Ascension. Sister Circumcision had come with the group in October 1844 and had made her profession at Bertrand March 25, 1847. She was serving as directress at Notre Dame. Sister Ascension had come with the 1846 group and was not yet professed. The title "superior" and the lesser title of "directress" seem to have shifted back and forth between Notre Dame and Bertrand. For most of the time there was only one real superior, and the house where the directress resided was what would be called today a satellite house. Sister Ascension was a strong person with qualities of good judgment and leadership, but at this time she was only twenty-two and still learning.

The council of the Sisters met the second, third and fourth of August 1848 to prepare the obediences, always "under the presidency of our Reverend Father Superior, of Sister Mary of the Assumption, Sister Mary of the Circumcision, and Sister Mary of the Ascension." At their next meeting, August 24, the name of Sister Assumption disappears and is replaced by that of Sister Redemption.

Sister Redemption (Rajot) was a member of the minor French nobility who had a checkered career in Holy Cross, moving frequently back and forth among France, Canada, Indiana, and New Orleans. She had some of the qualities of a good administrator but suffered from eccentricity and unpredictability. Like Father Sorin she could be brilliant, creative, loving, and self-investing, but also, like him, imperious, demanding, impetuous, and unwilling to admit mistakes. Their greatest difference lay in the fact that she could never be content anywhere for long; he threw his heart, soul, and life into Notre Dame and never wanted to see another horizon. Blessed Léonie Paradis, a Canadian[6] Holy Cross Sister who founded the Little Sisters of the Holy Family, saw all the good in Sister Redemption and kept her with her in her old age. Sister Redemption died at the motherhouse of the Little Sisters of the Holy Family and is buried in their cemetery. Meanwhile she wandered in and out of the history of the American congregation.

Desiring to have a firsthand report on the American foundations from someone not personally involved in them, Father Moreau sent Father Victor Drouelle from Le Mans to make an official Visitation, both in Canada and in Indiana, and to furnish a detailed report to the motherhouse. The problem of a superior for the Sisters was one of the things he was expected to look into.

Father Drouelle was greatly unimpressed by the four Sisters at Notre Dame.

> He reported that they observed silence "as ordinary women observe it." Obedience never bothered them and they were not scrupulous in their observance of charity. This general state of mediocrity was said to be due to the frequent changing of superiors, some of whom were altogether incompetent; to the excessive good-

> ness of the Father Superior, and to the bad spirit of several Sisters who had been admitted to the religious life without much preliminary investigation. He also remarked that the Sisters from France had only a tinge, a slight coating of the religious life.[7]

He found the situation in Bertrand more encouraging. Though he visited in summer and fall, he evidently heard stories about the winters in Indiana and Michigan, for he reported that the Sisters would have frozen in winter if they had not kept stoves constantly burning. "The poor Sisters," he wrote, "are obliged to get their water from the river, with great danger of breaking an arm or leg, especially during the winter."[8]

Bertrand at that time had

> eighteen Sisters in all: three professed and fifteen novices, almost all of whom were Irish and "as edifying as Carthusians." They sang while at work, and this was not regarded as a violation of the rule of silence. Their habit had been changed, because of the necessity of adapting it to circumstances; only the cord, the heart, and the rosary resembled those worn in the other houses.[9]

The chief circumstance to which the habit had to be adapted was probably the difficulty of obtaining proper materials on the frontier. The cord, heart, and chaplet of the Seven Dolors were made in France and sent from there (though four years later at her reception Sister Euphrosine specifically says that no chaplets were given to the novices). For the rest the Sisters had to improvise, and the results of the improvisation were startlingly similar to those of other communities on the Indiana frontier. In fact, Sister St. Francis Xavier, another of Father Sorin's friends among the Sisters of Providence, wrote him in 1847 protesting that she had heard that the Sisters of the Holy Cross had copied the habit of the Sisters of Providence. She told him tartly, "I have thus far prayed for your perseverance. If what I have heard is true, I must now pray for your conversion."[10]

Indeed, an 1855 picture of Mother Theodore and a picture of the 1841 Holy Cross habit in *Our Motherhouse*[11] show a similar pattern of white guimpe curving around the head and over the shoulders, with a black veil laid over it, a folded piece of white material worn shawl-like around the shoulders and crossed over the breast, and the square bib of a black apron pinned over this. The

Providence undercap curves just around the hairline, leaving the forehead uncovered, and a white cross is worn on a black cord around the neck. The Holy Cross band sits squarely over the eyebrows, covering the forehead, and the silver heart appears at the top of the bib line, but the picture does not show whether it was pinned there or worn around the neck. The 1845 habit in the same series of pictures (all of which were posed for many years after the fact) shows the guimpe shortened to a white bonnet under a black veil, and the neckerchief and apron bib replaced by a cape and a heart-shaped collar. The fluted cap appears in 1853. It is highly questionable that the Sisters on the frontier ever looked as good as those in the photographs — almost certainly they were never as clean. But it seems probable that the two groups of Sisters arrived independently at somewhat similar solutions to the problem of looking like a religious in the wilds of western Indiana in the 1840s.

Having looked over the establishments at Notre Dame and Bertrand, and having framed his own conclusions about the kind of superior needed, Father Drouelle was ready to act. The council minutes for September 4, 1848, give a succinct account.

> In the presence of all the members of the chapter, the Father Visitor declared that he was officially charged by the Reverend Father Rector [Moreau] to act together with Father Verité [Canadian superior who had escorted Father Drouelle to Indiana] and Father Sorin for the nomination of a superior. He declared furthermore to have consequently taken the advice of Father Verité, who told him he would approve the transfer of Sr. M. of the Savior to Bertrand, if Sr. M. of the 7 Dolors could be sent to replace her; and that Sr. M. of the Savior, consulted in her turn, had shown herself completely disposed to accept the said transfer if such should be the case. Father Sorin for his part has produced a letter from Rev. Father Rector bearing the date of July 22, 1848, the text of which contains the following proposition. "If I had the money, I would perhaps send you our superior to replace our deeply lamented deceased one." Upon which, the said Father Sorin, questioned by the Father Visitor, replied that he would voluntarily advance the money to pay the passage of Sr. M. of the 7 Dolors.

In view of all these considerations, the council decided that Sister Mary of the Savior would come to Bertrand, Sister Mary of the Seven Dolors would come from France to Saint-Laurent, and in the meantime, Sister Redemption, who had accompanied Father Drouelle from Canada and who had immediately begun serving on the local council, would remain in Indiana to serve as superior.

Father Drouelle then took up the matter of the Sisters who had been sent to Lebanon, Kentucky. It had not been possible to send any more priests or Brothers, and Sister Five Wounds was sending disquieting letters back. In April 1848 she had expressed misgivings about

> the worthy Father Saunier *(who does from day to day everything that it pleases M. Delaune to have him do)*. . . . For Heaven's sake, Father, deal yourself with the bishop [so that] there will not be any mistakes. If you can, come soon. Things are happening that you will not like.[12]

In August she complained about an incredible system by which the four Sisters, apparently with Father Sorin's approval, took turns as superior each for three months of the year. She supplied him with a long and wordy plan about how she planned to conduct the office when it became her turn. In a postscript she noted that "for a thousand reasons" she was glad to hear that Sister Redemption had arrived at the Lake. Another letter gives a long list of reasons why her scruples demanded that she not accept Father Saunier's twice-given permission but must seek Father Sorin's instead — to tear up an old piece of linen into dish towels! She repeatedly urged Father Sorin to come to Lebanon, sometimes citing the institutional situation, sometimes the needs of her own soul. She seems to have developed in Kentucky, if not before, a great craving for Father Sorin's attention and approval.

The *Marianite Annals* suggest that the Sisters in Kentucky were not only isolated, but that their superiors both in France and at Notre Dame were neglecting to communicate with them, and that Father Drouelle came to their rescue like a knight on a white horse.[13] The recently recovered letters of Sister Five Wounds do not uphold this theory. The Sisters were sufficiently in touch with affairs at Notre Dame to know that Father Drouelle was there and that he was coming to Kentucky. A postscript on an undated letter says, "Please be good enough to present my very profound respects to the worthy Father Drouelle. All the Sisters as well as I, will be very happy to see him."

Father Drouelle spent a week in Lebanon, concluded that the Sisters should be withdrawn, and wrote this recommendation in a detailed report to Father Moreau. He then planned to proceed to the island of Guadeloupe, on a mission as Apostolic Visitor. But he stopped in New Orleans for what was expected to be a quick passing visit and changed the history of Holy Cross in the United States. Bishop Antoine Blanc of New Orleans asked Father Drouelle if Holy Cross could take over St. Mary's Boys' Orphan Asylum. It occurred to Father Drouelle that if the Sisters left Lebanon, they and some Brothers who would have gone to Lebanon if it had remained a Holy Cross mission would be at liberty to come to Louisiana. This is what he recommended.

Father Moreau accepted the recommendation. The *Marianite Annals* state that "Father Founder at once notified the Sisters"[14] that they would be leaving Lebanon for New Orleans, but it was to Father Sorin that they addressed their pleas and "representations." They wanted, or at least Sister Five Wounds wanted, to come back to Notre Dame before going to New Orleans. She wrote:

> each of us intends to tell you privately, and I think I can tell you for all of us, that it is very necessary and very important that we come to Notre Dame to make a little retreat before being sent anywhere. There we will see you. . . . We will receive our obediences from your hands.[15]

She also hoped that the composition of the group might be changed.

> I do not feel in myself, thanks be to God, any repugnance for any employment or any Sister whatever. . . . But to begin an institution with Sister Mary of the Crucifixion. . . .
>
> Since I have been at St. Mary's [Lebanon] I have done all that I could to conform to her ways, and it is in vain that I have put my soul to the torture for that; I could never attain to it. She has suffered a great deal because of me, and I assure you she has not suffered in silence. . . . I will ask you, for the greater glory of God and good of the community, to send Sister Mary of the Crucifixion some Sister who can understand her and agree with her.

In another letter written before the departure from Kentucky she states that she still feels the same repugnance but is leaving it to God, "to inspire you with the salutary thought of changing something in the personnel of the Sisters whom you destine for this mission."[16] What God inspired Father Sorin to do was to recall, not Sister Mary of the Five Wounds, but Sister Mary of the Crucifixion, to Notre Dame. The Cattas in a charitable footnote in their biography of Mother Seven Dolors ascribe this to Sister Crucifixion's being "too worn out to continue."[17] The probability seems to be that she was removed from the group because, where her companions were concerned, she lived up to her name all too well.

After some weeks of making arrangements, which included preparing the Sisters of Loretto to take over domestic duties at the college, the Sisters were ready to leave Kentucky. Brother Theodulus called for them and they joined the Brothers on the river passage to New Orleans, where they arrived to begin a new ministry on May 1, 1849.

5

Maintain Your Independence, 1848–49

The fall of 1848 saw the beginnings of Saint Mary's Academy, Bertrand. The orphan girls who had collected around the Sisters from the beginning began to be augmented by a trickle of young ladies, daughters of farmers and merchants and of a few professional men, who came for a better education than their homes and local surroundings could offer. They seem to have formed from the first a separate group from the orphans.

A Miss Shea had the distinction of being the first secular teacher to work with the Sisters of the Holy Cross in America — the first of a long and honorable line. Miss Anne Molloy also arrived to teach music, but by the following February Miss Molloy had become Sister Mary of St. Francis. Sister Augustine (Murphy) was released from all other duties to give all her time to study and teaching.

It was about this time that the question first arose of canonical approbation for the Sisters. For a thorough consideration of this, we must, first, go back a few years; second, respectfully disagree with what have been considered unassailable certainties in community history; and third, take into account a factor never before seen as a matter of any importance in the history of the American Sisters — their relationship to the Sisters of Providence.

The Sisters of Providence predated Father Moreau's Sisters by almost forty years in the diocese of Le Mans. Their first two members, under the direction of Father Jacques Dujarié, began instructing children and caring for the sick in Ruillé-sur-Loir in 1806. Their first superior general, Mother du Roscoat, was elected in 1818. Two years later (1820) Father Dujarié also founded the Brothers of St. Joseph. In 1826 the Sisters received a royal decree of approval and permission to incorporate.

As the two communities grew, their temporal affairs had become more complicated. At first it had been easy enough for Father Dujarié to manage everything on one financial account, but in 1827 a separation of temporalities had to be effected. This left the

Sisters, even after they had paid all the debts of both communities, notably better off than the Brothers. They still, however, had no canonical status.

In 1833 Jean Baptiste Bouvier became bishop of Le Mans. It was to him that Father Moreau later had to apply for approbation for the "Association" of Holy Cross, and Bishop Bouvier simply would not give it with the Sisters as a part of the Association. The Cattas give the impression that he was leery of all women's associations which claimed or aspired to be religious.

> With regard to communities of women in his diocese, the Bishop felt it his duty to pursue a policy of extreme caution. The Providence Sisters of Ruillé had become well established during the episcopate of his predecessor, and he was very careful not to interfere with them. At Evron . . . the Sisters of Charity . . . gave every assurance of a successful future. Bishop Bouvier could not see new foundations thus appearing in rapid succession without experiencing certain misgivings.[1]

The fact is that almost as soon as he became bishop of Le Mans, Bishop Bouvier appointed himself ecclesiastical superior to the Sisters of Providence. He kept that position until his death and took a deep, active, fatherly interest in them. Their official history says:

> He continued as ecclesiastical superior of the Sisters of Providence of Ruillé-sur-Loir until his death, and no one stood nearer to the struggling community of Saint Mary-of-the-Woods. . . . Mother Theodore always looked on him as founder of Saint Mary-of-the-Woods. . . . He was never too preoccupied to listen . . . or to give . . . his wise, prudent, and learned counsel. One of the first authorities in Europe on Canon Law . . . not only his wisdom but his erudition gave Mother Theodore complete confidence in taking his decisions as final and in following them with fidelity and reverence.[2]

The first six Sisters of Providence, having been recruited in the diocese of Le Mans exactly as the Holy Cross missionaries were, arrived in Indiana in October 1840. They had expected to be located in one of the small but growing centers of population and were greatly disappointed to be domiciled literally in the woods. From the first they had extensive troubles with Bishop de la

Hailandière, as did most of his clergy. He tried to change their habit, then tried to change their rule, took their money for their wilderness property but would not give them the deed, sent them postulants who were clearly unsuitable for the religious life, forced four Sisters of Charity who wanted to return to their motherhouse to become Sisters of Providence instead, and tried to depose Mother Theodore when there was no one capable of replacing her. He insisted that they elect a new superior general (as Mother Theodore was known in America), though their rule allowed only Sisters ten years professed to vote in such an election, and only Mother Theodore and the Sister who was doing the cooking for the mission met the qualification. In the case of one saintly Sister, he refused to hear her confession or allow any of his priests to do so until, he said, she retracted the lies she had written about him to France. Since there were no lies to retract, the poor Sister was denied the sacraments for several months. He was the kind of administrator who would throw a tantrum and furiously demand that certain things be done in certain ways; when his subjects complied and the injudiciousness of his decisions became clear, he would just as furiously deny that he had ever made any such decisions and punish his subjects for their lack of prudence. After some years of struggle with Mother Theodore, he finally declared her dispensed from her vows, thus expelling her from the congregation. This happened when Mother Theodore was ill in Vincennes and could make very little response of any kind. By the time she was able to travel back to Saint Mary-of-the-Woods, the bishop had chosen to forget the matter.

Priests were leaving the diocese almost as fast as the leaky river boats could take them to Kentucky, Illinois, Missouri, and further.

It is clear that in the case of Holy Cross, Bishop de la Hailandière did the two most positive things he could possibly have done — he gave the priests and Brothers diocesan property located 215 crow-fly miles from his see city, and he refused the Sisters permission to have a novitiate in his diocese.

Against the harassment, the Sisters of Providence had one refuge besides God himself. While Bishop de la Hailandière was on his way to Europe in 1844, Mother Theodore was writing letters to try to protect herself against whatever charges might be made. "It was again to Bishop Bouvier's unfailing interest and kindness that she was pouring out the anxieties which harassed her night and day."[3] Bishop Bouvier did his best. He explained to the bishop of Vincennes that a bishop could not require a community to accept subjects whom it found unfit or to go against the rules and constitutions under which they had made their vows, even if these documents still lacked the final sanction from Rome. When Ruillé could do nothing, Bishop Bouvier could.

> If, as it appears, the French superiors proved equally unable to grapple with the difficult and momentous problems of the American mission, there came to their aid one who could and did so. Speaking with the clear and fatherly voice of the Church, one of the most learned and distinguished prelates in Europe, the kindly and devoted Bishop of Le Mans, Jean Baptist Bouvier, became their counsellor and protector. His figure looms as a tower of strength and encouragement over all these shadowed years.[4]

Eventually, in 1847, Bishop de la Hailandière resigned his see and returned to France. Rome never gave him another diocese. He continued to live on his family estate for thirty-five years, helping other bishops with confirmations and ordinations. He was present at the consecration of the Church of Our Lady of Holy Cross in 1857, and was one of the consecrators when the Reverend Pierre Dufal, C.S.C., became the first bishop of Eastern Bengal. Bishop Hailandière died May 1, 1882, the day before his eighty-fourth birthday.

Perhaps viewing things a little too narrowly, the Sisters of Providence have felt that Bishop Bouvier's intervention was instrumental in having the Sixth Provincial Council of Baltimore recommend that Rome accept Bishop de la Hailandière's resignation.

> That the prelates at the Council had decided to arrange for a change in Indiana was probably due in large part to Bishop Bouvier's letter to Archbishop Eccleston received at the opening of the Council, in which was detailed the refusal of Bishop de la Hailandière to approve the Sisters' rules or give them their motherhouse or permit their migration elsewhere. Bishop Bouvier's reputation for sanctity and learning was so great as to give immense weight to his plea for the community. "Estimable Bishop Bouvier . . . I venerate as one of the holiest and most learned prelates in Europe," wrote Archbishop Eccleston later.[5]

To substantiate the Sisters' opinion of the reputation for learning enjoyed by the Bishop of Le Mans, we may consult the 1907 edition of the *Catholic Encyclopedia:*

> The influence exerted by his *Institutiones Theologicae* (in fifteen editions), which was in use in almost all the seminaries in France, as well as the United States and Canada, gives Bishop Bouvier a unique and honorable position in the history of theology in the nineteenth century. His compendium had the distinction of being the first manual, and for many years the only one well adapted to that period of transition (1830–70) marked on the one hand by the death struggles of Gallicanism and Jansenism, and on the other by the work of reform undertaken in all departments of ecclesiastical learning.[6]

This is not the Bouvier who generally emerges from the pages of Holy Cross history. Though the Cattas, in their biography of Father Moreau, acknowledge Bouvier's intellectual gifts and contributions,[7] he is generally presented as vacillating, suspicious, temporizing, and somewhat unsure of himself. The Bishop Bouvier known to the Sisters of Providence had none of these problems. Far from "pursuing a policy of extreme caution" or being "very careful not to interfere with them," he was the person most actively concerned with the Sisters of Providence.

This provides us with an entirely new motive for his failure to approve the Marianites. There were already Sisters of Charity of Evron in the Le Mans diocese, besides his own daughters of Providence. It seems a permissible conclusion that Bishop Bouvier in the first place probably thought the diocese had as many congregations of women as it could do with; second, he may, without even admitting it to himself, have feared to approve a group that would compete with the Sisters of Providence either at home or abroad, or both; third, he may have feared, knowing that both Bishop Simon Bruté, first bishop of Vincennes, and Bishop de la Hailandière had appealed to Father Moreau for help, that additional religious from Le Mans in the Vincennes diocese, especially women religious, would only embroil him further with its bishop.

We also know now that Bishop Bouvier had no objection to women making vows. When he took over as ecclesiastical superior of the Sisters of Providence, they were making annual vows with permission granted to some to make perpetual vows after twenty-five years. He rewrote the rule so that they renewed vows only every five years and made perpetual profession at any five-year point where the bishop's permission could be secured. They also made a fourth vow to instruct children and care for the sick. In 1861, to obtain temporary approbation from Rome, the rule was changed to three years of temporary vows followed by perpetual profession, and the fourth vow was discontinued.

So it was not women's vows which constituted a problem for Bishop Bouvier but the vows of women in Holy Cross, probably for the three reasons given above. Bishop Bouvier permitted only private vows of obedience for Father Moreau's daughters. It was expected that in missionary dioceses they could make the usual three vows of religion with canonical approbation.

Father Moreau had foreseen that it might be more possible to secure approbation for the Sisters by going through an American bishop than by continued futile attempts in Le Mans. But by the time the first four Marianites arrived in America, Father Sorin had had thirteen months in southern Indiana and had taken the measure of the bishop of Vincennes. Bishop de la Hailandière had proposed separately to the Sisters of Providence on one hand, and to Father Sorin and the Brothers of St. Joseph on the other, that each group sever its ties with France immediately and completely. He then wished to reorganize them as a community of priests, Brothers, and Sisters which would belong exclusively to his diocese and be completely under his control. Structural, if not emotional, separation from France had been on the Providence agenda from the first, and there must have been some thought that if they had to separate from their Sisters at Ruillé, they could at least reunite with these Brothers with whom they shared a founder.

But Father Sorin and the Brothers would have none of it. Though Father Sorin later considered separation for himself, and eventually guided the American Sisters to autonomy, he knew that this was not the time for such ideas. He accepted the bishop's offer of land in the north and led the Brothers as far away from Vincennes as they could get without actually leaving the diocese.

Bishop de la Hailandière did not give up easily. Even after his resignation had been finally accepted and his successor named, and with the Marianite Sisters in Bertrand because he would not permit their novitiate in his diocese, he wrote again to Father Sorin, suggesting

> the consolidation of the two religious communities of Holy Cross and Providence with a consequent change of constitutions and of dress. . . . "This would take away your title of superior and founder," he wrote to Father Sorin, "but frankly I think that experience must have brought home to you that it would be an advantage for you."[8]

Bishop Hailandière also strongly pressed for having the Brothers' novitiate at Indianapolis, from where the Brothers would go out to be of service all over the diocese, with the assignments made by the bishop. This, too, was somewhat further than Father Sorin was prepared to go. Knowing it was unwise to give the bishop a flat refusal in anything, Sorin played a delaying game. He must also have known that Bishop de la Hailandière could not remain much longer in the diocese; hopeful rumors of his resignation circulated for many years before the event actually took place.

Meanwhile the bishop wrote contradictory letters to Father Moreau. He had originally asked for Brothers to work first in his diocese, "and then, if God permits, beyond its limits."[9] He soon forgot about anything beyond its limits and showed himself strenuously opposed to such an idea. He wanted the Holy Cross establishment dependent upon Sainte-Croix; no, he wanted it dependent upon the diocese but modeled after Sainte-Croix.[10]

Before Father Sorin and the Brothers sailed from France, after they had arrived at Vincennes, and later at Notre Dame, and still later after the Sisters had come, the arguments continued. The bishop wanted full control of everything. Father Sorin was attempting to follow Father Moreau's directive, "Maintain your independence."[11]

The Cattas have well outlined the step-by-step progress (or deterioration) of the situation. One note may be added.

As all this was going on, a gradual change took place in the self-identification of the Holy Cross religious in Indiana. They had come from Le Mans with the titles Father Moreau had given each branch of the Association in honor of the Holy Family — Salvatorists, Marianites, Josephites. In the first several years in Indiana these titles were gradually dropped in favor of an identification which stressed their unity — priests, Brothers, and Sisters of Holy Cross. This may very well have been deliberately chosen in order to make a statement to the world about them:

"We are one community. We are the religious of Holy Cross. We have a common founder, heritage, and purpose. The Brothers cannot be co-opted by the diocese. The Sisters cannot be amalgamated to another community. We have a responsibility in love and in justice to each other. What we have come here to be we will remain — the priests, Brothers and Sisters of Holy Cross on the Indiana mission."

6

I Saw a Man! 1849–52

Mother Mary of the Savior arrived from Canada in July 1849. Mother Compassion remembered her as "a noble woman in every sense of the word . . . an educated lady . . . just and straightforward in her dealings."[1] The novitiate increased under her and the academy flourished. The schoolgirls began to wear uniforms.

Like the novices, the students followed a no-nonsense schedule. They rose at 5:25 for morning prayer and study, but got no breakfast until 7:30. From eight to ten they studied arithmetic and English, had a break at ten, and went back at 10:30 for lessons in penmanship, drawing, and French. Dinner at twelve was followed by recreation, then they went to needlework and more study from five until supper at seven. From eight to nine in the evening they had classes in Christian doctrine, and from nine to ten they were trained in vocal music. Then they had to get enough rest to be able to start all over the next day at 5:25. Piano lessons were available at ten dollars a term for anyone who could find the money, time, and energy to take them; by 1851 the Sisters had at least three pianos.

In 1850 it was decided that "the orphans should spend the vacation here and not go out as in the preceding years."[2] This may have been to the orphans' benefit; the phrase "go out" rather than "go home" suggests that the orphans may have been sent around as hired help to local farmers in the summer.

Also in 1850 there were enough German Catholics in the settlement of St. John, Indiana, that they requested Sisters to teach their children religion, English, and as much else as possible. St. John is in Lake County in the western part of the state, almost on the Illinois line and about twenty miles south of Lake Michigan. The priests and Brothers also sent missionaries to St. John. For the Sisters it was the first non-Indian mission in Indiana outside the Notre Dame–Bertrand axis. Sister Francis (Molloy) and Sister Antoine (Trement), a German-speaking novice, were the first ones sent. The mission had a somewhat tumultuous history during its twelve or thirteen years of existence, changing Sisters almost every year. The old chronicle records that "of all the priests, Brothers, and Sisters who went to St. John, Mother Compassion was the only one who remained in the community."[3] Some of those who left, however, followed other apostolic paths. Sister (Mother) Alfred (Moes) left from St. John in 1853 and founded first the Sisters of St. Francis of Joliet, Illinois, and second the Sisters of St. Francis of Rochester, Minnesota. Her sister, Sister M. Barbara (Moes) went with her, as did Sister Alberta (Stockoff) and Sister Bernard (Peacord). Sister Bernard later returned to Holy Cross.

As the academy grew, Mother Savior tried to make sure that the quality of the teaching kept up with it. Sister Compassion and postulant Mary Sheehan were sent to study "arithmetic" at Notre Dame, becoming the first of an uncounted multitude of Sisters of the Holy Cross to pursue higher learning there. The same council minutes (February 19, 1850) which record the opening of the mission at St. John also record the departure of Sister Emily (Rivard) and Sister Cenacle (Joanneault) to study music and drawing with the Sisters of Loretto in Loretto, Kentucky.

These last two accomplishments quickly became a necessity on the frontier. Pioneers felt that they were not so far removed from civilization if their women had some artistic training. The Sisters of Providence, on their way to Indiana in 1840, had stopped in Frederick, Maryland, as guests of Mother Rose White, first successor to Mother Elizabeth Seton.

> This venerable Mother was able to give them information, valuable if a little disconcerting, on the requirements of the American schools, "various sciences hardly known in our French schools, but . . . music . . . is the indispensable thing in this country, even for the poor."[4]

Their chronicler also notes that "[t]he Sisters were surprised everywhere by the fondness of the Americans for music, which in France in boarding schools was generally taught by 'masters.' "[5]

In New York, Mother Theodore had noted in her journal that "[t]hey give a brilliant education here, offering a number of little things that the Americans greatly admire, notably drawing, painting, music, and various kinds of needlework, embroidery, etc."[6]

The Saint Mary's Academy prospectus for 1849 stated that

> A daily line of stages running from Niles to [South Bend], and passing through Bertrand, forms the connection between the Michigan

> Central and Southern Railroads, and renders access to the Academy easy from all parts of the country.[7]

Two years later the Northern Indiana and Southern Michigan Railroad, later part of the New York Central, completed its line through South Bend to Chicago. This brought immediate increase in enrollment to both Notre Dame and Saint Mary's Academy. On January 6, 1851, Father Sorin also managed, through elder statesman Henry Clay, to open a Notre Dame post office separate from South Bend's, with Father Sorin himself (by now an American citizen) as postmaster.

In spite of growth and prosperity, a certain amount of nervous anxiety was always present among the Sisters. There was anti-Catholic bigotry in northern Indiana, and some of the French Sisters had seen the damage mob violence could do. "Rough men from the neighborhood would gather on the road . . . and . . . hurl vicious threats of destruction against the Sisters."[8] The girls were instructed to admit no one to the grounds whose identity could not be vouched for.

One day when Mother Savior and Sister Emily, the prefect, had gone into South Bend for some necessary shopping, the girls were having dinner, and, for a change, were allowed to converse instead of being read to.

> In the midst of the talk and laughter, a sudden shrill scream cut its way. Then one of the girls sprang to her feet, caught up the carving knife, and jumped over a long bench, crying, "A man is coming in the gate. Oh, what shall we do?" Pandemonium broke loose. . . . [T]he girls . . . rushed from the room, carrying knives, forks, pitchers, umbrellas, brooms. . . . Down the avenue they rushed, to shout wildly at the astonished man, "Go away! Go away!" He, poor fellow, convinced that the wayside hotel he had been seeking was really an asylum, turned and fled, leaving his hat for a souvenir. On the way down the road, he rushed past the carriage containing the superior and the prefect, who straightway took fright and drove home at what was breakneck speed [for] their old astonished horse.
>
> [When they arrived] the superior . . . told the prefect to call for order. . . . But dinner was impossible; the benches were knocked over, meat was on the floor, gravy flooded the table, and coffee dripped from every corner. . . . Mother Marie du Sauveur

demanded an explanation. All eyes turned to the girl who caused the alarm. All she could say was, "I saw a man!"[9]

So it was a relief for all when Joseph Nicholas Loupp proposed himself as a permanent watchman. Joseph had originally, like many of the Sisters, come from France. He had three major hates, in order of intensity: the English language, women, and interference with his work. (Apparently the Sisters and academy girls didn't quite count as women.) He signed his services to Mother Savior for one hundred years, and in return was given his keep, but no wages. Thereafter Joseph and his big dog brought a new feeling of security to the place. His duties included gardening, carpentry, care of the horses, and driving the conveyance, whatever it was at the time. When the Sisters moved to Saint Mary's, Joseph and his dog came along. He served for thirty-six years. When his strength slackened and a new gardener and carpenter were hired, Joseph declared that this was "too much cross" [10] for him to bear, and he died in the summer of 1887.

In November 1851 the priests' council decided that Father Sorin should make another trip back to France. The Sisters' reaction to this was submissive but regretful.

> The Rev. F. Supr. having communicated to the chapter the decision . . . concerning his journey, the chapter of the Sisters has in consequence been forced to submit to the decision, humbly begging of the R. Father to shorten his absence as much as possible.[11]

This time they managed to avoid Father Granger's refusal of permissions which had marked Father Sorin's previous absence by simply not holding any council meetings while Father Sorin was away.

Misunderstandings and complaints between Indiana and France had multiplied, and Father Sorin was going to France to address them in person. A Catta footnote informs us that "Father Sorin . . . had received from his chapter the 'charge to re-establish confidence by all the means within his power, but at the same time with full liberty to discuss separation as a last resort.'"[12] The American Sisters' archives have no record of this charge, and the Cattas fail to tell us where the quotation comes from. But it seems probable that the idea of separation from France, so earnestly urged a few years before by Bishop de la Hailandière, had begun to show certain advantages for both the men and women of Holy Cross, especially since by 1852 Bishop de la Hailandière was gone and there was no longer danger of being co-opted or amalgamated. Many of the religious congregations in the United States were in the process of becoming independent of their European origins.

We have already seen, for instance, Father Dujarié's Sisters of Providence. They had sent their original six Sisters from Ruillé in 1840 and later sent one more but with the understanding that she was the last. She was escorted by Father Sorin and the Brothers on the voyage in 1842. "A later communication from Father Moreau revealed to the Bishop that . . . no more Sisters were to be expected from Ruillé."[13] The Sisters would have to accept American postulants and become an American community as soon as possible.

By 1852 the Sisters of the Holy Cross were developing along the same lines. There were forty-two Sisters of the Holy Cross on the Indiana mission (not counting New Orleans or Canada). Of these, only twelve had come from France. Sixteen had been born in Ireland, five in Canada, four in the United States, two in Germany, one in England, and there were two for whom the records do not give a place of birth. To put it another way, 38 percent of the Indiana Sisters, or slightly more than half of the non-French, had been born in Ireland. The potato famine of the forties had just ended in Ireland. There is no special evidence that any of these Sisters had been present during the famine or had come to America because of it. But it was the famine more than anything else that developed in the Irish, at home and abroad, a dread of and a hatred for an outside authority, especially one from "over the water." In 1852 no Irish Sister was in a position of authority, with the exception of Sister Compassion, directress at Bertrand. But their numbers and influence would grow throughout the 1850s and '60s, and there would be two of them on the council when the final decision had to be made for separation from France.

Father Sorin's 1852 trip certainly included other places than Le Mans. One of these was Laval, and there Rosalie Pepin was introduced to him.

Rosalie Pepin had first heard of Holy Cross from her pastor, who had been briefly a member of the community in France, and then from Father Louis Baroux, C.S.C., who preached in her parish about his mission at Pokagon.

> The description he gave of those two French Sisters' labors among the Indians, the good they effected by their zealous missionary spirit, thus alone with savages thousands of miles from their native land, fired my young imagination with the desire of joining them.[14]

A few years later, in 1852, when she was serving as a substitute teacher at a convent school in Laval, Father Sorin came to Laval. She made known her desires and was accepted as a postulant, along with three other young ladies. Sorin seems to have omitted one pertinent bit of information.

> I do not think that he mentioned Le Mans as being the seat of the motherhouse, or that any reference was made to it. I was completely ignorant that any connection would or did exist with any part of France and my future destination.[15]

Rosalie describes her fellow postulants as "three fine, respectable, and intelligent-looking young girls. . . . Like myself, they . . . were *certain* that by going to America they were to labor at the conversion of savages."[16]

Father Sorin left them together, telling them to meet him at the hospital of St. Thomas in Havre de Grace a few days later. When they arrived, they found him just getting over a flu-like disease which gave him "such [a] languid, dejected countenance that different impressions of him took at once possession of each one's heart; in mine sprang love and pity which always remained."[17]

It turned out to be a good thing that she had this personal sympathetic affection for Father Sorin in the many disappointments ahead of her. This reaction was not shared by the other three, but before they left "he showed himself so kind and considerate to them . . . that they felt quite reconciled."[18]

They sailed May 2, 1852, on the *American Union,* a party of two priests, a subdeacon, a seminarian, and four young ladies dressed in dark clothing and calling each other "Sister." Father Sorin "was the only one able to speak English and to him we each had to go in all our needs as to a mother, and he acted as kindly as one."[19] The passengers were required to supply their own food, which Father Sorin had done, but "cups, glasses, forks, spoons and knives had been overlooked."[20] Most of their fellow passengers were German, many of them Jews. None of the fine, respectable, and intelligent young ladies could cook, so a German man was hired to do so for the party, and later a Jewish woman offered to bake unleavened bread so they could have Mass. When they began to sing Vespers of Pentecost (in Latin, of course), a large number of German Catholics joined them, and the captain came to see what the "uproar" was about.

Father Sorin prepared coffee for the group each day.

> He pretended to be a good physician . . . and could always tell which one was in need of the first cup; as we had but one, we had to drink in turn. The men were never found to be sick, so they had to wait [till] last; and if I was not always found to be the worst, I was always, by the physician's verdict, found to be the next worst, so that I never had long to wait. Poor dear Father! How unwittingly you spoiled me in those days, and how much I have suffered from it since![21]

In their conversations, Father Sorin never quite cleared up the question of their future. They asked him if the people among whom he worked would not be surprised to see "white people"; he turned the question aside. Miss Bourdais showed him babies' bonnets with saints' names pinned to them, and asked if she could give them to the first babies she baptized; he replied that she would be permitted to do all the good she could. One day one of the men told them indignantly that he had just learned that "they kill oxen at Notre Dame, and eat about the same food we do! If they live like that, I shall not stay with them! I shall go and live among the savages!" "And *so he did,*" adds Sister Euphrosine approvingly, "a few months after his arrival."[22] Another of the men was even less sophisticated; he was bringing a cage of birds, including two pigeons, "thinking they would be the first in America."[23]

It was when Rosalie Pepin asked him if she could keep Rosalie as her religious name that the connection to Le Mans was revealed. Father Sorin told her that Indiana could only give out names beginning with A through G. Canada had another part of the alphabet, and New Orleans had the rest, with the motherhouse using the names of mysteries.

Part of the time on the ship was taken up with English lessons; the voyage ended before any of the young Frenchwomen could pronounce "beseech thee."

The food supply ran low and the little colony had to put itself on rations. At times this was not a problem, as some of the company still suffered from occasional seasickness. In fact Mary

Mathais, one of the postulants, was suffering from something unnamed but much more serious. She died at Notre Dame before she could receive the habit.

> [Father Sorin's] charity and kindness to us were not short of heroism. I saw him holding the famous tin cup over a lighted candle until the liquid it contained would be warm enough to give to [the] sick [person]. . . . Then he would sit for hours reciting the thousand Hail Marys and whispering words of encouragement.[24]

Land was finally sighted on June 28 and the passengers disembarked the next day. Rosalie's trunk and a bundle of "fine new blankets" were lost in the baggage transfer and never seen again; her umbrella had already blown away in mid-ocean. Her first reaction to New York was, "It certainly did not look like a country peopled only by savages."[25] But they took consolation in the idea that a place called Indiana must surely be the home of the Indians. On a wharf "we saw a couple of young women smoking cigarettes, a thing we had never seen nor heard of; if it was not the beginning of savagery, it was at least, to us, the end of civilization."[26]

By lake boat, by immigrant train, by ordinary passenger train, and by stagecoach, they arrived at last in Indiana, the "land of our dreams."[27] It was Saturday, July 4, and they found the general air of festivity encouraging (not knowing they had arrived on a national holiday), until Mother Savior rushed out of the Notre Dame convent to greet them, crying, "Ah, my poor children, why have you come here?"[28]

The weary postulants remained overnight at Notre Dame and went on to Bertrand the next day. The closing exercises of the academy had been delayed until Father Sorin's return, and at the sight of "a dozen or more large, fine young girls dressed in white with their hair hanging down to their waists . . . my good little companions were so disappointed and surprised that Father had to be called for to console them."[29]

Brought up against the results of his deception, Father Sorin tried to explain that the color and culture of the people they were to work with should matter little as long as they were doing God's work. Under the circumstances, the postulants had perforce to be satisfied, but the disappointment rankled for years. Fifty years later, in Sister Euphrosine's memoirs, the bitterness crept out in the form of a jealousy which had developed in Bertrand and endured a lifetime.

> [T]he labors of every minute's time seemed to be needed from all of us, except Miss Bourdais, who . . . was in possession of her . . . patrimony. In handing it over, she made a request to be put at study. She shortly entered the Academy as a student, and from that time to the [time] she left, the second of July, 1892, i.e., forty years later, she was always, at all times, treated differently, with more favors than the rest of us.[30]

This is, of course, a very subjective judgment, and it should be noted, in fairness to Sister Arsene (Bourdais), that after many fruitful and respected years in Holy Cross, many of them as a general councillor, she left to seek a more penitential life and died a Trappestine in France.

The mission at Pokagon, which had originally sparked Sister Euphrosine's desire to serve, was closed in 1852, as the Indians were drifting into smaller and more widely scattered bands. Another mission was opened, perhaps imprudently. In an effort to answer as many calls as possible, Father Sorin allowed the new Sister Cenacle to open a mission in Mackinaw, Michigan, three hundred miles north. This was the same Sister who had already spent a year in Kentucky studying music and drawing. She was still a novice, but the measure of Father Sorin's esteem for her is his allowing her to have Mother Cenacle's name. With her went another novice to help teach and a postulant to do the cooking and housekeeping. One Brother was also sent to open a boys' school. At the end of the year, according to the chronicle, "Brother John and Sister Cenacle, instead of returning to Notre Dame, went off and got married. This scandal caused the establishment to be closed July 1853."[31]

The other novice in this ill-fated adventure was Sister Frederick O'Reilly, who had just received the habit, July 16, 1852. Five months later, on December 12, her father, Thomas O'Reilly, also received the habit of Holy Cross and the name Brother Alphonsus. In the final count he persevered, she didn't. Brigid O'Brien, the postulant housekeeper, died nineteen years later as Sister Angelica, the only one to live through the Mackinaw experience and remain in the community.

The glamor was gone from Rosalie Pepin's life, but she was

beginning the long hard path that eventually brought her to something better — self-knowledge.

> My obedience was to mend the stockings of the two places, Notre Dame and Bertrand, and to do the darning of the white linen. Quite a comedown from my evangelizing dreams!! That I was not happy, is most certain; and that I was jealous and envious of learning English, is equally so. I showed my feelings on my countenance and was disliked for it. My Mistress of Novices and Father Superior were kind to me, they seemed to understand and sympathize with me; but they did nothing for my improvement.[32]

Lent was early in 1853, and Easter came on March 27. A few days before, Rosalie Pepin and her companion Miss Nail were finally told to prepare to receive the habit. Long as the wait had seemed to them, Miss Bourdais, now studying at the academy, had to wait even longer; and Miss Mathais was dead. Rosalie went to the clothesroom and found Miss Nail searching for something suitable to use as a habit.

> We had not a single new piece of clothing except what composes the headdress and collar. Miss Nail's habit was a combination of [cotton] cloth, merino, and alpaca. The skirt of mine was from a grey marino dress dyed black, the waist from pieces of cloth, the sleeves from a black apron, and the cape from a black shawl. No black [under]skirt, mine was brown and white, no beads, no directory or office book, but a leather belt in which we could, if we wished, pass our five-decade beads.[33]

On that Easter all the Sisters put on the new fluted caps for the first time, and the blue cords. That afternoon Father Granger proceeded with the reception ceremony. Father Sorin arrived after it had started and, said Rosalie, "preached, we were told, a beautiful sermon, of which, being in English, I did not understand a sentence."[34]

> We went into the gallery [she continued] . . . put on the habit, and then came down to receive our names. Beautiful, great saints' names were at his disposal, which have been given since, but to us, the first postulants he himself had brought from France, he gave the names Eugenie and Euphrosine. Sister Eugenie consoled herself at not having received mine . . . and the following September I had

> the chance of consoling myself to have received mine instead of Arsene, which our . . . companion, Miss Bourdais, received.

It was dark when the community returned to the convent after the ceremony. Next day, Easter Monday, the two new novices received their obediences, Sister Eugenie as directress and Sister Euphrosine as assistant in a newly purchased house in Bertrand where the orphan girls were to learn "whatever we could teach them."

7
Here Will I Dwell All the Days of My Life, 1852

When Father Sorin returned from France in the summer of 1852, he found everything in Indiana in good order.[1] The school year started peacefully, but where Sorin and the men's and women's councils were concerned, the peace was soon shattered. On September 13 a letter arrived from Father Moreau commanding what was in their eyes the worst thing that could possibly happen — the departure of Father Sorin from Notre Dame and from the North American continent.

Father Sorin had been named superior of a new mission which Holy Cross was accepting in Bengal, and the plan was that he would eventually become bishop of Dacca (now Dhaka). He was forthwith ordered to wind up his affairs at Notre Dame, name a successor, depart for Bengal without returning to France, and report for duty there.

The easily reportable part of the story is simply told. Father Sorin refused the assignment. Father Moreau insisted. There was a prolonged struggle. Finally, after more than a year of correspondence and the arrival of an official Visitor at Notre Dame, Father Sorin submitted and went to France, prepared if necessary to continue to Bengal. But by then Father Moreau had at last reconsidered and Father Sorin returned to Notre Dame.

For the Sisters in Indiana, the fear of losing Father Sorin underlay the anxious weeks and months, at least for the council members (it is not clear that the other Sisters knew anything was going on). On July 15, 1852, the council consisted of Mother Savior, Sister Circumcision, and Sister Ascension. This group functioned until September 28, 1853, after which there are no recorded council meetings for over a year, until July 16, 1854. It was on these Sisters that the burden fell of trying to imagine their mission without the strong guiding presence of Father Sorin.

The matter was not simple. It concerned authority; it concerned finances; it concerned the complex personality of Father

Sorin and the overly rigid views of Father Moreau. It probably involved a difference in sense of mission and of the needs of an enormous developing country to which Father Sorin had committed himself, not just as citizen but as son, and the scope of which Father Moreau was never able to realize, even after he saw it. It concerned the workings of places outside of both France and Indiana, and it touched the ministries of many people other than Sorin and Moreau.

The three Sisters who made up the council received a letter from Father Moreau the evening of October 7, 1852, asking for suggestions as to a new ecclesiastical superior to replace Father Sorin. They seem to have reacted with a kind of controlled panic. They wrote at once, "this evening," to Father Moreau telling him that there was nothing they would not do[2] to get the order revoked. They were so anxious to impress Father Moreau with the necessity of leaving Father Sorin in place that they offered contradictory reasons, first dwelling on the toll taken of Father Sorin's health and resiliency by his "twelve years of hard work in the foreign missions," then pointing out the "misfortune from which the establishments in the United States" would suffer by the change. They deplored the consequences to themselves if Father Sorin should act from "a spirit of obedience pushed too far." This undoubtedly reflects on the quality of the religious training they had had (though all three had begun their training in France, and the motherhouse considered Mother Savior an outstanding religious and leader of religious). But their anxiety was genuine. They were really afraid that Father Sorin might go, and they saw this as a betrayal of the personal bonds between Father Sorin and themselves: "may they not think [speaking of themselves in the third person] that the attachment to them to which he has borne witness was nothing but a dream. . . ." It was much more unusual for a religious of the mid-nineteenth century to speak in terms of personal attachment for another religious (especially one of the opposite sex) than it would be for one of the late twentieth century. It was not a good argument, but it was a cry from the heart.

They felt that if the motherhouse could deal them this blow, its protestations of affection and concern were revealed as perfunctory and essentially meaningless.

"How could we believe that the motherhouse wished us well from now on?" [reverting to first person in their confusion]. They ended by begging Father Moreau to reconsider in view of their "fully justified feelings" and closed, they said, with profound respect and humility. Sister Ascension, as the one with the neatest penmanship, copied the letter and signed it as secretary. The letter is contradictory, abrupt, impertinent, frightened, and heartfelt. It is not defiant, as the Cattas try to make it. It gives no evidence whatsoever of having been dictated by Sorin or anyone else. A dictated letter would have been much better constructed and reasoned. This one was composed on the spot ("this evening") and mailed at once.

Father Moreau composed an answer to it as soon, clearly, as he received it. The Sisters' letter is dated October 7, as is a letter on the same subject from the men's chapter at Notre Dame. Father Moreau's reply is dated October 29, only three weeks later. If all dates are correct, the eastward bound vessel bearing the letters of the two chapters must have been helped by winds of almost hurricane proportions. Father Moreau addressed the Sisters as "my dear daughters" and proceeded to destroy their hopes. First, he informed them that he had not been consulting them as to Father Sorin's future. Second, he pointed out that "minor chapters" were not empowered to give advice to major chapters or major superiors, though they might offer their "respectful observations." Third, he told them that suggestions as to Father Sorin's successor were "the only point on which I was expecting you to express yourselves." It is hard to say from a point of view of a hundred and forty years later whether he was being firm but gentle or stiff and haughty.

He took up most of their rather hysterical objections and disposed of them quite reasonably. Unfortunately, utter reasonableness was not what the frightened Sisters on the American mission needed.

> Have you recalled [he asked them] what the Divine Master replied to his disciples, namely, that it was expedient for them, that He should deprive them for a while of His visible presence? Do you think that God will abandon you, because He deprives you of an instrument of His Providence, which He wishes to use elsewhere for the salvation of other souls? Would you really love God, and would you be showing toward Him the confidence inspired by simple faith, if you opposed a sacrifice which He is asking of you, and which, sooner or later, He will demand through death?[3]

Good theology, well reasoned, but somehow not going to the mark.

In contrast, Sorin reassured them by ignoring the existence of the problem and proceeding with business as usual. In early December he had to go by river to New Orleans. Just before the boat reached Louisville he wrote to Sister Ascension, the local superior at Bertrand. Sister Ascension had taken charge of an English class almost as soon as she arrived in the United States, so she must have had considerable preparation in English before she left France. He wrote to her in English.

> Louisville
> December 6, 1852
>
> My dear daughter,
>
> I was happy to find a moment of leisure to write a few lines before we reach a P office where I can mail news for St. Mary's.
>
> We left yesterday at 6 o'clock on the *Queen of the West* after a sojourn of three days. We saw the German congregation where I trust we shall soon have a new establishment for orphan boys and perhaps also for girls. Indeed it would give me much pleasure to see the Association once introduced in this [indecipherable]. However there is nothing yet of any definite character. But tomorrow I think we shall know it by a dispatch at . . . Evansville.
>
> On Thursday I took dinner with Father Badin and spent a few hours with him very pleasantly. He desired me to remember him to the Sisters at Bertrand and wishes to give them his likeness. On my return I shall call on him for it.
>
> I trust the health of my dear St. Mary's has now been improved to such a degree as to leave no uneasiness in your mind. Pray give my affectionate remembrance to all your good Sisters and pupils. I think of you all every day, nay, every hour. I would be delighted to find some letters from St. Mary's on our arrival at New Orleans or at least shortly after. My secretary must have written you but a few days past. He is now well also.
>
> We expect to reach the end of our journey in about six days hence. The wheather [*sic*] is very mild, even warm here.
>
> E. Sorin

Perhaps reflecting life on a riverboat, the letter is pleasant, calm, unhurried, and unworried. The mention of a possible expansion into a "German congregation" must have been most reassuring.

Father Sorin was apparently absent from Notre Dame for some weeks after the Bengal turmoil began, leaving the chapters of both men and women to contemplate the difficulties they would face in his permanent absence. He was back by early February 1853 and on February 10 wrote again to Father Moreau.

There has been a tendency among present members of Holy Cross, both male and female, none of whom ever knew Father Sorin personally, to see him in a bad light. No one denies that he did great things at Notre Dame and Saint Mary's. But there is an idea that he did them by demagoguery, dictatorship, trickery, sometimes ruthlessness, and an eye for the main chance. His religious spirit is called into question and there is a strong suggestion that he was more politician than priest.

Most of this seems to have arisen about fifty years ago, at the time of the community centenary, when all of the communities of Holy Cross were concentrating on the great objective of the beatification and ultimate canonization of Father Moreau. Unfortunately, the objective was sometimes pursued by tearing down anyone who may have looked like a competitor, anyone who may have opposed the founder; and chief of these was Father Sorin. It is no bar to canonization to make occasional mistakes in judgment, and Father Moreau's present-day followers must recognize that this occasionally happened. The error has been greatly compounded by the dependence placed by Etienne and Tony Catta, Father Moreau's chief biographers, on the life of Father Basil written by his nephew, Father Charles Moreau. Of this work Father Gilbert Français, fourth superior general of the men of Holy Cross, said that it contained "on every page regrettable insinuations, unwarranted assertions, unjust accusations made in a lamentable tone; and a patently absolute predetermination to admire and justify everything on one side and to depreciate and censure everything on the other."[4]

Two things are certain about Father Sorin: his work in America has been abundantly blessed, and the Sisters who knew him loved and revered him almost to the point of worship. There is nobody still living today who worked with him but there are many Sisters at Saint Mary's today who were mission companions of those who had known Sorin when they were young and he was old.

They can testify to the honor and love in which he was held. His own extant correspondence testifies to the gentleness, courtliness, thoughtfulness, and consideration he felt for them. But the later view has been that on the Bengal question, he was "disobedient." Legalistically this was so. Quite early in the dispute, on October 13, 1852, Father Moreau wrote, "If you are waiting only for a formal order from your superior, I command you, in the name and virtue of holy obedience." It is probably quibbling to say that the "if" clause in this sentence is inoperative because Father Sorin was *not* "waiting only for a formal order." (Though a legalistic claim deserves a legalistic reply.)

Father Sorin based his refusal on two points: first, that he was, according to the Holy Cross constitutions, free to refuse a bishopric; second, that the demand was unreasonable because it would ruin the work at Notre Dame. The second point has often been challenged because Father Sorin himself made a point of how well things were going at Notre Dame. The first question, then, is, would his absence really have ruined the Notre Dame mission? Father James Connelly, a Holy Cross historian who has turned much of his attention to Father Sorin, thinks that Sorin had a valid point. The priests at Notre Dame at the time were responsible for the budding "university," for circuit riding to bring Mass and the sacraments to scattered Catholics all over northern Indiana and southwestern Michigan, and for some of the personnel needs of New Orleans.

> To serve all these commitments there were in September 1852 only eight Holy Cross priests in the United States, including Sorin. One of them, Baroux, . . . [went] to France at the beginning of the month, whence he set out for Bengal in December. Baroux's departure had necessitated the closing of the Indian mission at Pokagon, Michigan, because there was no other priest available. Three others, Schilling, Shortis, and Voors, had been ordained that year and were inexperienced. Another, Fourmont, had arrived in the U.S. from France in the summer of 1852. He may not have spoken English. He certainly knew little of the United States.
>
> Father Cointet was sick in New Orleans. Father Gouesse had been assigned to New Orleans but in the fall of 1852 he was still in Canada. Moreover, when Moreau had named Gouesse superior in New Orleans in 1851, Sorin had vigorously objected and had re-

placed him with Cointet as soon as he could. Sorin knew what Moreau would learn only later, that Gouesse had a problem, probably alcoholism, which rendered him unsuitable as a local superior. Among all of the Holy Cross priests in the U.S., only Sorin, Cointet, and Granger had much experience of religious life and of pastoral ministry in their adopted country. Granger had spent his life in houses of formation and had already begged Moreau to leave him in that work, a plea which had been heeded. If Sorin were removed and sent to Bengal, who among these men would lead the Holy Cross community in the United States?

Sorin had become an American citizen by the end of 1850. He had come to the U.S. as a young man of twenty-seven. By 1852, he had been in the country eleven years. He had grown to maturity on the American frontier and he had made the Holy Cross mission in America his life's work. Now, at thirty-eight, he was being asked to start over again in another part of the world and in another climate. Admittedly this was a difficult thing to ask of a man. It was being asked of him, moreover, by a superior who himself had scarcely been outside of France. Sorin and the other Holy Cross religious in the United States could well have doubted that Moreau understood what he was asking.[5]

The question of the cost to Sorin personally is secondary but also needs to be looked at. In all of Sorin's references there is a suggestion of something beyond the ordinary in his attachment, his total dedication to Notre Dame. It began with a pre-attachment to America before he ever saw it. We can only understand him by taking quite literally, not at all metaphorically, what he wrote to Bishop de la Hailandière before he ever left France: "I no longer breathe except for my dear brothers in America. *That is my country,* that is the center of all my affections and of all my pious thoughts."[6] The day after he landed in New York he wrote Father Moreau: "This will be my part of the inheritance; it is here that I will dwell all the days of my life."[7] This was not just a quotation: this was a very literal statement of fact. Father Lemarié remarks, "[T]he first twenty-seven years of his life were like a time of exile for Edward Sorin. . . . He had *finally* found his homeland in the last days of the summer of 1841."[8]

He thought he had found the exact spot within the homeland when he arrived at Vincennes, but that total fulfillment was reserved to his second place of settlement, Notre Dame du Lac. Then the vow went into full effect: "Here will I dwell all the days of my life." Useless to try to move him. There was a mystical connection between Sorin and Notre Dame, and Sorin clearly believed that God was part of the connection. It seems presumptuous and futile for anyone today to try to deny it.

Was, then, the command unreasonable? There seems to be a good case for an affirmative answer. Religious are required to obey a formal command in all that is not sin; would it have been a sin to obey? Sorin claimed in his letter of January 10 that it would have been a sin of scandal and injustice. Is an unreasonable command binding? Father Moreau himself supplies the answer.

During the financial difficulties of the congregation in 1868, after Father Moreau had ceased to be superior general, Bishop Charles-Jean Fillion of Le Mans wrote to him:

> A formal order has been given to you, and you have not obeyed. You have not even seen fit to make known the reasons which courtesy as well as obedience make it your duty to manifest. Hence, you are either in open revolt or are a victim of an illusion which I find it difficult to explain.[9]

Father Moreau replied to this in a long letter of his own, of which the main point appears in two sentences.

> First of all [he told the bishop] not even legitimate superiors can command in virtue of the vows of religion except insofar as their orders inflict no grave harm on truth, justice, and charity. Now, in the actual circumstances, I could not obey without violating these three virtues.[10]

Father Moreau was giving the bishop the same reasons Father Sorin had given him, and he felt himself totally justified in doing so. This, of course, was sixteen years later. Had Father Moreau always known that such reasons were to be respected, or had he learned it, possibly from this encounter and others? It might be significant that in the same letter he lists eight causes of grievance against Father Sorin (who was then his superior general) but does not mention the Bengal matter.

The details of the settlement of the problem do not seem to have involved the Sisters much. The council members knew that Father Sorin continued to decline to leave Notre Dame permanently, though he was absent in New Orleans for part of the next several months. They knew that a Visitor came from France almost a year after the original letter had arrived, that an agreement was reached, and that Father Sorin went to France in November 1853 and returned to Indiana in January 1854. Readers interested in a detailed chronology are referred to chapters 32 and 33 in the Catta biography of Father Moreau.

But with the Sisters, especially the very influential Sister Ascension, there arose from this matter a distrust of the motherhouse which never quite died away and which made its way into the thinking of those who came later. And it was in the Bengal matter that the word "separation" first arose. Since it was in the end not the Holy Cross men in Indiana but the women who actually separated from the authority in France, the appearance and development of this thought needs to be followed.

8

This Question of Final Separation, 1852–53

Though Bishop de la Hailandière had his own ideas about the purposes and status of the Holy Cross Sisters, he had no objection to their making valid vows within the diocese of Vincennes. Nor did Bishop Le Fevre of Detroit object to professions at Bertrand. By 1853 thirty-six Sisters had been professed on the Indiana mission.

Permission for profession in North America had to be obtained from Le Mans. At first this caused no problem, but as the number of American postulants increased, the feeling seems to have grown in Indiana that Father Sorin, the Sister superior, and the members of the Sisters' council were better able to judge the suitability of candidates than a group of people in France who had never met nor seen the candidates.

Furthermore, the American members stayed on the Indiana mission. There was no constitutional reason why they could not have gone to France, Canada, or New Orleans, but with very rare exceptions, they simply did not. On the other hand, of thc total of forty-four Sisters who came to Indiana from France, only twelve died in Indiana. Most of the others went on to Canada or Louisiana, or returned directly to France.

Nevertheless, the idea of separation first arose in connection with the Holy Cross men. When Father Sorin wrote to Father Moreau on February 10, 1853, refusing quite clearly to go to Bengal, "after having faithfully reflected, consulted, and prayed," he also asked, in the name of himself and his chapter, that Father Moreau "would declare our majority for five years, at the end of which we will submit without fear into the hands of M. Heurtibize, along with yourself, this question of final separation or reunion."

Canon Heurtibize was a theologian attached to the cathedral in Le Mans. Father Sorin wrote to him as well. In addition, Father Sorin was in correspondence with the archbishops of Cincinnati, Baltimore, and New Orleans, all of whom replied with guarded negatives, advising caution and patience.

Sometime during March or April, probably earlier than later, Father Sorin also wrote the Most Reverend Maurice de St. Palais, Bishop Bazin's successor in Vincennes, requesting a temporary dispensation for himself and his community from their vows of obedience to the authority of Sainte-Croix. It is likely that this request was presented before Canon Heurtibize's reply, dated March 5, 1853, arrived sometime around the first of April. For the reply contained a shock that Sorin clearly had not foreseen. Heurtibize wrote: "If you separate, I do not see by what right you could continue to remain in a house which, as I see it, would cease to belong to you by the very fact that you would no longer belong to the Congregation of Le Mans."[1]

This was an authentic deciding argument. Sorin was putting on the line all that he had, including his vocation to Holy Cross, for the right to remain at Notre Dame. If this ultimate sacrifice should result in his actually having to leave Notre Dame, it would be counter-productivity both ironic and fatal. "Here will I dwell all the days of my life." If Sorin's will to fight was not destroyed by this letter, it must have been severely damaged.

The bishop replied April 30 with a reluctant, hypothetical dispensation. Father Sorin wrote to Father Moreau both in May and in June, both times mentioning the proposed separation, but leaving the threats vague and any concrete action utterly unmentioned. He may have been hoping to push Father Moreau into sanctioning the temporary separation, which would then have turned into a permanent one, and under which Sorin could have claimed that in giving the Indiana group their "freedom," Le Mans had also given them Notre Dame.

It didn't work, and by the time the Visitor arrived in September Sorin probably didn't want it to. He capitulated[2] and agreed to go to France for possible re-assignment. This was a genuine risk, though not as great a one as it would have been a little earlier. The Holy Cross missionaries to Bengal had arrived at their stations by that time and were getting along without him.

Two other considerations underlay Sorin's reluctance to leave Indiana. One was the problem of Father Gouesse. This young priest had already become a problem, through some unfortunate bad habit or set of bad habits, part of which, as Father Connelly has demonstrated, was almost certainly alcoholism. Sorin was adamantly opposed to even having Gouesse in his province, much less allowing him to serve as a superior anywhere. Sorin struggled with both Father Moreau and Bishop Blanc of New Orleans in his efforts to keep Gouesse out of any position of authority.

At no point, however, does Sorin seem to have named the problem plainly to either Father Moreau or Bishop Blanc. Perhaps confessional matters were involved. Sorin devotes several pages of the Notre Dame *Chronicles* to complaining about Gouesse, and again never states the exact nature of Gouesse's offenses, except that when Gouesse was in charge of New Orleans he remained completely out of touch with Notre Dame, never even reporting the deaths of religious.[3] That it is more than a personal matter is borne out by the fact that Father Granger and Father Cointet also wrote to Father Moreau commenting on Gouesse's unsuitability.[4]

Another fear in Sorin's mind seems to have been that a second and pro-French province might have been set up within the United States, with New Orleans and later New York as focal points. He was not seriously concerned with the strong French elements in Canada, with which he had little to do; Canada was, after all, a foreign country. But Americans (meaning residents, not only citizens of the United States) should, in his point of view, be striving to cast off the views, attitudes, customs and even languages of their countries of origin to become the people of the future, the Americans. His loyalty to his adopted country called him to remain on the spot and protest, where Holy Cross was concerned, the tendency to cling to the old.

Separation for the men of Holy Cross had become a dead issue. But the possibility had been considered. The issue had been awakened for possible application to the Sisters. Not only the Sisters of Providence, but women's communities all over the United States were separating from their European roots, or were being "re-founded" in America.[5]

Father Sorin eventually envisaged for the Indiana Marianites, or the "Sisters of the Holy Cross," as he was now beginning to call them, an autonomy from European supervision, but he seems to have had no vision of their ever achieving autonomy from his own supervision.[6] The Sisters themselves would have been terrified at such an idea. As he had become the most American of Americans (he became a citizen before 1850), and as he, correctly or otherwise, saw himself as the founder of the Sisters in America, he wished them to be a thoroughly American community. European-written constitutions would not suit them, even if the areas of difficulty were few and small.

To Sorin only two kinds of French Sister superiors were acceptable: the quiet, humble and subservient kind, and the bright and practical ones — Sister Ascension is one of the few examples — who were as eager to become Americanized as he was. The others, cut more to the pattern of the European superior, he simply got rid of. Sister Heart of Jesus, expelled to Canada for the crime of going to a doctor in Detroit (though Sorin readily agreed to Mother Cenacle's going to a doctor in Fort Wayne); Sister Calvary, sent to Lebanon for an unrecorded offense; Sister Five Wounds, sent to beg in France and then kept moving from Lebanon to New Orleans to New York in spite of her pitiful pleas to be allowed to come back to Notre Dame and talk with him;[7] Sister Immaculate Conception, who was actually Visitor rather than superior, though her Visitation lasted fourteen months; Sister Redemption, adored by the French in New York but unsuitable for Indiana. He seems to have truly loved and appreciated Mother Cenacle, but she died after nineteen months on the American mission. There are no recorded problems with Mother Savior, but she returned to France as soon as she could be replaced, after about two years. Mother Seven Dolors aroused his hostility, not in herself, but in her position. He saw her as the greatest threat to his own authority over the American Sisters. He objected to sending names of profession candidates to her in France, and when she moved to Canada, he flatly refused to send the names there. When Father Charles Moreau sent her the Indiana profession list in 1882, Sorin abruptly resigned as superior of the Sisters.

There is no way of knowing how much of all this was a conscious plan on the part of Father Sorin. But by the spring of 1853 it was clear that if the American Sisters were to become an indigenous group, they would have to have American leadership. Mother Savior had the Sisters praying for educated subjects. Father Sorin was praying for a good leader. The answer to all the prayers was at hand.

9

The One I Have Been Praying for, 1853–54

It was the morning of Easter Monday, March 28, 1853. The Sisters of the Holy Cross in Bertrand were donning and still covertly admiring the fluted caps and blue cinctures which they had worn for the first time the day before. The two new novices, Sisters Eugenie and Euphrosine, were beginning to adjust to the new names which neither of them liked. Father Sorin was probably addressing himself to his heavy correspondence, which had had to yield time to the observance of Holy Week.

In Lancaster, Ohio, Eliza Marie Gillespie and her mother, Mrs. William Phelan, were setting out for Chicago. Eliza came from a family of impeccable Catholic credentials, with American roots back to 1765.[1] In 1853 she was twenty-nine years old and well educated, with experience both in nursing the sick and in teaching children. She had decided that God was calling her to the religious life and had applied to and been accepted by the Sisters of Mercy in Chicago.

Eliza's brother Neal, six years younger, had been one of the first graduates (some sources say the very first) from Father Sorin's college in the wilderness. Now he was in the Holy Cross novitiate at Notre Dame, preparing for the priesthood. His letters home during his years at Notre Dame had mentioned the Sisters twice, once merely to relate what they did at Notre Dame and Bertrand, and later, when Eliza had decided to enter the convent, in a different and somewhat prophetic strain:

> I could say much more, my dear Sister, but I will wait until I see you. . . . I am afraid that the reason you did not choose at first to join our Sisters, is perhaps that my letter to you, some years ago, when I was a senseless youngster, may have tended to give you a very wrong impression of them. If you have not fully determined to become a Sister of Mercy, do not make any final arrangement, but wait until you have seen me here and have visited our Sisters.[2]

Eliza had no expectation of being deflected from her Chicago-bound path, but both she and her mother were eager to see Neal. They broke their journey at South Bend and hired a carriage to take them out to Notre Dame. Near the entrance to the college they met Father Sorin starting for town. He immediately recognized Mrs. Phelan, stopped his own carriage and theirs, and dismissed their driver. The ladies moved into his carriage, and he turned his "two beautiful cream-colored horses"[3] around and reentered the grounds, pointing out the sites of interest as they passed. Mrs. Phelan answered him politely, but Eliza was silent, gazing at the buildings. Some were of bricks made of marl taken from the local lake, some were of logs, all were spattered with spring mud, forming a contrast to the handsome buildings she had seen as a student at Georgetown Academy in Washington and as a teacher in Maryland.

Nor was Father Sorin's own mind entirely on his conversation. In the midst of the tour he suddenly turned to Eliza and said, "You are the one I have been praying for for so long." What reply would she have given? She was not called upon to frame one. They had reached the little Notre Dame post office and out of its door came Neal himself. Surprise, excitement, and greetings effectively changed the subject.

For the rest of the day, Eliza and Mrs. Phelan visited with Neal. That evening they met priests and professors and two Sisters, probably Sister Bon Secour (LeDuc) and Sister Patrick (McGookin), who showed them to sleeping quarters in the infirmary.

The next morning Father Sorin returned to the attack. While he was insisting and Eliza was resisting, her train for Chicago came and went from the South Bend station. Mrs. Phelan declined to take sides, though she later confessed to having thought that it would be ideal to have both her children in the same religious community. Eventually Eliza agreed to make a short retreat at the convent in Bertrand.

According to Mother Elizabeth's recollections, Father Sorin asked the Sisters to lend Eliza some suitable reading matter — one wonders what was considered suitable for a young lady who wanted to be on her way to another community — and that he also suggested that she spend her meditation time "in the chapel or in the garden or in the nooks along the river." Mother Elizabeth's recollections (she wrote her memoirs as a very old Sister) do not seem to allow for the fact that this was late March in Michigan, not a time for wandering in empty gardens or by thawing rivers.

> On the day the retreat ended, while Father Sorin was standing on the small stoop in front of the door giving some directions to the Mother Superior and to Sister Eugenie, he saw the ladies approaching. Motioning them to enter the house, he told Joseph to bring the carriage round in half an hour, that they might have time in which to say their farewells to the Sisters. Mrs. Phelan was greatly surprised when her daughter, instead of saying goodbye, knelt at Father Sorin's feet and asked permission to enter the community of Holy Cross.[4]

Eliza made one of the shortest postulates in the history of the religious life, somewhere between a week and ten days, depending on how long she had been on retreat. The records say that the new Sister Mary of St. Angela received the habit at Notre Dame on Sunday April 17, 1853. Considering the difficulties the Sisters had had three weeks before in putting together enough pieces to clothe Sisters Eugenie and Euphrosine, it could hardly have been much of a habit. She took it off the next day to begin a journey to France for her novitiate. Sister Emily (Rivard) accompanied her, also in secular dress.

After mentioning the reception ceremony, McAllister says, "In the meantime, Father Sorin received permission from the motherhouse to have the new postulant . . . make her novitiate in . . . France."[5] This is clearly impossible. Even if Father Sorin had sent off a message to France the day Eliza arrived at Notre Dame, it would not have been received at Le Mans by the time she left for France, much less would an answer have been returned. This was thirteen years before the Atlantic cable was laid, and seven weeks was a good time to get a message from Notre Dame to Le Mans and back. Eliza was on her way to France three weeks to the day after she left her home in Lancaster, Ohio.

It seems more likely that it had already been planned to send two Sisters to France. Sister Emily had been one of the first American Sisters sent away to study when she and Sister Cenacle (Joanneault) had gone to Kentucky in 1850 or 1851 to study art and music with the Sisters of Loretto. A talent for the kind of art that could be taught to academy girls — drawing, painting, fancy work and flower making — was highly prized in those days, and Sister Emily had it. After a year or so back in Bertrand, she was going to France, with a companion, to develop her talents further. Sister

Angela simply replaced the companion. In France she did not go to the motherhouse, which would have been the logical place for a new novice, but to the Good Shepherd monastery in Caen, where she learned sign language for teaching the deaf along with her spiritual formation. These facts, together with the whirlwind haste with which she was received into the community and packed off to France, all suggest that the travel plans had originally been made for someone else.

A few weeks after Sisters Angela and Emily left, another reception of the habit was held, this one in Bertrand. All the Sisters except Sister Euphrosine were in St. Joseph's Church for the ceremony on Sunday May 15, when a spring storm of unusual violence blew up. The convent was struck by lightning, taking off a part of the roof, and "rain fell in torrents into the building,"[6] which probably prevented a fire. After that the Sisters were favored with a peaceful summer.

In September, with the arrival of Father Pierre Chappé, the Visitor sent from Le Mans, Father Sorin's struggle regarding his Bengal assignment was concluded. Though Father Chappé found Father Sorin and his council totally opposed to Father Sorin's departure, Father Chappé received a different impression from that which prevailed in Le Mans. Things were "not as bad as he had expected."[7] Only the council knew that a problem existed; "outside of it, all was silence and peace." Perhaps he also felt the Spirit working, or perhaps he just knew Sorin well enough not to push. He kept his own calm, refrained from strong-arm methods, and prevailed. Two days after his arrival, Father Sorin unexpectedly submitted and agreed to go to Le Mans for possible re-assignment. It took him until early November to arrange affairs at Notre Dame satisfactorily.

There is no record of his having told the little community at Bertrand that he might not return, but a general uneasiness at his departure seems to have infected them all:

> It was rumored that their beloved Father was going back to France on special business. What would become of them without Father, who never failed to come every week, when all ran down to meet him. . . . [They suffered from] all sorts of imaginations . . . the greatest of all culminated by one of the larger girls crying, "Perhaps he will remain there for good, and then what shall we do?"[8]

Father Sorin came to Bertrand one evening to say that he was leaving the next morning for New York, to ask their prayers, and to remind them to be good while he was gone. " 'Yes, Father,' was the simultaneous cry, 'only come back!' His answer was by a look upward for a moment, and all knelt for his blessing."[9]

The story, of course, has a happy ending from the Indiana point of view. By the time Father Sorin arrived in Le Mans, Father Moreau had decided not to send him to the struggling Holy Cross community in Bengal. In all, five Holy Cross priests eventually refused the assignment as superior there, although only Father Sorin seems to have incurred the historical indignation of the community.[10]

In 1858, following the death of Father Vérité, the Reverend Pierre Dufal became superior in Bengal. His name was proposed for the vicariate of Eastern Bengal in 1859, and he was consecrated in Le Mans on the last Sunday of November 1860. He later served about twenty-two months as Father Moreau's first successor in the office of superior general.

Shortly after Father Sorin's arrival in France, Sister Angela and Sister Emily concluded their courses of learning in Caen and came to the motherhouse. Both made religious profession on Christmas Eve[11] at a ceremony presided over by Father Moreau.[12]

Father Sorin must have written to his council that he would be returning to Notre Dame and would leave France in January 1854. The Sisters in Bertrand knew that he and their two Sisters would be on the seas at the most dangerous time of the year, and they kept perpetual adoration in the chapel at Bertrand for the safety of the travelers. Sister Euphrosine writes:

> As we were so few, we could only go one at a time. On one occasion, Sister Francis left the chapel by the garden door, gave no notice of her leaving, and did not put out the burning candles. Through inspiration, doubtless, a Sister opened the door and saw the whole altar on fire. She called the Sister sacristan, who, at the sight of it, fainted, and thus left alone the poor young novice had to do the best she could. She, fearing to frighten the superior, who was sick, took a bucket of water and dashed it at the altar and succeeded in extinguishing the fire.[13]

The prayers were answered by the safe arrival, on February 2, 1854, of Father Sorin, Sister Angela, Sister Emily, and two new arrivals. Sister Mary of the Immaculate Conception (Prévert) came to make the regular Visitation from the motherhouse. She remained fourteen months, superseding the local superior, Sister Ascension, and "making a number of changes and dismissing several novices."[14] Sister Mary of St. Liguori (Chrétien) was assigned to Notre Dame as another clotheskeeper and seamstress. Within a few years she had become American provincial, and toward the end of her life she served a brief term as superior general of the Marianite Sisters in France.

The frightful discomforts of a winter voyage rendered the passengers freezing cold, soaked through, and usually seasick. Yet in the midst of all this Father Sorin and Sister Angela had found time for a lucid examination of the educational policies at Bertrand. Among other things, they were hoping to build up the music department. In this regard, the names of Mrs. Redman and Mrs. Lilly were mentioned.

Mrs. Harriet A. Redman, a widow, had been Eliza Gillespie's music teacher in Lancaster. She was descended from a family named Arnold, court musicians who had moved from Germany to England with the accession of the Hanovers to the English throne. Her daughter, Harriet Lilly, also a widow, was about Eliza's age, and the two young women were close friends. Like her mother, Harriet Lilly was a fine musician. Both women were converts to the Catholic faith.

Sister Angela suggested these two to Father Sorin as the nucleus of a new music department. With his approval, she wrote and invited both of them to come to Bertrand. It seemed to fit their own desires perfectly. They auctioned off their furniture, though their pastor mistakenly announced to his congregation that "a whole family was going to the convent and would give away their furniture."[15]

From their home in Lancaster, the two women went north to Columbus, bringing with them Mrs. Lilly's two children, Eddy, ten, and Edith, six. In Columbus they were joined by the Misses Amanda Anderson and Mary Caren, and by Mr. Thomas B. Ewing, a relative of Sister Angela's who would act as escort to the party. They arrived at Notre Dame on the evening of June 9, 1854. Mrs. Phelan, who was visiting her seminarian son, Neal Gillespie, was there to greet them along with Father Sorin. An animated conversation began over a serving of cake and wine. In the course of it,

Father Sorin looked out the window and remarked, "Here comes good Brother Vincent, a model of saintly obedience. There is something very singular about him for a Frenchman; he cannot touch wine, for it makes him very sick." But when Brother Vincent had entered and placed the mailbag on the table, Father Sorin startled the ladies by pouring a glass of wine and giving it to Brother Vincent with the words, "You must drink this to pledge these ladies, that they may always remain with us." The Brother paled, but bowed to the visitors and raised the glass to his lips, whereupon Father Sorin took it from him before he could taste it, put it back on the table, and said, "Thank you, Brother, that is all. You may go now." When the Brother had left the room, Father Sorin turned aside Mrs. Redman's indignant protest with the explanation that he had merely wanted them to see an example of perfect obedience.[16]

The next day, after a tour of Notre Dame conducted by Neal Gillespie, the party went to Bertrand. A few weeks later, Mrs. Lilly was accepted as a postulant, while her mother took charge of the children and taught music to support herself and them. Mother Elizabeth (as Harriet Lilly became known in Holy Cross) outlived every other member of that day's party, including her own two children, both of whom became religious of Holy Cross.

By the time Harriet Lilly entered it, the novitiate had probably been moved back to Notre Dame. Bishop de St. Palais had no objections to the location of the Sisters' novitiate in his diocese, and Sister Immaculate Conception, the appointed Visitor from France, had found the novitiate too closely connected with the academy in Bertrand. The council minutes for 1854 do not record the date of the move and the old memoirs disagree wildly, but one thing all the diarists did remember: when the novitiate went back to Notre Dame, it was, on the orders of Sister Immaculate Conception, very strictly enclosed, in a fenced-off corner of the property, with a grille in the parlor. Sister Ascension became mistress of novices, since Sister Emily could not be spared from her classes at the academy.

When Sister Immaculate Conception concluded her Visitation and left to take over a superiorship, probably at LaPorte, Indiana, in 1855, Sister Angela became religious superior in Bertrand in addition to her duties as directress of the academy. Sister

Ascension held the title "Mother Superior" and presided at the council meetings.

Years later, Mother Compassion, a young Sister in those days, remembered Mother Angela as superior:

> Sister M. Angela was very much loved by the Sisters and pupils. She was sunshine to all. Full of zeal and fervor, she imparted her spirit to others. She was very mortified, ready for any kind of work, and when we had to sleep on the floor she rejoiced over it. One morning she was called away before she had time to gather up her bed, and, as the beds had to be put away before the workmen came, a Sister in putting up her bed found a package of nettles in a thin cloth, one of the many ways she had to mortify herself. The children loved her very much. She was very kind and had the gift of gaining hearts. She tried to inspire all with the love of God and to do all for him.[17]

Mother Compassion continues into a matter for which Mother Angela has been both praised and blamed.

> Mother Angela regarded Very Rev. Father General [Sorin] as God's representative and obeyed him as such, and taught all her Sisters to do the same. No matter how much it cost her or how different her opinion was, as soon as she learned his will she submitted to it without a murmur. All who knew her intimately knew how much it cost her when, later on, the novitiate for manual labor Sisters was opened at Notre Dame. She silently submitted but it crushed her.[18]

These are the words of a wise community elder, written when Mother Angela had been dead five years and Father Sorin was in the last year of his life. Mother Compassion obviously regrets the pain occasionally caused to Mother Angela by her lifelong loyal seconding of Father Sorin. But her words do not suggest that she would have had it any other way; she herself, after all, was one of the Sisters who were "taught to do the same." Angela's was not a blind and dogged following; it was the devotion of a fine intelligence and a disciplined will to the one whom she saw as the mediator of the voice of God. It was, in fact, very similar to the devotion that Mother Mary of the Seven Dolors accorded Father Moreau. For this Mother Seven Dolors has been rightly commended, while Mother Angela has been questioned and attacked, sometimes by her own spiritual daughters. Those who find a holiness in Mother Seven Dolors which they judge to be lacking in Mother Angela should consider the identity of approach with which each came to her duties.

10

The Marsh between the Lakes, 1854

Harriet Lilly received the habit of Holy Cross July 23, 1854. Sister Immaculate Conception was still in charge, and for once Harriet's musicianship deserted her.

> She trained us for the ceremony, and the singing belonging [to it], having a loud voice. . . . For my part, I forgot, in the importance of the great step, all about singing.[1]

There were other reasons besides the importance of the step why the new novices were sadly distracted. Their retreat was barely opened on July 18 when Barbara Wurtz, a postulant not yet eligible for the habit, was stricken with violent pains and died within hours. The next night a thirteen-year-old apprentice at Notre Dame was found dead by his own father, who had come to visit him. Two days later two students died, and a day after that, in a death unrelated to the epidemic, a Brother drowned in the lake. The Bertrand Sisters hastened back to Michigan at the close of the retreat, but the specter followed them. Sister Aloysius Gonzaga (Rivard), a sister of Sister Emily, died August 15. Sister Dominica (Feagan) died three days later. Sister Antoine (Tremant), a novice, died August 29.

The epidemic continued into September. Father John Curley, C.S.C., a young Irishman ordained only one year, died September 7. Sister Anastasia (Byrne) died at Bertrand September 9. Five Brothers and three Brother postulants died, and another student, and a priest postulant.

> Notre Dame was one vast hospital, in which there were few who were not patients, but those who were not so bad helped to take care of the others, whose suffering cannot be described. It was called the epidemic or plague, and seemed to be a combination of dysentery and typhus fever, though some thought it was nothing less than the cholera, which was at that date prevalent in the United States.[2]

The worst was yet to be suffered.

> Ten days after the burial of Fr. Curley, Fr. Cointet himself fell sick on his return from a mission. It would be useless to attempt to describe here the fears, the terrors and anguish of the whole house during the eight days of his illness. . . . To preserve such a precious life, each one in the house had considered it a duty to offer his own life; but God willed this great sacrifice.[3]

It was the greatest loss the American community of Holy Cross had suffered so far. Finally, on September 21, Miss Mary Morris, a postulant assigned to work at Notre Dame, became the last one to die in this phase of the epidemic. Cooler weather came, and the sickness receded, but those who had contracted the illness and survived were many weeks returning to their normal energy. "Survivors looked more like skeletons or the walking dead than living men."[4]

Bigoted neighbors suggested that their fundamentalist God was showing his wrath at the Catholic institutions among the Indiana and Michigan farmlands, ignoring the fact that there had been a nationwide outbreak of "cholera." The Indians warned against a kind of poisoned fish in the local lakes. Some blamed the drinking water. "The greater number, and they were the people of most sense, attributed to the marsh between the lakes . . . the first cause of all the illnesses."[5]

The obvious solution was to drain the marsh, but the drainage path lay through land west of Notre Dame owned by a Mr. Rush. This man had dammed the St. Joseph River in such a way as to force the back-up between the lakes. Father Sorin had tried to buy the land, but Rush was demanding $9,000 payable in installments impossibly close together. Negotiations were discontinued.

Meanwhile the American Sisters had become a definite majority in the Indiana community. In Bertrand there were twenty-three Sisters, eighteen American (many of Irish birth) and five French. At Notre Dame there were twelve American and three French, plus a fluctuating number of American postulants which averaged about fifteen. Of the three French Sisters at Notre Dame, one worked in the washhouse, one in the clothesroom, and one was in charge of the infirmary. Thus the council minutes for October 19, 1854, note:

> Sister Marie de la Misericorde, sent from the motherhouse to be directress of the kitchen at Notre Dame, not being able to discharge

> this employment on account of the language, having no French Sisters with her, had on her own request been sent to Bertrand, where this difficulty was removed.

About the same time three Sisters were sent to Michigan City, Indiana, to take over from one Brother who had been teaching the children of the Irish and German railroad laborers. In a short time they had over seventy pupils.[6]

The habit was given on five different occasions in 1854, to a total of twenty-three novices, and during the year eight Sisters made their profession, four of them in July. This would have been a group of six except that Le Mans refused the professions of Sister Eugenie and Euphrosine, two of the French postulants whom Father Sorin had brought over in 1852. They had learned of the existence of the French motherhouse only when they were in mid-ocean. Now they were being asked why they had not entered properly through Le Mans. "Father Superior Sorin," says Sister Euphrosine in her memoirs, "whose order we had simply obeyed, had to give whatever excuse he could on the subject."[7] The French Sisters made profession in November, not knowing that their ceremony was historic because of the single postulant who received the habit that day. She was Amanda Anderson, who had come with the Lilly party from Lancaster, Ohio; and she became Mother Augusta, the first superior general of the Sisters of the Holy Cross.

Meanwhile, at the same time that the Bishop of Vincennes had become more friendly, the Bishop of Detroit had become less so. He would no longer allow Father Sorin to be confessor to the Sisters at Bertrand, and for undisclosed reasons he disapproved of the removal of the Sisters' novitiate to Notre Dame. Father Sorin was therefore looking for someplace on the Indiana side of the state line where the novitiate and academy could again be located together. Mishawaka, a small town east of South Bend and not too far from Notre Dame, looked like a possibility. It was decided to begin by moving the orphans and other dependent children to a house which could be purchased there. This move was effected December 8, 1854, and the place became known as the Manual Labor School. Sisters Augusta, Liguori, and Bethlehem made the move with the children. (Also, on that day, in Rome, the doctrine of the Immaculate Conception was promulgated.) In Mishawaka, a three-story hotel was purchased, fitted up for school purposes, and named Holy Angels Academy. Sister Circumcision left her duties as head of the students' infirmary at Notre Dame to become directress; Sister Euphrosine constituted the entire staff.

At Christmas of 1854 Joseph the handyman made a sled out of a wooden box nailed to runners, and in this contraption Sister Angela went to Niles to purchase small treats for the Sisters and students. It was a memorable Christmas in Bertrand, perhaps made more so in retrospect by the fact of its being the last one.

The Manual Labor School had been in its new home less than three weeks, and Christmas had barely gone by when the disease of the summer before returned to claim Sister Bethlehem. She died December 30. She had gone to Mishawaka as her first and only move from Notre Dame since arriving there as one of the original four in 1843. For all but one of those eleven years she had had charge of the cows, pigs, and chickens. "She would sooner have deprived herself of the necessaries of life than allow one of those animals to suffer. . . . She was constantly speaking affectionately to them."[8]

There was sickness in the area all winter. Father Sorin, convinced that Mr. Rush's dam in the ravine was a major contributing source, intensified his efforts to buy the Rush property.

With the first spring breezes of March 1855 the illness reappeared. On March 15, Louis Devos, a 25-year-old priest novice who was teaching at the college, a man "of great talents and of much promise"[9] died at Notre Dame. Two weeks later Brother John of the Cross (King) became the next victim. But the day after Brother John's funeral, Mr. Rush came forward and offered to sell the property for $8,000, payable in four years. After four days of negotiations, "all the papers had been signed by both parties and nothing remained but to exchange them."[10] At this point Mr. Rush abruptly broke off the negotiations and left town. It was Wednesday in Holy Week.

Enough was enough.

> On Thursday morning, before mass, Fr. Sorin sent for five or six of his stoutest men with strict orders to listen to no one and to tear down the dam; they were especially charged to answer anyone who might attempt to stop them that they received no orders from anybody except their master and that the land was his. Never was an order more promptly carried out.[11]

Mr. Rush returned and went through with the sale. The property now belonged to the religious of Holy Cross. On April 24 Father Sorin walked the one mile from Notre Dame, past the ravine through which the stagnant water had already flowed freely into the river, and formally blessed the property. It is now the site of Saint Mary's General House and College.

In May at least one of the Mishawaka buildings was removed to the Rush property and the Manual Labor School took up residence. Holy Angels Academy was absorbed by Saint Mary's Academy. Their short period in Mishawaka had not been happy, and the Sisters especially must have been glad to get away from the scene of Sister Bethlehem's sudden death. Thus it was that the novice Sister Augusta, later first superior general, and her co-worker Sister Liguori, later superior general of the Marianites, became the first Sisters to reside at what is now Saint Mary's, Notre Dame.

The last school year at Bertrand was coming to a close. On one otherwise pleasant evening, Father Sorin announced that he was bringing several professors from Notre Dame to examine the graduates next day. It is reported that the evening study hall was a model of decorum, as the young ladies crammed furiously. Next morning when the carriage from Notre Dame rolled onto their avenue, the whole school knew it at once, including the deaf students, across whose blackboard someone quickly scrawled, "College men here."[12]

Father Sorin went to examine the music himself (Mother Elizabeth, the music teacher, whose memoirs relate this day in great detail, would especially remember that) while the other examiners went together to the graduates' classroom. They started with math problems, done on the blackboard, a different problem for each girl, and Professor Denis O'Leary found the students so proficient that when noontime came they were still doing math. They stopped for a turkey dinner, at which everyone watched "to see that Mr. O'Leary should carve the turkey numerically." Examinations continued in the afternoon, beginning with history, at which students "were deprived of the small assistance of even passing from one Reign to another; questions were asked without connecting links." At the end of the day the visitors had one warning for Father Sorin: " 'You must arm yourself well,' " they told him, " 'against being too proud of your dear children.' Father's eyes sparkled with pleasure."

There was a final play, a gypsy thing with "large bushes from the woods near, and grass scattered thickly on the floor," in which "the imagination of the audience no doubt filled out what was wanting in the scenery."

There remained the commencement ceremonies, presided over by Bishop Joshua Young of Erie, Pennsylvania, another old family friend of Angela's. Here they either started or continued a Saint Mary's tradition — the ceremony was held outdoors, and it was rained on. Saint Mary's is still holding graduations outdoors, and they are still being rained on.

In July the Sisters went to Notre Dame for retreat, then returned to Bertrand. It seems incredible that they did not know they were to move, but that is the way Mother Elizabeth remembered it.

> Of course all worked to prepare and beautify, according to our poverty, the house and grounds, when to our surprise Father Sorin announced we should pack up and prepare to move to the then small clearing of ground . . . on the river embankment, still surrounded by forest trees; that all of the buildings were to be moved, whole or in parts, by ox teams from Michigan into Indiana; that Brothers Stephen and Lawrence, with carpenters, would begin next morning to haul away the first cleared out.

The flabbergasted Irish Sisters "would not believe houses could be moved in America or any country," and were offended at what they thought was a joke at their expense. But when the teams arrived and the buildings began to disappear down the road, they "began to think it might be true, but Americans were certainly queer people entirely."

The Sisters in Bertrand crowded into smaller space and tried to find time for such regular summer tasks as gardening, preserving, and jelly-making.

On August 15 the whole community went to Notre Dame to celebrate the great feast of the Assumption. The four youngest had been left behind because there was no room for them in the wagons, but they hitched a ride with a neighbor and turned up in time for Mass. (Recall that Mass in those days was necessarily before breakfast.) After several Masses and dinner, there were processions around the grounds, singing hymns at and between the various chapels and shrines, and then Vespers. Finally, as the other

Sisters were preparing to go back to Bertrand, Father Sorin escorted Mother Angela and Sister Euphemia along the path across the fields to Saint Mary's.

> The original Rush property covered a site of 185 acres lying west of the college [Notre Dame] on the bank of the St. Joseph River. . . . It covers a magnificent plateau bounded on the south by the river, at a depth of seventy-five feet, and on the west by a rich prairie almost at the ordinary level of the waters of the St. Joseph.[13]

Its advantages are listed by Sister Emerentiana as

> the health of the congregation, the cultivation of some thirty of the richest acres around the college, the monopoly of the chalk and marl, a most valuable water privilege, and finally a beautiful site for the Sisters.[14]

By this time two buildings had been moved from Mishawaka. One, known as the brown house, was to be the residence of the first Sisters who would come from Bertrand, but it was still unfinished and only one room was plastered. The other was the Manual Labor School across the ravine, where Mother Angela and Sister Euphemia spent the night.

Next day they went back to the brown house and began the task of following the plasterers and carpenters, scrubbing floors and washing windows as the workmen moved on. By the third day a pair of beds and rudiments of other furniture were brought in, and they took up residence. Gradually the twenty-five Sisters from Bertrand began to arrive, along with some of the boarders who had spent the summer at school. The building where the deaf students lived and were taught (which had started its existence as a chicken coop) came from Bertrand, and its occupants with it.

The money for the moving and improvements came chiefly from a fund provided by Mr. and Mrs. William Phelan, the mother and stepfather of Mother Angela and Father Neal Gillespie. They had signed over extensive property in Ohio to the congregation, in return for Father Sorin's assuming certain mortgages and meeting other easy conditions.[15] When the little building that had served as a priest's house at Bertrand was moved to Saint Mary's, the Phelans occupied the front two rooms, while Mrs. Redman and her grandchildren had the two in the rear.

As Bertrand was abandoned, the bigots among the neighbors fell on the ruins

> to find the *secret corners* . . . as they hoped . . . peering into cupboards formed in the walls and sounding the remaining partitions . . . going down to the bottom [where they] found only a few potatoes, instead of underground horrors. . . . [They were greatly disappointed] to find this mysterious convent to be like ordinary houses, not even a chain . . . [to] bind a delinquent nun . . . nothing to create their alarm of "Popery revealed."[16]

Chickens, pigs, cows, barns and stables were moved, Joseph and his house and dog. At last nothing was left to come. The original convent building, a thousand feet from the church, was not demolished, and must have been quickly occupied by someone, possibly the pastor. It remained in good repair and is still standing and occupied today (1993).

The displaced buildings afforded shelter and not much else at first. The boarders slept on a floor above the Sisters, washing in tin basins set along a bench. As the floorboards did not fit together, this wash water often dripped down on the Sisters' pallets. At first the new plaster was still wet, and the Sisters set out buckets to "gather the damp."[17] Mother Elizabeth makes a proud point of the fact that no one took cold.

By the end of the first week of September, 1855, the new location, while far from finished, had reached a stage of sufficiently decent occupancy that they were ready for the ceremony that was at once climax and inauguration.

> By the Feast of the Nativity [of the Blessed Virgin, September 8], we made preparations for a high Mass. A large empty room on the second floor had been scrubbed. The old Bertrand altar was dressed with flowers and homemade tallow candles, with two small ones of wax near the tabernacle. We had borrowed Mr. Gillen's squeaky small melodian. De Monte's grand Mass had been practiced by the choir, and . . . Edward Lilly played the violin cello, thus supplying chorus and base solo parts. Mrs. Redman played and her daughter led the choir. Sister Angela and Mary Sweeney (afterwards . . . Sister Columba), Miss Fitzpatrick and Miss McDonald were the main soloists, and a full chorus of voices trained by note. Father Sorin sang the Mass, and preached one of his animated ser-

mons, and then intoned the *Te Deum*. Reverend Father Granger and his seminarians alternated with all the Sisters in this heartfelt expression of thanksgiving, while tears of gratitude flowed.[18]

Later that day, Mother Angela handed out the Sisters' assignments for the new academy — teachers, prefects, dormitorians.

Before the end of 1855, the academy held sixty boarders and thirty Sisters. In December the novitiate's quarters were habitable, and the postulants came over from Notre Dame. Also by December the Manual Labor School had been enlarged to accommodate thirty students and their teachers.

Saint Mary's Academy, Notre Dame, had become a living thing. It stood on the edge of history, looking forward.

11

Thinking I Was Coming to Certain Death — New Orleans, 1849–52

The troubles which revolved around New Orleans and New York in the early fifties were central to the separation of the Indiana Sisters from the motherhouse in France. Although they are well documented, there is such a strangeness about them that from a distance of a hundred and fifty years it is difficult to see into some of their aspects. The situation turned on four cogwheels — the attitude of Father Sorin, the problem of Father Gouesse, the desires and understandings of the Sisters, and the disastrous Visitation by Mother Ascension and her companions in 1855.

Certain facets of Father Sorin's character stood him in good stead in an attempt to build a university in the wilderness, minister to the settlers and Indians, administer the affairs of a rapidly growing community, and deal with a varied group of pioneer bishops. But some of the same qualities occasionally took over his whole personality, and Sorin himself fell victim to them.

He could not bear to feel he had been cornered or placed in a situation where he had no alternative. This may, for instance, explain his unduly harsh treatment of Sister Heart of Jesus when she went to consult a doctor in Detroit. If she had been denied the permission before Sorin left for Europe, and then, under the shadow of Father Badin's encouragement, had nevertheless made the trip while Father Sorin was away, he would have felt that he had been disobeyed, crossed, thwarted, and presented with an accomplished fact — and the anger and punishment followed.

Sorin also had a stubborn persistence of bulldog proportions that tended to become more stubborn when it was opposed. The simple fact is that he *did* have better judgment, most of the time, than most other people, and it was a judgment backed up by a tremendous faith, the "priceless spirit of faith" that he endlessly recommended to his religious.[1] So even on the occasions when he was wrong, he was incapable of perceiving his errors and felt that an attack on his decisions was an attack directed against both Sorin and God. He was not the only religious superior in history to suffer from that delusion.

Third, his strong, almost mystical loyalty to his new country could run away with him. He believed that everything in America should be American and that religious houses in America should be governed by those residing there. In the case of Holy Cross houses, this meant himself; but to be fair to him, he also intended it to continue beyond his own lifetime or capability. This attitude was fully supported by the "American" (mostly Irish) recruits in the north; but the religious in New Orleans were mostly French, and they felt as strongly about remaining French in that very French city as Sorin did about turning them into Americans.

The religious who left Lebanon, Kentucky, went down to New Orleans without returning to Indiana. They arrived by river boat May 1, 1849, and immediately applied themselves to bettering the conditions of the children in St. Mary's Boys' Orphan Asylum. An Irish priest, Father Adam Kindelon, had founded the establishment in 1835, and it had grown and then declined under a succession of administrators. By the spring of 1849 the children were living in "most frightful misery."[2] The five Brothers and three Sisters took hold.

> [E]very morning a Brother went out with a cart to beg from the hotels the leftovers of the day before. The collection was thrown pell-mell into large paper bags, and often included, besides the bread, meat, and vegetables so badly needed, a fair amount of fruit skins, cigar stubs, and an occasional knife, fork, or dishtowel. But this food, properly cleaned and well presented, was their "first sizable resource."[3]

When the local people saw that the orphanage was being capably administered, their gifts began to arrive. At the end of the first month Sister Mary of the Five Wounds could write to Father Sorin that they were already seeing changes for the better. She says in the same letter that she has been hoping that a Sister directress would come with the Brothers and that she cannot in conscience hold that responsibility. She suggests that Sister Mary of St. Anne and Sister Mary of the Compassion be sent, and asks Sorin to remember that it is important that they have only Sisters "who know how to support one another," "in view of the fact that we depend on an administration in a foreign country."[4]

In August she wrote again. "Everything concerning temporal affairs seems to grow and develop satisfactorily," she said. Some of her fears of the place had not materialized.

> I tell you frankly that . . . I only accepted this mission of New Orleans thinking I was coming to certain death, which is what they told us at St. Mary's [Kentucky]. But, to my great astonishment, I still feel perfectly well, and I have been only slightly bothered by the heat.[5]

But then obscurity descends on her language. Immediately following the last sentence above, she continues:

> So it is that I find myself in the presence of the difficulties which I foresaw, and which I feared too much to try to challenge them. God grant that He may soon deliver me from them!

Sister Mary of Calvary, who suffered intermittently from malaria, "has been a little better, and then for the past two days she has become worse." Apparently the state of Sister Calvary's health occasionally became a source of irritation to Mary of the Five Wounds. In January 1850 her comment was tart, not to say catty.

> Sister Mary of Calvary is in the kitchen. . . . One day she is fairly well . . . and another day she feels she will probably die before spring. However, you know quite well that she has never done anything she said she would do.[6]

Sister Five Wounds tells Sorin of the proposed new addition on the house and mentions casually that of course that means they will need four or five more Sisters. And then another six for a project suggested by a Father Jackson, which would be "supported by the state" and "would not present the problems of poverty, which never fail . . . to cause much concern." Almost as an afterthought, she observes that the project includes a novitiate for the Brothers and one for the Sisters.

Through this first year, Sister Mary of the Five Wounds, though she deplored the task, seems to have served as superior of the Sisters, with Brother Vincent in charge of the Brothers and Brother Theodulus administering the orphanage. Having to go outside the institution for Mass and the sacraments added to the difficulties of the religious, and there was constant illness in the house among both the religious and the children. "As there was no priest attached to the house, they lived in constant fear of dying without the sacraments."[7]

They saw the solution as having a Holy Cross priest for superior, but, as has been pointed out, Holy Cross priests were not thick on the ground anywhere in North America. In the late winter of 1850, however, Sorin sent young Father Gouesse as Visitor. On first sight, he met with Mary of the Five Wounds' enthusiastic approval.

She wrote to Sorin on May 4, 1850, that Gouesse had started by giving them a little retreat and that he "was quickly brought up to date on my uncertainties past and present on the subject of my vocation."[8]

The report of another Sister was somewhat different. Sister Mary of the Angels (Couillard or Conyard) had been one of a group who accompanied Father Gouesse on the river journey. By the time they arrived she was worried, but she acknowledged that Father Gouesse had been well received by the community in Louisiana.

> He seemed to me to have the general affection of the members here; I think that each one will readily submit to all these decisions. He asked us for our obediences; after having read and reread mine, he said in front of all the Sisters that he didn't understand it, which produces a singular effect. . . . I think the needs of the sick are enough to keep one person busy. I am thinking of submitting it[9] to you. Sr. M. of the Nativity was always in charge of it till now.[10]

Having said that much, Mary of the Angels apparently decided to tell Sorin a few more things about the new chaplain.

> With reference to the action that P[ere] G[ouesse] took toward me during our trip, it was extraordinary; my companions noticed it, and . . . were shocked by it. He showed a coldness, an air of contempt with a certain mistrust. . . . When I absolutely had to say a few words to him, he never answered the first time; it was necessary to repeat and he often made me no answer at all. . . . He was very friendly with my companion, and showed a great confidence in Sister Mary of St. Agnes. . . . On several days he paid us a visit, without addressing one word to me, always speaking English.
>
> [I]f P.G. had the shadow of an idea that I was going to make known to you what went on in his conduct . . . I would be putting

myself in such a false position that it would not be tenable. I have no doubt that you will understand it. . . .

In the end, Sister Nativity was left in the obedience with the sick, "according to the feelings of the Sisters," remarks Mary of the Five Wounds.[11] Little was found for Mary of the Angels to do but fill in wherever useful; hers seems to have been the only obedience from Sorin that Gouesse changed.

> Father Gouesse [wrote Mary of the Five Wounds] has not wanted to change anything that you yourself had set up . . . except the stewardess, Sister Mary of the Angels, who cannot just at present be of any use because of the measures which have been established.[12]

One wonders if those measures were established precisely to keep Mary of the Angels from being of any use.

François Gouesse had come to the United States with the first four Sisters in 1843. He was then a seminarian and was later ordained by Bishop de la Hailandière. When the rowboat capsized on the occasion of the first postulants' final visit to the island chapel, just before they were to leave for Bertrand and noviceship, it was young Mr. or Father Gouesse who jumped into the lake and pulled them all to safety.

He seems to have been a man of difficult character, though the exact nature of his problems goes unnamed in all the early documents. This seems to have left the Cattas wondering, though they acknowledge that he was "a bit odd and very independent,"[13] that "if he were not handled prudently he would end up in revolt,"[14] and that his utterances were "marked with the spirit of exaggeration."[15] At the same time, however, he was temporarily able to improve conditions at the asylum, and the archbishop, who probably did not see a great deal of him, testified to his zeal and energy.[16] He covered long distances in shifts of obedience, from France to Indiana to New Orleans, back to France, back to New Orleans, to Canada, back to France. It was during his second assignment in France that he was dismissed from the congregation by Father Moreau. Father Sorin had developed an absolutely implacable hostility toward him. He fought fiercely against the idea of Gouesse being superior in New Orleans, or anywhere — of his even being a member of the community. But Father Sorin does not ever seem to have given Father Moreau a reasonable explanation of his attitude.

Recent scholarship[17] has concluded that Father Gouesse's flaw was almost certainly alcoholism. This would be perfectly consistent with making the Sisters nervous, calling down the wrath of Sorin, doing a certain amount of commendable work and keeping in the archbishop's good graces, and finally incurring dismissal. At some time after his departure from Holy Cross, he returned to the United States, and his name is on the priests' necrology of the archdiocese of Indianapolis.

In the spring of 1850, however, Father Gouesse completed the formalities of the Visitation and showed the religious his obedience from Father Sorin, in which, says Mary of the Angels, "his powers were prolonged after the Visit ended, until the mother-house at Ste.-Croix delivered to him a new obedience, which he hoped would be shortly."[18] But no new obedience came, and the weeks stretched into months, with Father Gouesse more or less adequately performing the functions of superior of New Orleans. Then in December, Father Moreau decided to confirm the obedience, to give Father Gouesse a minor chapter with which to govern, and to make New Orleans dependent on Notre Dame for official Visitation and admission to profession.

The two-volume biography of Father Moreau by Etienne and Tony Catta is something of a Bible of Holy Cross history, and we now need to look at it very closely. Father Moreau was in Rome when he made the decision about Gouesse's superiorship and on December 4, 1850, he wrote, not to Father Gouesse or Father Sorin, but to his own council in Le Mans to tell them what he had decided. If either Father Moreau or his council wrote at that time to tell either Father Gouesse or Father Sorin about the decision, neither the letter nor any record of it has survived. In the travel conditions of December 1850, it would have taken a letter at least six and probably closer to ten days to go from Rome to Le Mans by land, sea, or any combination of the two. The council would need at least a day or two to read and discuss the decision and conclude that, in the absence of Father Moreau, they should notify Fathers Sorin and Gouesse. The letter for Indiana would need at least two days to reach the port at Le Havre. The next ship for New York, whenever it sailed, could take it — a four or five weeks' winter voyage. If it then came by train to South Bend, it could make it in two or three days; the lake steamers, if the lakes were passable, were cheaper but slower.

Even with miraculously good connections, a decision taken in Rome on December 4 could hardly have triggered a reaction in South Bend on January 7; yet the Cattas treat this as if it were not only possible but obvious. They quote the terms of Father Moreau's decision. Their next sentence is, "This arrangement was not acceptable to the Superior at the Lake,"[19] and they go on to quote a letter of January 7 to Archbishop Blanc of New Orleans (which had become an archdiocese in June 1850) in which Father Sorin denounces Father Gouesse as incompetent and unworthy, and adds that "We no longer consider him as one of our own."[20]

The Cattas' idea is that Father Moreau's decision inflamed Father Sorin into an outbreak against Father Gouesse. Considering the near impossibility of Father Sorin's having learned of the decision by that time, a much greater likelihood is that Sorin really believed that the archbishop needed to be warned, and yet, like most of his contemporaries, or for personal (possibly confessional) reasons, he declined to call the problem by its right name. The word "unworthy" is especially revealing; it is the kind of word that would have been used against an alcoholic, rather than a mere incompetent.

In Father Sorin's Notre Dame *Chronicles* he says that Father Moreau had given permission before the end of 1850 for Father Gouesse's dismissal from the congregation.[21] The *Chronicles* were not kept day to day, journal style, but written up in large segments at intervals of several months; so this could be a case of creative memory. At any rate, the statement "We no longer consider him as one of our own" can have several meanings and is definitely not a formal statement of expulsion or dismissal. But it shows clearly the direction of Sorin's thinking and that of the Indiana council.

It was on January 13, a week after Sorin's letter to the archbishop, that Father Moreau wrote to explain to Sorin how Father Gouesse's accounts would be handled. This letter, which arrived March 30, was the only explanation Sorin got of Gouesse's status, as far as the records show.

At the same time that Father Sorin wrote to the archbishop, he also wrote to Brother Vincent, telling him that the Brothers were released from obedience to Father Gouesse. Brother Vincent did not relay this information to the Brothers.[22]

By April 1851, when Sister Mary of the Five Wounds wrote again, there were various bits of news to be passed along (some plainly and some cryptically), Father Gouesse was no longer so high in favor, and the Sister's own tendency to tartness was increasing. The whole letter, written at the end of Lent and on a day when a shocking tragedy had occurred, suggests a certain amount of strain. After telling of the efforts of a benefactress, Mrs. Jourdan, in the matter of fund-raising, the letter continues:

> This good Mrs. Jourdan has just been submitted to the most cruel test. This very morning, the youngest of her daughters, Miss Anastasia, after having worked till eleven o'clock last night to fix the flowers to decorate our repository for Holy Thursday, was seized at five a.m. with a vomiting of blood, which carried her off in ten minutes, without anyone being able to call a priest. . . . Her poor mother was wild with grief. We went to see her after Mass. . . . I cannot tell you the impression it made on me, the sight of this young woman whom I had seen laughing and chatting the evening before . . . cold and inanimate, insensible to the caresses as to the tears of her poor mother.[23]

The letter continues on other topics. The council at New Orleans, apparently composed of Father Gouesse, Brother Vincent, and Sister Mary of the Five Wounds, had considered having Brother Vincent go to France on "some important business," but the last discussion of it had seriously alarmed the Sister. "[A]s I could not understand anything of the opening discourse heatedly pronounced by Father Gouesse, I was afraid of my inexperience, of my ignorance. . . ." For "heatedly" should we read "incoherently"?

A priest who was having trouble on another mission, and, surprisingly, Sister Mary of the Angels, who helped Father Gouesse without permission, come in for a share of sarcasm.

> Father Superior [Gouesse] has received a letter from Father Gratien in which Father Gratien goes into pompous detail on all the miseries they have gone through and perhaps also those which they have not gone through. After making known the contents of this letter, Father G. said he was going to send it to France. Nobody answered anything. However, the generous soul of my dear Sister Mary of the Angels was the first to come to his help with that praiseworthy design, by copying that letter herself, a work which took her two days and even had to be started again. This of course without

> my knowledge. I owed the knowledge of it to another providential circumstance, and this was for me only another sorrow.

Poor Mary of the Angels seems to have been caught between two fires, bound to displease somebody no matter what she did.

Mary of the Five Wounds continues by mentioning "some interesting news from Rome," which she shared with Mrs. Jourdan, "conform[ably] to your intention." Then she became afraid that the Ursuline Sisters and the vicar general, Msgr. Perché,[24] would be offended if they heard the news (she does not say what it was) before being informed by the religious of Holy Cross; but she was afraid that if she mentioned it, "I would be reproved because it was for the Father Superior to do that." She let the matter go for some time, but reflected that, "[M]any times already, when you have expressed the desire to make known something capable of elevating the society in the eyes of the public, he always has some special reason for hiding it." Definitely Gouesse was beginning to make her uneasy.

It was in this same month of April 1851 that the council at Le Mans considered sending a Visitor to Notre Dame and New Orleans, and again we must take a close look at the chronology as handled by the Cattas.

Father Louis Baroux, the chief missionary to the Potawatomis, had been on a begging tour in France and would be returning to Indiana the end of April. There was some thought of sending a Father Houdebourg with him as Visitor. The Cattas write:

> Even though the news reached Notre Dame as the result of an indiscretion, the forthcoming visitation unleashed a new storm. Father Champeau, who was responsible for the indiscretion, advised the motherhouse of Father Sorin's ill humor. Following the advice of the Father Founder, the council at Ste. Croix dropped the idea of the visitation.[25]

The sequence is clear. First the decision to send the Visitor. Then Sorin's unofficial notification by Champeau. Then Sorin's furious reaction, directed at Champeau. Then Champeau's relay to the council of Sorin's response. Then the second decision by the council, calling off the first one.

But the footnotes of the same episode tell a very different story. The actual chronology is that on April 13, having considered sending Father Houdebourg to America, the council decided not to do so. On April 25, *twelve days later,* Father Champeau, who had not been present at the council and was not even living in Le Mans, wrote to Father Sorin what could only have been a rumor at best, and was, in fact, not true. Then, *four days after writing* to Sorin, Champeau probably regretted stirring up a possible hornets' nest and wrote to Le Mans to warn them that he had sent Sorin unwelcome news. Champeau's letter to Sorin was barely on its way, possibly not yet out of France, when Champeau wrote to the council, only to find that the whole idea had been dropped long before. There is, in fact, no evidence that Sorin ever replied to Champeau's letter at all, yet the Cattas present for our belief the idea that "a new storm," "unleashed" by Sorin, scared off the council at Le Mans. The "storm" existed solely in the imaginations of the Cattas.

Even though Archbishop Blanc told Father Sorin that he thought Sorin had "greatly exaggerated the danger,"[26] the archbishop took it seriously when Father Sorin told him a second time, and somewhat more formally, that Gouesse was "no longer a member of the Association of the Holy Cross in the United States."[27] Sorin was not speaking for the Association in France. Gouesse did not argue the matter; he wanted out from under Sorin as much as Sorin wanted him gone. Father Cointet arrived from Notre Dame in June 1851 and Father Gouesse sailed for France.

About the time Father Cointet arrived, Sister Mary of the Five Wounds was taking note of the condition of poor girls, aged twelve to fifteen, too old for the girls' orphanage of the Sisters of Charity, but certainly too young to make their own way in the city. With the help of Mrs. Jourdan and other benefactors, Sister Mary set up a "workroom" on the French model, where the girls could learn the plain and fancy sewing by which they would later be able to support themselves. Food, shelter, and clothing would be provided at the workroom, as would religious instruction.

With the blessing of the superiors and the help of the benefactors, Sister Mary opened the workroom in August 1851. Nine girls formed the original group. They had been allowed a six months' trial by the archdiocese. At the end of that time, with all bills paid, there was a remaining fund of two dollars. Sister considered her point proved. The girls would not have to depend on public charity. Furthermore, she tells Father Sorin in a letter of

September 15, she thinks she sees among the girls "two good postulants."

The letter goes over a number of the writer's routine topics, including her continuing struggle with Mary of the Angels: "[Since] you wouldn't give me a sweet and docile person to put with her, I have had to take care of the laundry myself to prevent more big trouble."

She wants two more Sisters for her workroom, "and it would be well if you would be good enough to install them yourself in a house of which you will consider yourself founder and director." If factions were forming, or had been formed, by this time in Louisiana, Mary of the Five Wounds was still with Sorin.

She mentions a problem which

> Father Cointet did not tell you for fear of causing you pain, he said. . . . The Reverend Father still has not addressed a word to him; this leaves this good Father in a void and a painful uncertainty, which only a virtue such as his could support with patience. . . . On the other hand, Father Gouesse has written to many people, especially Brother Theodulus, announcing his return as certain. The Bishop and Msgr. Perché almost seem to expect it.

Sister Mary expects Father Sorin to know who the taciturn "Reverend Father" is.

On November 10, 1851, Father Moreau wrote to Father Sorin that the council had decided to send Father Gouesse back to New Orleans. He had been gone only four months. Father Sorin had not attended the general chapter of the previous summer, which had rebuked him for overstepping his authority in the Gouesse matter.

Again, and again to the detriment of Father Sorin, the Cattas find a sequence which does not exist. First, "It is easy to imagine," they write, "the reaction provoked at Notre Dame by Father Gouesse's return to New Orleans."[28] It is indeed easy to imagine, but much less easy to find any documentation. The reaction at Notre Dame would have been the more contained because Father Sorin was not there when the news arrived.

Second, "Word came to Le Mans," they say,

> that Father Sorin was sailing for France, coming as a delegate of his chapter, "to take up with Notre Dame de Sainte-Croix everything bearing on the welfare of Notre Dame du Lac, with a view to insuring solid and lasting peace."[29]

The authors are quoting a meeting of the council at Notre Dame du Lac on December 2, not any "word" that arrived in Le Mans. In the chronological register of documents in the General Archives in Rome, there is nothing from anyone at the Lake to anyone at Le Mans until January 1, 1852, when the religious at the Lake wrote to Father Sorin, a letter which would have arrived no sooner than the end of January, and probably some time in February. If the decision for Father Sorin to go to France was taken December 2 and he left immediately, there was no point in sending a letter, since it could not have traveled faster than he did. This also calls into question the Cattas' further remark:

> According to the account in the Chronicles of Notre Dame du Lac, which could have been written by none other than Father Sorin himself, the Father Rector was greatly surprised by the unexpected arrival of the traveler from America.[30]

This is a case of having it both ways. Either word arrived that he was coming, or Father Moreau and the others were greatly surprised by his arrival. Not both.

Third, with their usual judgmental attitude toward Sorin, the Cattas go on:

> Thus, Father Sorin, who had felt that he could not leave America for the General Chapter in August, did not hesitate to leave on the spur of the moment as soon as he learned of Father Gouesse's return to New Orleans.

Fact: the decision to send Gouesse back was taken November 10, 1851. If promulgated immediately, it could not have reached Notre Dame until mid- or late December. But the decision for Father Sorin to go to France was taken December 2 and acted on at once. If the dates given by the Cattas are correct, he was actually at the motherhouse, making a presentation to the council, on December 31, a flying trip indeed for those days. It would have been just about then that word of the council decision reached the Lake.

Sister Mary of the Five Wounds wrote to Father Sorin in New York before he sailed (at least she and Father Cointet each wrote letters which they hoped would catch him), telling him that she would send her accounts to him in France and that from now on she is going to begin "serious work with the orphans."[31]

Her last letter from New Orleans is dated January 13, 1852. She speaks of another building put at her disposal by the Ursulines and offers a long quotation from a letter of Msgr. Perché to the faithful of New Orleans, urging their support for the orphanage. Then she takes up the topic of the other Sisters, some of whom have recently arrived. Sister Mary of Calvary and Mary of the Angels, she says, will be writing to him themselves, Sister Mary of St. Anne is well and busy in the kitchen. That seems to be the end of the good news.

> Our English-speaking Sisters are always the same, not very capable but good enough. The family has just grown by two Sisters, Mary of St. Bridget and Mary of the *Presentation.* The first cannot be very useful here because of her lack of capacity; however, she has not a bad character. . . . As for Mary of the Presentation, I am not going to tell you anything about her — what good would it do?

She then complains at some length of having sent two very superior postulants to Bertrand.

> And I admit I was not expecting Sister Mary of the Presentation in return. Mother told me she wanted to send . . . Sister Mary of St. Aubin and Sister Mary of Providence. . . . To do myself justice, I received them . . . with respect and politeness.

But they, or at least Sister Mary of the Presentation, have turned out to have "colossal pretensions, fantastic and bizarre character, capricious and very officious, all in short exactly fitted to raise a tower of Babel."

She begs not to have to put any of these Sisters with the girls. She will find some lay teachers, while awaiting the arrival of "some fairly virtuous as well as capable subjects." She fears to expose the girls to "some Sisters capable of making them lose the esteem they have for us."

And then there was the continuing problem.

> Thanks to the help of good Father Cointet, peace and harmony are maintained among us, but to tell you the truth, I dread beyond all expression having Father Gouesse around. . . . This good Father, having very little to do, wanders around the asylum and pays me visits which never last less than two hours. . . . If I did not respect him as one of our Fathers, I would already have had a word with Monsignor.

It certainly seems logical that the reason why Father Gouesse changed from a praiseworthy and trusted confessor to an object of dread must have lain with Gouesse himself.

This, however, was the year in which the Sisters succeeded in opening a foundling home, so in spite of all their problems and the strains of incompatibility, they were increasing the scope of the apostolate.

12

Many Changes and Troubles—New Orleans, 1852–55

Father Gouesse's second stay in New Orleans was a short one. He arrived in December 1851 or January 1852, and by February the council at Le Mans had decided to send him on to Montreal. He left in the late winter or early spring of 1852, but, as we shall see, his journeyings were not over. Father Sorin was in Europe during this time. Father Cointet was superior in New Orleans, so Gouesse's departure did not leave the group without a superior.

In March 1852 two Sisters and fifteen girls moved into the new building, a house which the Ursulines had owned, repaired, and donated. The workroom and the orphanage were doing well, but the sickness that was the curse of the city was still prowling about. The *Marianite Annals* tell us that fifty boys and two Brothers were stricken with cholera during 1852 (they don't say how many survived), while three Brothers, one Sister, and several children became victims of yellow fever.[1] Deaths of parents created new orphans, and more children kept coming into the orphanage, either bringing the infection with them or risking being infected after they arrived. The Sisters opened a separate foundling home for infants, and Sister Mary of the Five Wounds wrote to Archbishop Blanc, July 22, 1852, asking his blessing upon it.[2]

It will be remembered that 1852 was also the year of the Bengal controversy. Father Moreau's letter to Sorin of September 13, 1852,[3] not only announced Sorin's assignment to Bengal, but also informed Sorin that Father Cointet would have to return to Indiana because of his health and that Father Gouesse would immediately resume the duties of superior in New Orleans. Father Moreau must have felt that this would now make no difference to Sorin, as he would be leaving Notre Dame anyway. As we have seen, Sorin refused the Bengal assignment and the struggle went on.

We do not know on what date Father Moreau's letter arrived

at Notre Dame. The Sisters were notified of the Bengal matter on October 7 and wrote immediately to Father Moreau. The letter is extant and the date, in Sister Ascension's neat handwriting, is perfectly clear: 7 8bre 1852. ("8bre" is a French abbreviation for October.) If it were not so clear, it might be possible to say that perhaps it was dated for October 17, for a mystery sets in ten days later.

Father Sorin wrote to Archbishop Purcell of Cincinnati on October 16 from Notre Dame, "I leave tomorrow for New Orleans, whence, God willing, I shall return in a month." The Cattas quote this and add, "He was still there on December 14,"[4] implying that Sorin was overstaying his time. But the letter to Sister Ascension[5] indicates that he did not reach New Orleans until some time in the second week of December; on December 6 he was still two or three days out of New Orleans. For some reason he changed his mind within twenty-four hours of telling Archbishop Purcell that he was leaving October 17. Later, he may have gone to see Purcell in Cincinnati, for he speaks of visiting with Father Badin, who had retired to that city.

So it is not clear where Father Sorin was during October. On November 6, Father Rézé, superior in Canada, wrote to Father Moreau that Sorin had wired Gouesse to remain in Montreal. Father Rézé acted as a kind of chorus from his post in Canada, offering Father Moreau various bits of anti-Sorin commentary; or at least these are what the Cattas choose to quote.

The Cattas put the next stop this way:

> Father Sorin went personally to New Orleans, and, both before the Archbishop, and before the priests, Brothers, and Sisters at the Asylum, declared himself formally opposed to the new arrival taking over his functions as superior, even though he had been sent under orders from the highest authority in the Congregation. Confronted with this delicate situation, Father Gouesse wisely asked Father Moreau either to confirm his obedience or to give him another assignment.[6]

We must again, however, correct the Cattas' chronology. Father Gouesse wrote to Father Moreau on November 27. Father Sorin did not get off his riverboat until December 9 or 10. Father Gouesse did not request the clarification because he was "confronted" (he was still in Montreal) with a "situation" of Sorin's making. Again the order of events has been deliberately twisted. The Cattas continue:

> Consequently, on December 9, in a letter to Archbishop Blanc, Father Moreau confirmed the order already given to Father Gouesse. [Consequent to what? Not to Gouesse's request of November 27, which could not have reached Le Mans by December 9.] . . . When this letter reached its destination, Father Sorin was already on hand, as he had left for New Orleans about the middle of October. He had declared to the Archbishop and to the priest whom he had ostracized that, since he "had refused the office to which he had been assigned in Bengal . . . things should have been left as they were."[7]

The only way to know whether Father Sorin was in New Orleans when Father Moreau's letter arrived would be to know, not when he left Notre Dame, but when he left New Orleans. We know now (from the evidence of the letter to Sister Ascension) that he arrived there December 9 or 10, when the letter of December 9 was just starting its journey to America. That he was there when it arrived a month later is unlikely from his letter of December 20 to Sister Ascension.

At any rate, Father Moreau did confirm Father Gouesse's return to New Orleans as superior and asked that Father Cointet be allowed to return to Notre Dame for reasons of health. (Ironically, Father Cointet died of cholera at Notre Dame less than two years later.)

On December 18, perhaps having had time to discuss the matter with Sorin and not yet having received Father Moreau's confirmatory letter, Archbishop Blanc wrote to Father Moreau suggesting Gouesse's removal. On December 22 Father Moreau wrote again, "expressing his astonishment," say the Cattas, "that Father Cointet had not yet left for the Lake, as he had been ordered to do."[8] The part where the astonishment is expressed is not quoted. The question arises, how did Father Moreau know, on December 22, that his order of December 9, which could not possibly have reached America (three full weeks was the portal-to-portal record in the best of weather) would not be fulfilled? Are the Cattas imagining, not only the astonishment, but the basic contents of the letter? They continue:

> But in the meantime, through an abuse of his authority as provincial, Father Sorin had already ordered Father Gouesse "to leave as soon as possible, and for good, not only the asylum, but also the Archdiocese of New Orleans and the Province of Notre Dame du Lac, without awaiting any further orders."[9]

It should be noted that the Cattas are here quoting, not Sorin, as they purport to be, but Gouesse. And whether this constitutes an abuse of authority is open to question. There is again no suggestion of dismissing Gouesse from the congregation at large, merely from the province of Notre Dame du Lac. Sorin as provincial probably had the power under the somewhat obscure canon law of the day.

Father Sorin left New Orleans after a stay of about two weeks, not two months. He wrote to Mother Ascension on December 20 that he would probably not have another opportunity to write before starting for home. He says that everything has been satisfactorily arranged in New Orleans, but he may be referring only to the Sisters, who were adjusting their staff to the requirements of the newly opened workroom. Most of the letter asks Mother Ascension to assure everybody that in the matter of his going to Bengal, the question is settled and they can stop writing him letters begging him not to go. He closes with very affectionate regards to the postulants, the young ladies of the Bertrand academy, and the "dear Sisters." There is no mention of Gouesse or of any friction in New Orleans.

But, as we have seen, the Bengal matter had not been laid to rest, and the New Orleans problem merged with it for a while. The story of the struggle and eventual reconciliation (chapters 7 and 8) ended with Father Sorin's trip October 1853 to France, his return to a state of friendship with Father Moreau, his witnessing of the profession of Sister Angela (and possibly of her companion, Sister Emily) and their return to Indiana over the uncomfortable winter seas of 1854. Father Julien Gastineau apparently made the same trip with the object of replacing Father Gouesse in New Orleans. He went first with the rest of the party to Notre Dame and spent the rest of the winter there, reporting to New Orleans about the first of April 1854. There something caused him to panic. He stayed one week and fled to Canada. The poor religious in New Orleans were again without a superior.

The next appointment was Father Pierre Salmon, who had come from France by way of the Lake. He had been named steward to Father Gastineau and now found himself in charge. Archbishop Blanc kept Father Gouesse in the city, though Gouesse had been recalled to France by Father Moreau. Father Moreau wrote asking for the return to New Orleans of Father Cointet. By this time two Brothers were supposed to be on their way from France to New Orleans. They would stop at Notre Dame. It seems to have been decided that whatever priest would be going from there would wait for them.

They did not come. Meanwhile the summer of 1854 arrived and sickness set in at Notre Dame. From then on, no matter how often he heard about the plight of New Orleans, Father Sorin was both physically and psychologically unable to spend any time on the problems of the South: physically because he was on twenty-four-hour duty, replacing the sick teachers in the classrooms, ministering to the dying, and burying the dead; psychologically because this was one of the times when his horizon shrank, as Father Lemarié points out,[10] to the present moment and the spot where he was. Nothing else existed.

There was cholera at New Orleans, too, and on September 6 it took Father Salmon. On September 10 the long-awaited Brothers arrived at Notre Dame, but by this time Father Cointet had come down with the disease. He died at Notre Dame September 19.

Poor Father Gouesse had to gather the reins again in his less-than-capable hands. Guided by him, the chapter at New Orleans wrote to Father Moreau October 1 formally requesting that the house be closed as soon as possible. Since the contract between the archdiocese and the congregation required seven months' notice before the closing of a house, this earliest possible date would have been May 1, 1855. Archbishop Blanc followed with his own letter to Father Sorin, October 16, asking that the house be reorganized but not closed. This crossed a letter from Father Moreau saying that he was doing what he could for New Orleans and that Sister Mary of the Five Wounds, who had been in France, would be returning to strengthen the staff of the workroom. Father Moreau also wrote on October 23 to Father Sorin, gently mentioning that New Orleans should be helped if at all possible. Sorin, who by November was finding a little time to write letters again, replied that the only way he could help New Orleans was by having total control. Otherwise he recommended complete withdrawal and "draw[ing] an iron curtain[11] over our stay in New Orleans!"[12]

It is hard to understand what control Father Sorin wanted that he did not already have. Father Moreau had acceded to his wish not to have Gouesse as superior; Gouesse had returned to New Orleans to serve on the archbishop's staff because the archbishop either had no objection to him or felt able to control him. It was through Providence, not through Father Moreau, that Gouesse resumed the superiorship after the flight of Gastineau and the deaths of Salmon and Cointet. Father Sorin had asked that Le Mans help supply the personnel for New Orleans; when it did, he complained about newcomers who didn't know what they were doing. He had rights of Visitation and of the approval of professions, and accounts were to be submitted to him. Surely he was being unreasonable.

At least we can see that the two years from the late summer of 1852 to the autumn of 1854 were not comfortable times for him. First came the totally unexpected blow of the Bengal obedience. He had sincerely thought he had found his life's work in Indiana, and he could scarcely believe that Father Moreau did not think so too. While that struggle was going on, the New Orleans problem came to a head.

First, the problem with Gouesse. Sorin himself testifies in the *Chronicles* that he could not endure the thought of having to leave the United States himself while Gouesse, with all his faults, remained in charge at New Orleans. Second, the drain that New Orleans represented on Notre Dame resources, especially in personnel. In Sorin's mind, Notre Dame came first and there really was no second. He resented having to give time, attention, and resources to any other place, particularly one whose connections with the Indiana foundation were necessarily rather loose (though the calm pleasantness of his 1852 letters to Sister Ascension suggests that he could usually hide the resentment even from himself). He was especially reluctant to share his priests, though he could proudly send out the Sisters and Brothers, as their numbers grew, to various new missions. But the priests were never as numerous as the Sisters and Brothers, and they were much more needed for the academic success of his university. And New Orleans was becoming a death trap for priests.

Third and probably the worst aspect of the situation was the determination of New Orleans to remain French. Perhaps the determined loyalty of many of the New Orleans religious to the motherhouse acted, even unconsciously, as a reproach to his rejection of his first motherland in favor of the new, and true, homeland. At any rate, Sorin wanted control of the people in New Orleans because he wanted to Americanize them or to re-absorb them into the Indiana personnel, or both. He never seems to have articulated these goals.

Finally came the second severe shock in two years, the horrible cholera epidemic which hit New Orleans and Notre Dame at the same time, and at the end of which Edward Sorin, defenses down and shatterproof composure at least cracked, was openly demanding the one thing he could settle for: total control of Holy Cross in the United States.

Father Moreau replied quietly and calmly. In the next several months there was a sudden overabundance of superiors for New Orleans. Father Moreau sent an obedience on December 22, 1854, to Father Francis Voors (Moreau gives the name as "Force") to proceed to the post. Father Voors did not go, because before this letter arrived, Father Sorin, mollified by Father Moreau's mild, conciliatory attitude, had sent Father Michael Rooney, a young Irishman from New York state, to take over the asylum. Father Rooney seems to have been a well-educated man and probably spoke French, but he also seems to have been most obnoxiously superior to everything and everybody around him. On February 6, 1855, he wrote to Father Sorin that the religious in New Orleans

> are so heartily sick of the many changes and troubles they have had, that . . . they care not by what house they are governed if only they knew for a certainty . . . upon whom to look as their superior. Notre Dame, however, is not extolled to the skies, nor are its superiors in the best odor among the religious creoles down here. All, with the exception of Brother Ignatius . . . have a peculiar and perceptible leaning toward "la Maison Mere," and imagine everything goes wrong if not done according to its fashions. I have given them to understand, however, that I would reserve to myself the interpretation of its Rules and ways.
>
> As for Brother Francis — in what *he* says much faith is not to be reposed. If he only kept within the confines of sobriety you might forgive him all his peccadilloes. What spite the poor Sisters have against me, I cannot discover; their firm attachment to Father Gouesse, however, will explain all. . . .

> [T]heir desire, ultimately, is to have this a province, entirely distinct and separate from any house in this country, as soon as their novitiate is formed, and when they are strong enough to depend upon themselves.[13]

Meanwhile Father Moreau had changed his mind about Father Voors even before that letter reached New Orleans and was sending Father Isador Guesdon from Le Mans. The records indicate that this priest left France February 16. He did not arrive in New Orleans until sometime between April 8 and May 17.

On April 8 Father Rooney wrote another negative and sardonic report to Father Sorin, though he seems to have felt one small touch of pity for the Sisters.

> [T]his is a much God-forsaken, Lord-abandoned place, and the sooner you wash your hands of it the better. . . . Among the Sisters I do not believe there is one who does not grieve the change [to a new superior], as they come to me every day in tears begging me not to go. The poor old creatures, for old they are with much care, expect another season of trouble, verily they have had enough.

The Sisters seem to have shifted some of their "firm attachment to Father Gouesse" over to Father Rooney, probably only in hopes of gaining a little stability. He has no such affectionate feelings for them, especially for Mary of the Five Wounds, of whom he says, "Time alone can remove the injuries which that woman has done the community in this quarter." Now "everyone is disgusted with her," "she has no friends," and Father Perché "thinks her about as capable of conducting a novitiate and an *ouvrier* as a superannuated old cat to raise a brood of chickens." Rooney's final judgment on her is that she "wants that most essential and indispensable ingredient in the human economy — brains."

The letter notes that there are ten Sisters with three postulants, and six Brothers with three postulants, "between 12 and 14 years old." Father Sorin has apparently suggested sending a seminarian to help Rooney, but he replies, "[L]et him not come on my account, for perhaps as he arrives I myself will be in another latitude, in a more congenial sphere, singing 'Te Deum' for my deliverance."

Rooney got his deliverance May 18. The night before, Father Guesdon, who had finally arrived, wrote to Sorin that many of the religious (he names five Sisters and two Brothers) are longing to leave as well. He thinks two, and possibly three, will go with Rooney in the morning, permission or no permission; but he has persuaded most of them to write to Sorin for advice, and now he begs Sorin to tell them all to stay — they are badly needed. He thanks Sorin for sending them a Brother Commissionaire, who will be a great help.

He wrote again sixteen days later. The opening sentence is heartbreaking: "The Divine Providence took away from us, on May 30, at one o'clock in the afternoon, the excellent Brother Clement, whom you had the goodness to send us as Commissionaire."[14] No wonder the poor religious in New Orleans thought God himself was against them!

In spite of this blow, attitudes were improving. "No one, I think, regrets staying, and many perhaps would regret leaving."

Though the sickness continued during the summer, under Father Guesdon's direction the house gradually settled down to some peace and religious regularity. The little community dared to breathe cautiously and begin to expect the stability they had so long prayed for. Sending in the accounts on August 28, Father Guesdon took a firm line on financial matters with Father Sorin. He also denied sending any religious back to the Lake (seven had gone, counting Father Rooney).

> I never sent anyone, they all left of their own accord, taking all the responsibility for their move. As I had made up my mind not to keep anyone who was not devoted to the place, I left them free, and it will be the same in the future. If the occasion ever arises again, you are free not to take them in, which is what I would probably do myself.

"It will be the same in the future." Father Guesdon did not know that his future consisted of three weeks. On September 18, he, too, was dead of yellow fever.

13

An Entirely Different Style—New Orleans, 1855

Early in the existence of the community, Basil Moreau told his religious, "The work of Holy Cross is not the work of human beings but the work of God." No clearer example of the truth of this statement could be provided than the early story of New Orleans. Had it been a human establishment, this mission would have disappeared in the series of calamities which afflicted it.

Once again, following the death of Father Guesdon, the Brothers of St. Joseph and the Sister Marianites found themselves a flock without a shepherd. It was almost the last straw, even for so strong a faith as Father Moreau's. He had received word of the death of Father Voisin, superior in Bengal, and immediately thereafter the further word of the drowning deaths of Father Montigny and Sister Mary of Victory within sight of the mission in Bengal where they were awaited. He wrote:

> I have never been so disheartened. . . . We had hardly recovered from the shock of this sad news when letters from New Orleans announced the death of Father Guesdon and Brother Martial, who fell victims to yellow fever . . . on the eighteenth and twenty-eighth of September.[1]

There was no one left in France to send to New Orleans. Father Moreau notified Archbishop Blanc[2] that Notre Dame would have to take the responsibility. He must have notified Father Sorin, probably about the same time.[3] Sorin, having seen this coming when he heard of Father Guesdon's death, was understandably reluctant to send another superior down to be swallowed up like one of Sara's husbands in the Book of Tobias. He decided on a long-range assessment of the situation and called upon the people who could do it.

Sister Mary of the Immaculate Conception (Prévert) and Sister Mary of St. Liguori (Chrétien) had come to America when Father Sorin returned from France in January 1854. Other members of the party had been Sisters Angela and Emily, who returned to Bertrand, Father Gastineau, who went on to New Orleans and stayed one week, and probably Sisters Mary of the Passion and Mary of St. Claire, who were made of sterner stuff than Father Gastineau and were still there.

Sister Immaculate Conception had come as Visitor from the motherhouse and had undertaken the already difficult task of recasting the Indiana houses into a more French mold. She had moved the novitiate back from Bertrand to Notre Dame and put the novices behind a parlor grille, had sent several novices home, and had changed the obediences of a large number of professed. She was French, conservative, and high-handed, but if Father Rooney's perception was correct — that the Sisters in New Orleans "have a particular . . . leaning toward 'la maison mère' and imagine everything goes wrong if not done according to its fashion" — she should have been just what the Sisters in New Orleans would have welcomed. She had taken fourteen months to complete her task and was serving as superior in Michigan City when Father Sorin summoned her to this continuation of her American Visitation. Sister Mary of the Passion was then serving as superior of the asylum, superior of the workroom (at a different location in the city), and mistress of novices. Sister Immaculate Conception was to replace her at the asylum.

Sister Liguori had started her American apostolate as a seamstress at Notre Dame, had gone to Bertrand to take charge of the Manual Labor School, had moved that school first to Mishawaka and then to the Rush property at the new Saint Mary's, and was still there when Father Sorin added her to the team. She also was thoroughly French (but more flexible than Sister Immaculate Conception), devoted, intelligent, and emotionally responsive. She was expected to stay in New Orleans and take charge of the workroom, an assignment very similar to her work with the Manual Labor School. Thus Sister Mary of the Passion would be free to devote herself full time to her work as mistress of novices.

Sister Mary of the Ascension was the third and chief member of the Sisters' part of the delegation. She had served as mistress of novices and as local superior both at Bertrand and at Notre Dame. She had been the copier, if not the chief author, of the Sisters' letter to Father Moreau protesting Father Sorin's assignment to Bengal. She had kept pace with Sorin in learning not only to speak and write but to think in English. His letters to Father Moreau and to bishops were often recopied in her neat and readable handwriting. Most of the Indiana Sisters were fully devoted, not to say emotionally attached, to Father Sorin; Sister Ascension all but adored him. Whatever he did was right, whatever he commanded was to be done. A modern psychologist might find something strongly sexual in this; so be it. Whatever its ingredients, her devotion to Father Sorin was the ruling passion of her life.

Sister Ascension's task as chief Visitor was to examine the situation as a whole and report back to Father Sorin. This was not to be a hasty business; she was not expected back in Indiana until the following April.

Two Brothers also made the journey. Brother Stephen, described as a "good administrator," was the official delegate to the Brothers. He had a shadowy companion about whom no information has survived, not even his name.

The New Orleans group had been expecting, optimistically if somewhat unrealistically, another kind, efficient, model superior like Father Cointet, capable of healing their wounds, relieving their bone-deep fatigue, and guiding their work forward. They may be forgiven for losing sight of the fact that there are never very many Father Cointets in the world. At any rate, they seem to have thought that the supply of priests at the Lake was inexhaustible. They did not expect three Sisters and two Brothers. The extent of their disappointment can hardly be imagined.

The Visitors saw at once that they were far less welcome than they had expected to be. They had hoped to be helpful, but it was clear that only one kind of help would be acceptable — a priest superior. The New Orleans religious saw the failure to send a priest as one more manifestation of Sorin's unconcern toward their mission. The travelers, who were hungry and tired, were thrown on the defensive by the hostile reception. By the time the Visitors got across the threshold, the Visitation was doomed.

The accounts of what happened do not agree in all particulars. There are four main voices reporting the event to Father Moreau: Mother Ascension and Sister Immaculate Conception from the Visitors, and Father Gilbert Raymond and Sister Mary of the Passion from New Orleans.

In spite of the lateness of their arrival and the length of time they seem to have been kept up, Mother Ascension and Sister

Immaculate Conception both wrote to Father Moreau that very night. Sister Immaculate Conception wrote again the next day, and Mother Ascension submitted a full report through the Saint Mary's council after she returned home.

The question of validity of authority on both sides was the first problem that arose. Since the death of Father Guesdon, the New Orleans establishment had been getting along as best it could, apparently with the most authoritative people taking the most responsibility. Sister Immaculate Conception wrote:

> We are still amazed to see Sister Mary of the Passion display the full authority of a superior, when she is only in charge of the postulants. Well, blessed be God, she believes she has the duty to act that way in the face of all those who know perfectly well she has no authority.[4]

Father Raymond, the diocesan priest who had been representing the archbishop's authority at the orphanage, considered someone else the Sisters' superior. He wrote to the archbishop before he had seen any of the Visitors that he hoped they would not take away a certain Sister whose absence would be "a mortal blow to the house. . . . I am not speaking," he added, "of the Sister Superior, Mother Mary of the Desert, for I am sure no one would dare touch her."[5]

Among the men, Father Raymond himself was more or less regarded as the superior, though he was not a member of the congregation. Father Moreau had known him in France and had apparently asked him to look after the religious in New Orleans. The archbishop had sanctioned Father Raymond's functioning as orphanage chaplain and a sort of superior pro tem. Father Raymond seems to have feared from the beginning that the Holy Cross religious were going to be removed from the New Orleans area altogether. Since he had just secured some Sisters for his own parish in Opelousas, that would have been a personal blow to him. He panicked when he first heard of the Visitors and wrote to the archbishop that "three young Sisters, one professed, coming from France, and two Irish novices" had arrived "to replace the Sisters who are supposed to make their vows in New Orleans."[6]

Mother Ascension wrote:

> [W]e learned that the community would finish the annual retreat the next day, and . . . that this retreat had been given by Mr. Ray-

> mond, according to an invitation from Your Reverence, which established him as superior of the institution; and he was, in fact, presented as such to Brother Stephen, when, according to the Rule, he asked who the superior was in order to present his obedience.[7]

When Mother Ascension declined to present her own obedience to Father Raymond on the grounds that he was not a member of the congregation but said she would show it to the Sisters,

> they would have Brother Elias come in, and see with him what could be done (I still didn't know at that time that he had been acting as superior since the death of Father Guesdon).[8]

A meeting of the Brothers' council, however, which took place during the Visitation (but which does not mention the matter), lists Brother Ignatius as the presiding officer; he subsequently refused to sign the minutes, and they were signed by Brother Elias and Brother Valentine.[9]

If the authority in New Orleans was diffused to the point of evaporation, the authority from Notre Dame was simply unacceptable. The New Orleans religious, especially the Sisters, had found that in spite of heat, yellow fever, and lesser inconveniences, the atmosphere of New Orleans was congenial because it was French. Most of them had experienced the northern climate and the strongly Americanized environment of Indiana, and they wanted no more of either one. They feared being reinserted into both if they submitted to the authority of the Lake.

They cited special arrangements with Father Moreau and the canonical technicality of Visitors having to be appointed either by the superior general or the general council (which, as a matter of fact, Sister Immaculate Conception had been, for all the houses in America). The Visitors presented a letter from Father Moreau himself, explaining that he was asking Father Sorin to take over responsibility for them, and enjoining upon them obedience to him or whomever he would send. The local community insisted that this would mean only the sending of a superior, not Visitors.

As Mother Ascension's lines quoted above had noted, the community was finishing a retreat and preparing for the reception of six postulants and the profession of four novices. This coming ceremony constituted the next problem. During the superiorship of Father Gouesse, Father Moreau had given Father Sorin the right to approve professions in New Orleans. The power had been ignored rather than rescinded; New Orleans had continued to apply to Sainte-Croix for permission to grant professions, and Father Moreau had continued to send the permissions. It is possible that the Visitors registered a technical protest since Father Sorin had not been consulted, but there is not much evidence one way or the other. The Cattas claim that the Visitors "changed the obediences [and] stopped the professions scheduled for the following day."[10] *Both these charges are negated by every contemporary source.* Mother Ascension, having noted that the retreat would end with reception and profession, says no more about either. Sister Immaculate Conception objects not to the ceremony but to one of the participants. In a short list of people the mission would be better off without, she mentions, "Sister Mary of Ste. Claire, who had the unfortunate fault of drinking — she is nevertheless going to make her profession tomorrow morning."[11] Sister Mary of the Passion, writing on December 5, merely says, "I have the consolation of seeing six new novices and four professed going along in good spirit."

Father Raymond couched his comment in a convoluted French double negative which the Cattas seem to have read too quickly. "*Ils n'avaient dit qu'absolument ils ne s'opposeraient pas à la profession et à la prise d'habit de ce matin.*" "They merely said that they were not absolutely opposed to the profession and the taking of the habit of this morning." In other words, they had some reservations but would not pursue the issue.

What did the Visitors do the next day?

Father Raymond says, "They did not attend the ceremony; they went out in the morning without speaking to anyone and are not back yet. It is now four-thirty in the afternoon." In a midnight postscript he adds:

> The Visitors went out and stayed out until seven in the evening. They ate in the city; they went to see the administrators, and dined with one of them. One could call it an electoral campaign. Besides, they have sulked all day long with all the Sisters, they have not attended one exercise with them.[12]

This is overkill. It is hard to see how people who were out from early morning until 7 P.M. could be accused of "sulking all day long with all the Sisters," or expected to attend religious exercises.

Mother Ascension says that she "went next day, with Brother Stephen and one Sister," to the residence of the vicar general, Father Rousselon. They were coldly received and told that the members of Holy Cross were constantly bickering and quarreling and that he wanted nothing to do with them. They withdrew in confusion. She does not say whom else, if anyone, they visited. It would have been logical for them to call upon the lay administrators to get their views of the local situation.

The return of Archbishop Blanc to his city brought some order into the situation. He settled the authority question by deciding that the Visitors could remain as observers but could not make an official Visitation. Mother Ascension had been told to send a report to Father Sorin after ten days but to remain in New Orleans until the report had been forwarded to Father Moreau and a reply received from him, which would have been several weeks. Instead Archbishop Blanc told her to take the ten days for observation but then to return with Sister Liguori to Notre Dame.

Had the Visitors really come to be helpful?

There seems to have been some tact exercised in the selection of Sisters. All were capable missionaries and all were French. Sister Mary of the Passion, with the care of the orphanage, the novitiate, and the workroom, could have been replaced in one or two of those tasks. But instead of feeling relieved, she felt threatened, and the mission, if there was one, failed. The idea, however, that the Indiana contingent simply stomped in and took over the house is not well borne out. They arrived at eight in the evening after traveling several days, were kept up until midnight attempting to account for themselves, and were offered rather precarious hospitality.

Mother Ascension relates that after their arrival, Father Raymond was sent for, and she was interviewed by him. When she declined to present her obedience, the Sisters' local council was called together, and she gave them her obedience, Father Moreau's letter, and an explanation of the purpose of the Visitation. Brother Elias was then called in, though she protested that the Brothers and Sisters had no authority over each other. They told her that they did things differently in New Orleans, "So," she says,

"I kept quiet and asked if we could have some supper, which we greatly needed."[13]

After the meal, there was another meeting with Father Raymond, then with Brother Elias, then with the Sisters' council. Then, "As the night was getting on," she says, "I begged them to at least accord us ordinary hospitality, so we would not have to make our affairs public by going to look for it elsewhere."

Father Raymond, on the other had, tells quite a different story.

> What was surprising from the first was the manner in which they announced themselves. It was their excessively offensive and imperious tone. One would have thought it was a place taken by assault, to which the conqueror had come to impose his laws.[14]

He gives no examples or details of this imperious conduct. Mother Ascension's long account, paragraph by paragraph, of each of the inquisitions to which she was submitted on the first evening is the more convincing. On the other hand, it is likely that she was being selective when she accounted for the second day, mentioning only the visit to the vicar general and saying nothing about seeing any lay administrators.

Within a few days, Sister Mary of the Passion had picked up Father Raymond's language, and wrote to Father Moreau, "Father Sorin . . . does not treat us like a father, but came to take us as one takes a place by storm. I don't need to tell you any more; Mr. Raymond was here; he has written to you."[15] The coupling of Father Raymond's name with the imagery is significant.

Unfortunately, but not surprisingly, this is the language the Cattas adopted, so that the impression given is that the Visitors went about like roaring lions seeking someone to devour. The Cattas either did not know that there was a possible alternative view or chose to ignore it in pursuance of one of their chief aims — always to make Father Sorin look as bad as possible.

The Cattas seem to have depended heavily, if not entirely, on Father Raymond's account and the matter of Father Raymond's reliability has never been questioned. But it may be noted first that a small group of Sisters had just begun work at his parish in Opelousas, so that he had a personal stake in whatever happened to the New Orleans religious. Second, there is some inconsistency between his view of the matter when reporting to Father Moreau and of the same matter when writing to his own archbishop. Writing to Father Moreau, he paints an extremely rosy picture. Having described the reception and profession ceremony, and the "twenty-one Sisters or aspirants who make up a magnificent house," he goes on to the Brothers, naming each and his occupation. Of Brother Valentine he merely says, "Brother Valentine is in charge of the shoemaker's workshop." Writing to his own ordinary, he says what he would not say to Father Moreau:

> I was obliged to go a little more often this week to the orphan asylum, to try to calm down poor Brother Valentine a little. He is standing on his head, and such a poor head it is! The devil makes use of him like a Pirouette; this time it is purely pride which is the cause of it.[16]

To Father Moreau he writes,

> Brother Elias, whom you know, very hot, very ardent, but an excellent heart, takes care of the discipline of the children, and has them in hand amazingly well. But he also takes charge of more or less everything; for you know he is very enthusiastic and full of good will.[17]

But to Archbishop Blanc, "Brother Elias, for his part, is always meddling, but I won't worry about it too much. I think it will finally be necessary to get rid of Brother Elias."[18]

The very hot Brother Elias supervising the children's discipline is probably the source of Mother Ascension's report that the Brothers struck the children, even in church.

Another central problem is the question of whether there was a real need to send anyone, superior or Visitor, or whether Father Moreau had been in any way misinformed, or whether he had misunderstood the reports from New Orleans. Certainly the mission had had a most unfortunate history in its superiors. Gouesse had been sent away after a long squabble; Cointet had been sent back to Indiana for the sake of his health; Gouesse had returned and been sent away a second time; Gastineau had fled after one week; Salmon had died of yellow fever after five months; Cointet had been re-appointed and died at Notre Dame before he could come; Gouesse had once more filled in for about two months; Rooney had served under protest for three months; and Guesdon had died of yellow fever after five months. From Father Gouesse's first arrival in February 1850 to Father Guesdon's death in September 1855, six different men had served as superior in five and a half years. That alone would have been enough to put any mission off balance, even without the ravages of yellow fever and other problems. But the religious in New Orleans had kept asking for priest superiors, though Father Raymond had noticed that the line was getting thin when it reached Father Rooney.

It should also be remembered that the fall of 1855 was the time of Father Moreau's great spiritual trial. It had been coming on for some time during the spring and summer, but the trial itself began in October. It ended when Father Moreau was reading a letter from his benefactress, the Countess de Jurien, which contained a particularly felicitous sentence comparing Father Moreau to St. Peter walking on the water. The letter is dated October 30 but we do not know when Father Moreau read it.

While he was still in the grip of the trial, feeling utterly deserted by God, Father Moreau may have been inclined to view things more pessimistically than usual or necessary. We do not know in what terms the requests were made, or how the situation had been described, but Father Raymond at least regretted that the picture had been painted so darkly.

> First, you believed them [the members at New Orleans] to be in great distress, lacking subjects, incapable of proceeding, perhaps obliged to suspend operations. . . . You therefore asked Father Sorin to come to the aid of a house in distress.[19]

One wonders where Father Moreau would have received this impression if not from the New Orleans members themselves. But under threat of a return to Father Sorin, the rhetoric changes. Father Raymond now writes, "It is inconceivable how good God is to His children! The whole house gets along as well as it possibly could since the death of Father Guesdon, and finds itself as steady as ever." He then assures Father Moreau that a Jesuit priest comes every week for confessions, a diocesan priest offers Mass for the community several times a week, the archbishop is always ready to lend a fatherly ear, and he himself is more than willing to get involved in the details of administration as needed. What need have they of help from Indiana?

> [Sister Mary of the Passion] may have her little faults, but at bottom she is a good Sister. . . . Sister Nativity could . . . direct the asylum, and Sister Mary of the Desert the workshop, both without her. You will have to tell her to have great charity for these two Sisters, as well as for Sister Holy Angels; to have great kindness, and to be very united with them; to work things out together, when that needs to be done; to instruct the novices well, and to give them an example of everything that she tells them. That's the right way.[20]

The fact that Father Raymond found these suggestions necessary makes its own statement.

Sister Mary of the Passion herself strongly seconded the idea that if help could come only from Father Sorin, then no help was wanted. She wrote to Father Moreau that the New Orleans religious were not only surprised to learn that they had been placed under Father Sorin, but "we felt it was the worst thing that could happen to these establishments, which could develop under the motherhouse, and under Father Sorin would certainly be finished."[21] She agreed that Father Raymond was sufficient superior for the present. She also felt that if the Visitors were any example, the Rule was not properly kept in Indiana.

> I am pained to see here the superior from the Lake with her assistant live as if she had no Rule at all. If one judges them according to what they are doing here, one would believe that at the Lake they observe the Rules very loosely, and if one of them stays here as superior, very soon everything we have done to establish the spirit and practice of the Rule will be destroyed.

She may have been aware that the Visitors had made the first complaint. Sister Immaculate Conception had written the first night, "[T]he religious spirit does not seem to reign here, and the manner in which your orders have been received gives me . . . very little hope."[22] Mother Ascension wrote, "All resistance was useless with people of so little religious spirit."[23] Is this mere name-calling? Or have we reached a fundamental disagreement? Father Raymond seems to have found the answer without knowing that he had found it.

> All the time, the Sisters were thinking that, if you had known the actual state of the house, you would never have written to Father Sorin, especially if you had known the ardent desire of all the

> Brothers . . . and . . . Sisters to remain dependent on the Motherhouse . . . particularly considering the innumerable inconveniences for a house in a hot, feverish climate inhabited by people of a special kind of character to be mixed with a house of an entirely different style.[24]

This is very revelatory. What has happened here? Back in their native France the New Orleans religious had not been accustomed to a hot, feverish climate; nor had those of Indiana been accustomed to a vista of hundreds of miles of lakes and woodlands, where the Indians for whom the state was named were drifting away as the pioneers rolled in. But each group had now become "people of a special kind of character." The New Orleans group had seen just enough of Indiana to have felt its strangeness and to have been grateful to be received back into the French atmosphere of Louisiana, heat, disease, and all. The Notre Dame group, following Sorin's lead at every step, had begun to meet the problems of their post-frontier society with an independence which both France and Louisiana found shocking and sometimes offensive. The two groups lived "an entirely different style," and for that century and decade, the styles would not mix. To a degree they were reflecting the North-South problem agitating the whole nation, but only to a degree, because even in the South, New Orleans has always been more special than typical.

There is another account, taken from the local Marianite Chronicles, which differs in several particulars from the letters written at the time. It gives the impression of having been written some time after the fact, or by someone who was not there and who gained information at second hand and after the stories had had a chance to grow in the telling. It needs to be examined, as it has till now served as the only account retained in either Louisiana or Indiana of what happened on the visit.

The chronicler does not seem to be aware that the Visitors arrived at eight o'clock at night. She relates that Mother Ascension presented the letter from Father Moreau and does not mention that any objection was raised to it at first.

The matter of the next day's professions came up. Mother Ascension registered her objection, it was duly noted, but the plans were not changed. There was a further discussion with the Sisters' chapter about the legitimacy of the Visitors' authority. No mention is made of Brother Elias or Father Raymond, or of the Visitors having to ask for something to eat. In fact, in this version they have arrived before dinner, which leads to further complications.

> In setting aside the power of her obedience, she [Mother Ascension] did not seem to be willing to take second place. Her companion (who had no official status) and another Sister of the house who was too attached to the Lake, led her to the superior's place in the refectory. When the two superiors entered the refectory, the local superior, knowing nothing of all this, went to her usual place, which she found occupied. She was ready to yield it when a Sister, as usually happens in these disagreements, said, "No, you must not yield as superior of the house; you must keep your place!"
>
> Another contest followed this first: a Sister, the same one mentioned above, with the same Sister from the Lake, found it would be necessary to give the local superior's bedroom to the superior from the Lake. Then the same Sister who had stood up for her superior, so that the superior from the Lake should not replace her without legitimate authority, refused her the use of the room and the local superior took the key of it.[25]

While this has a certain ring of authenticity, it is impossible to place it within the known chronology. It could not have happened the first night. Dinner in New Orleans would have been over by 8 P.M.; and whether the travelers were welcome or not, the only sensible explanation for their not being offered a meal is the probability that the New Orleans group assumed that the travelers had already eaten. The Visitors requested and were given some food around 10 P.M., by which time all the New Orleans religious who were not members of the council would have been in bed.[26]

Nor could it have happened the second day, as all the accounts agree that the Visitors were out of the house all day; also the question of who slept where would already have been dealt with. From the second evening on, the Visitors had become mere observers and were neither expecting nor receiving the honors of the visit. The story provides an interesting human view, but it simply does not fit into any contemporary account.

The account goes on:

> Mother Mary of the Ascension showed a purported document from the Superior General, but Mother Mary of the Passion had a

> real one from him. She showed it and said, "Yours is false; this one contradicts it." Mother Mary of the Ascension and her companion did not dare argue any further nor show their forged document.

There is no suggestion in the on-the-spot documents that any letter was forged or false. It was the kind of a case which arose quite regularly from Father Moreau's efforts to keep peace among his children. Each group was told what it wanted to hear, and though the versions may not actually have been contradictory, they often sounded that way, and no attempt was made to explain how they worked together. The complaint made at the time was not that the letter from Father Moreau which the Indiana group presented was false, but that it should have been sent on sooner to New Orleans, and that anyway they had special arrangements with Father Moreau which it did not abrogate.

The document also claims that during the Visitation Father Sorin was in St. Louis, waiting for a telegram which would tell him to come and take possession of New Orleans. This seems to be part of the "take by storm" idea but is the least likely point of all. There is nothing in Father Sorin's correspondence to indicate that he was anywhere but at Notre Dame at this time. Nor does St. Louis form a good lurking place for jumping out at New Orleans. Even by today's superhighways, St. Louis is 695 miles from New Orleans.

There are positive elements in the document, however. It accounts for Sister Liguori on the second day, when Mother Ascension says she took her "assistant," Sister Immaculate Conception, and went to see the vicar general, and the other documents indicate that they also visited the administrators. Sister Liguori attended the professions. "The young professed Sister kept in the background and gave no trouble."[27] It gives the names of two administrators, Mr. De Armas and Mr. Layton. It explains how Sister Mary of the Passion's duties would have been reassigned if she had been willing, with Sister Immaculate Conception serving as superior of the orphanage and Sister Liguori in the workroom. And it begins to account for Sister Presentation.

Poor Sister Presentation, whose mental capacities apparently began to deteriorate soon after she made her profession, was an unwelcome troublemaker wherever she went. She was the one who had been characterized by Sister Mary of the Five Wounds as having "a fantastic and bizarre character," among other things (see chapter 11). According to the document, when Sister Immaculate Conception left New Orleans, Sister Presentation decided to go with her. Sister Mary of the Passion forbade her to go and told her that if she went away, she would never be received in New Orleans again. Sister Presentation left anyway. In Indiana her condition continued to become worse and she was eventually committed to a mental institution in St. Louis, where she died.

Finally, the document mentions the bill which Father Sorin asked the New Orleans house to pay for the Visitors' travel. This was and is standard practice in religious houses. The New Orleans religious might have been willing to pay for these five Visitors, even without recognizing their authority. But they were also being billed for the journeys of Father Gastineau and Father Rooney. Sister Mary of the Passion had told Mother Ascension, "The establishment of New Orleans is not obliged to pay what members who have been expelled or those who have seen fit to run away have taken with them."[28] The matter was referred to Father Moreau, who eventually told Mary of the Passion to pay the whole bill.

The major points of the problem thus present themselves.

Father Moreau told Father Sorin to send "someone" to New Orleans. He told the religious in New Orleans that a priest superior was coming. New Orleans got a nasty shock when the "someone" turned out to be a team of observers, at least three of whom were prepared to remain in New Orleans and assume some authority. The Visitors were shocked not to be received in a more friendly fashion. The Visitors did not attempt (Cattas to the contrary notwithstanding) to change obediences or stop the reception and profession ceremonies; they did, however, voice some objections.

Each group had developed its own way, in response to its own mission situation. The situations were totally different and so were the responses. We will never arrive at the full truth of what happened on this Visitation, but it makes no difference. Whether it was a rescue mission or a takeover, whether the Visitors were subjected to an inquisition or took the house by storm, whether one side or both or neither sent an accurate report to Father Moreau, the visit from the start had no chance at all of success. Indiana and Louisiana had grown too far apart. The life-styles would not mix.

14

Through the Intermediary— New York, 1855–56

The first Marianite venture into New York City lasted only about a year, and closed because of a failure to draw clearly the lines of authority among the archdiocese, the motherhouse in Le Mans, and the Province of Notre Dame du Lac.

The brothers Catta in their two biographies of Father Moreau and Mother Seven Dolors, the *Marianite Annals* published in 1947, and Sister Eleanore Brosnahan's *On the King's Highway* all tell substantially the same story. The records of the Sisters of the Holy Cross in Indiana tell a curiously different one which has so far never been presented in public.

The majority report first.

Backed by some French Catholic ladies of the city, the Fathers of Mercy in New York asked that the Marianites open an orphanage and workroom similar to those in New Orleans. But even before these projects were undertaken, they wanted the Sisters to establish a novitiate to ensure continuity to the work. Space would be provided by the French parish of St. Vincent de Paul. It should be noted that wherever there is a novitiate, there is the possibility of a province being established. There is also the possibility of break-off, either into an autonomous group or into a diocesan community. Father Rooney saw this second possibility forming in New Orleans and warned against it. In view of the restlessness among the Indiana Sisters, this may have been in the minds of the Roman authorities a few years later when they ordered that all the Sisters on the North American continent should form one province; bulwarked by Louisiana and Canada, the Indiana group was less likely to break away.

Sister Mary of the Five Wounds discussed the plan for the new venture with Father Moreau during her visit to France in 1854. In August 1855 she went to New York to undertake the work. The Reverend Benedict Madeor, S.P.M., was to be superior and chaplain for the project, and many of the expenses were underwritten by a Catholic businessman named Mr. Devlin. According to the *Marianite Annals* his terms of "pay when possible and without interest" made the venture financially failure-proof.[1]

Sister Mary of the Five Wounds requested that Indiana, Canada, and Le Mans send two Sisters each to staff the foundation, and each did, the Sisters from Le Mans arriving somewhat later than the others. Not all the names of these original six are known, but from Canada came Sister Mary of the Redemption (Rajot), a full-fledged eccentric, capable but unpredictable; and from Indiana, where she had been convalescing, came the once-adventurous Sister Calvary, now somewhat subdued by the trials of life.

In December 1855 Father Madeor wrote to Father Moreau, explaining the New York concept of a "workshop," assuring him of diocesan support, and stating that the backers required the New York foundation to be dependent on the motherhouse. The *Marianite Annals* state that by that time, with the New Orleans episode just over, "Father Sorin made up his mind not to allow any new houses in the U.S. which would be beyond his jurisdiction."[2] This is a fair assessment. For whatever reasons, Father Sorin was determined that all American houses should be responsible to the same superior, the superior at Notre Dame.

The house prospered. "Providence was lavish in its gifts," say the *Annals;* "postulants, novices, boarders, and a sympathetic public — what more could the Sisters desire!"[3] But at this point Father Sorin "summoned" Sister Five Wounds to Notre Dame and tried to give her a new obedience. She showed her obedience from Father Moreau and returned to New York. Sorin then wrote to Moreau that he wanted to handle the New York house all by himself and sent Sister Angela to look at it.

In February 1856 (the *Annals* date of September 8, 1855, seems very unlikely) Archbishop Hughes of New York and Father Madeor drew up a document and sent it to Father Moreau, stating among other things that "the house in New York will depend directly on the motherhouse in France. No other authority will be recognized." Father Moreau, who was then in Rome, did not get around to signing the document until April 10. When he did, he changed "directly" to "through the intermediary of the Provincial at Notre Dame du Lac."[4] This only muddied the waters. "Through the intermediary" was a vague phrase which could have meant any of several things. In February the council at Le Mans had declared themselves "willing to strengthen Father Sorin's authority as far as possible, but . . . not to subject Canada and New Orleans to his jurisdiction."[5] Sorin therefore assumed that this phrase gave him control over accounts, obediences, receptions of the habit, professions, and Visitations. The Sisters at the workshop and the authorities in New York did not know what it meant. Nobody wanted a repetition of New Orleans.

The standard story goes on that Sorin did not find the Sisters in New York sufficiently obedient to him and complained about it. Father Madeor wrote to Father Moreau, May 23, 1856, that the archbishop still wanted the project to depend entirely on the motherhouse and suggested that after eighteen months a Visitor from France should be sent, with the possibility of erecting the house into a province. Before that letter could have reached France, Father Sorin, having visited the place, wrote warning that the archbishop intended to take over the orphanage and have it depend on no one but himself; this would effectively make the Sisters there into a diocesan community. Madeor wrote that Sorin's visit had caused difficulties. Moreau wrote reiterating that the house was to depend on Father Sorin. (The Cattas call this a "reply,"[6] but Madeor wrote on June 10 and Father Moreau on June 19; not a reply.)

On July 12 Father Madeor wrote again saying that the archbishop would fight his case against an intermediary all the way to Rome if necessary. Surprisingly, however, when Father Shortis came from Notre Dame that same month to serve as superior, the archbishop approved the appointment.

Father Moreau wrote again to Father Madeor on July 29, repeating that the house should be governed through the intermediary of the superior at the Lake. On August 18 he wrote to Father Sorin, "If the house at New York does not function in dependence on Notre Dame, recall the Sisters."[7] This was not merely an "unfortunate phrase," as the Cattas suggest. This was what Father Moreau had been reiterating in letter after letter.

In October Sister Angela returned, found the situation not to her liking, and immediately closed the house.

> Boarders were dismissed, orphans were returned to their protectors. The novices, as well as the twelve postulants ready to receive the Holy Habit, were sent either to St. Mary's or to Phila-

> delphia where the Sister Visitatrix had rented a house, all provisions were sold, and the furniture was moved to the Indiana houses.[8]

So the good work of fourteen months and the first Marianite venture into New York City came to nothing.

Thus the majority report.

There is a different account.

Sister M. Emerentiana (Nowlan), the first official archivist of the Sisters of the Holy Cross, entered the community in 1868, the year before the Indiana Sisters became an autonomous congregation. She personally knew many of the pioneers, including Mothers Angela and Augusta, and it was she who persuaded Mothers Compassion and Elizabeth and Sister Euphrosine to write the memoirs which have saved so much community history. She also had access to written material now lost. Unfortunately she provides little documentation, but for each early mission she managed to gather a detailed and coherent account.

She never interviewed Sister Mary of the Five Wounds, who left the community in 1856, so her account of the beginning of New York, following the Notre Dame *Chronicles*, states that Sister Five Wounds "somehow or other obtained an obedience"[9] to open a house in New York similar to the one in New Orleans, that she requested Sisters from Canada and Notre Dame, and that she brought up a novice from New Orleans. (There is no mention in this account of Sisters from Le Mans.) They rented a house on 29th Street for a thousand dollars a year and concentrated on the novitiate first. They soon had twenty-five postulants. But troubles began almost at once.

> The Sisters who came from Canada could not agree with her. . . . Father Madeor and the archbishop were made acquainted with the miseries with which the work was beginning. After some weeks of quarreling and some disagreeable and offensive letters had been exchanged with the superior of Canada, Sister Redemption was obliged to return to St. Laurent, but not before she had inflicted an almost irreparable injury, by decrying the superiors and the Society, even in the presence of those who should have esteemed it the most.[10]

At this point Father Sorin received a letter from Father Moreau saying that the New York foundation would depend upon the Lake. As a business trip took him to Canada and the East, Father Sorin stopped at New York to see the establishment for himself.

> It was evident to him that neither the archbishop nor Father Madeor nor the Sisters themselves knew on whom the establishment depended, and that everybody was tired of this uncertainty, which threatened everything with speedy and inevitable ruin. In this emergency, Father Sorin thought he was authorized to take the house under his direction and assume the responsibility. He spent three days there, and before departing promised to send the persons necessary for the work.[11]

But he had hardly got back to Notre Dame when the Visitors returned chastened and disheartened from New Orleans. Like God, Father Sorin seems to have made a point of testing his favorites occasionally. Still smarting from the New Orleans episode, Sister Ascension was told to go and make the Visit in New York. She could take her report on New Orleans with her and work on it there, and then send it directly to Sainte-Croix.

She did go, spent "some weeks" there, and concluded that

> the good superioress and foundress of this house [Sister Mary of the Five Wounds] was not a person to manage it properly. Every day there were new projects, new journeys hither and thither, and nothing permanent but a constant state of endless changes. Then there were quarrels, dissensions, and sullenness altogether unbecoming in a religious house. This good Sister had not the remotest idea that her chimerical projects could be condemned, and had made up her mind to go in person to Notre Dame du Lac in order to have an understanding with Father Sorin.[12]

Some of this is reminiscent of Father Rooney's conclusions about the same Sister: she "is everything by turns, and nothing long;" and she "wants that most essential . . . ingredient . . . brains."

We know from her previous correspondence with him that Sister Five Wounds had been begging Father Sorin for years to let her come back to Notre Dame. This, and the fact that she "made up her mind to go in person to Notre Dame," take some of the authoritarianism out of Father Sorin's ensuing "summons" to her. He did, however, call her to Notre Dame, and a confusing situation followed. First Father Sorin

> sent her an order by telegraph, being fully resolved to put an end to troubles she had been giving in New York.
>
> But the very next day, having received the famous answer of the chapter at Sainte-Croix, condemning all his proceedings in New Orleans, he telegraphed a second time in the contrary sense. Unfortunately . . . Sister Mary of the Five Wounds [had] left immediately for Notre Dame. Father Madeor was well pleased at her departure.[13]

Sister Five Wounds got her trip back to Notre Dame. She showed her "new" obedience, "recently sent her from Sainte-Croix," along with copies of the obediences of her two assistants, a stewardess and a mistress of novices, and messages from Mother Seven Dolors "not to give the habit to anyone without the approbation of His Reverence [Moreau], even if the Postulants had already been admitted by the Lake," and "the positive declaration by the foundress [Mother Seven Dolors] that the Reverend Father would no more cede New York to the Lake than he would New Orleans." From the evidence of his own correspondence, Father Moreau must have been telling Mother Seven Dolors something different from what he was telling Archbishop Hughes, Father Madeor, and Father Sorin. Faced with these documents, Father Sorin sent Sister Five Wounds back to New York, recalled Sister Ascension, and notified the authorities in New York that "it appeared that Sainte-Croix wished for the future to take charge of the establishment."[14]

> Father Sorin's letter had hardly reached Father Madeor, and by him been communicated to the Archbishop, when the Reverend Father [Moreau] again manifested intentions altogether contrary to those reported by the colony of Sisters from Sainte-Croix. He maintained that this establishment depended on the Lake, and letters in his own hand came pouring in, in this sense.
>
> . . . the Archbishop . . . answered . . . that for the future he wanted to have no other intermediary between him and the Superior General but the person who should be the local superior of the establishment.[15]

It was at this point that the contract was drawn up which

Father Moreau amended to read, "through the intermediary of the superior of Notre Dame du Lac." This hopelessly confused Sister Five Wounds, who asked Father Sorin to come and straighten it out. He went to New York in May 1856 but "found His Grace inflexible."

Sister Emerentiana, still following the Notre Dame *Chronicles*, says that Father Sorin then wrote a report to Father Moreau which included a strong recommendation that a province be established in New York. This conflicts with what we know of Sorin's views about other provinces in the United States and, without Sorin's own statement behind it, would seem most unlikely. Father Moreau received a letter written at this time and urging such a step, but it came from Father Madeor.[16]

> No answer was returned, but the Very Reverend Father [Moreau] insisted the Sisters should rather be returned to the Lake. During this time Father Madeor acted as superior, gave the habit to thirteen postulants, several of whom had not even been accepted by the chapter. On his side, the Rector [Moreau] reiterated his decision.[17]

In July 1856 Father Shortis was sent as superior and accepted by the archbishop. In August Sister Five Wounds made another trip to the Lake to say that the archbishop was ready to change his mind. This was backed up by a letter from Father La Fonte, one of the founders of the project, to the same effect. Both reports were wrong. Father Shortis

> saw this misunderstanding, but remained silent for three weeks. Finally it became evident that the Archbishop had not changed his mind, and that consequently the formal orders of the Very Reverend Father Rector must be carried out.[18]

Sister Angela was in Philadelphia, setting up a house similar to the one in New York. She came to New York, examined the situation, and concluded that the house must be closed. Her reasons are not detailed but related to a general air of dissension, misunderstanding, and mismanagement.

The records in the *Chronicles*[19] go into considerable financial detail about the closing. The dowries of the postulants and the board bills of the pupils had been spent for furnishings and food. Mr. Devlin claimed a debt of $950. The furniture was not sent to the Indiana houses; it was assessed at $808 and taken by Mr. Devlin in partial payment of what was owed to him. That left the house still more than $2,000 in debt. "And yet," concludes Sister Emerentiana, "there was no lack of industry and of economy, but the good Sisters were slaves in the hands of a man who whilst protecting them was ruining them financially."[20]

These are the contrasting reports. The one which has found its way into the books is better known. The other is more detailed, and this gives it a ring of reality. The chief difference between them is in the interpretation of Father Moreau's several letters saying that the house was to be subject to Notre Dame du Lac. The Cattas say it was to placate Father Sorin. The *Annals* in English uses stronger language, saying that Father Sorin "finally succeeded in extorting the authorization of recalling the Sisters if they failed to submit to his orders,"[21] whereas the Cattas, quoting Father Sorin quoting Father Moreau, give it as "If the house in New York does not function in dependence on Notre Dame, recall the Sisters," changing it from a personal to a structural context. Father Moreau's letter no longer exists.

The Indiana version interprets all the letters as simply expressing Father Moreau's decision and desire. The extant letters themselves offer nothing to contradict this interpretation.

15
Wonderful Unheard-of Event, 1857

By 1857 the Holy Cross effort in America was sixteen years old and still Father Moreau had not seen any of the missions. He had been planning to come for some years, but one circumstance or another had always forced him to postpone the trip.

Father Moreau's circular letter of May 25, 1856, had brought to the whole community the news of the papal approbation of the priests and Brothers of Holy Cross. This was not the final ecclesiastical word, but Father Moreau found in it a confirmation that the congregation was going in the right direction, walking in the ways of God, and pleasing in the eyes of the Church. "My heart swells with gratitude," he wrote; "I cry out joyfully."

There had been one problem in securing the approbation. It first came in the form of approval of "the Institute according to its primitive form and limits." Father Moreau declined to accept this approval because he simply did not understand it. A conversation with Pope Pius IX cleared it up. The primitive form of the Society meant Brothers directed by priests. The Sisters were a later innovation and could not be part of the same society. Father Moreau wrote:

> When I saw that the question of the Marianites was causing the Holy Father some concern, I hastened to assure him that I was ready to sacrifice everything rather than occasion worry to His Holiness. He, in turn, deigned to reassure me and added, "You will govern them separately. I bless them also, and later on you will submit their rules to the Sacred Congregation."[1]

With this condition, the priests and Brothers were approved. Father Moreau ordered that the joyful anniversary be kept every year by the singing of the *Te Deum,* and that this first year the observance be fulfilled as soon as the letter reached each house.

He never understood the reaction at Notre Dame, which was one of dismay rather than delight. How could the priests and Brothers rejoice when their close co-workers, the Sisters, were not included in the celebration? The council at Notre Dame decided that for the time being, the approbation would simply not be announced.

Nevertheless it had happened, and no matter how long it took to get the Sisters separately approved, they were no longer part of the original society, and the matter had to be financially and canonically straightened out. There had to be a "separation of temporalities" — money, property, possessions.

In January 1857 Father Moreau had convoked for June a general chapter of twelve priests, at least nine Brothers, and seven Sisters, including Angela and Ascension.[2] Official approval of the men's congregation intervened on April 27 to prevent the Sisters' attendance. The statutes under which the new congregation was approved were promulgated, and the men set themselves to begin the separation of temporalities, first in France.

Father Moreau finally embarked for America on July 28, arrived in New York August 11, and went directly to Saint-Laurent. According to the Cattas, the whole Visitation was an unqualified success. Father Moreau took part in the exercises of the Canadian community, saw each member in direction, gave the habit and received professions. Finally

> he proceeded to separate the financial interests of the Sisters from those of the priests and Brothers. No objections were raised. The division of property was effected on the basis of equal partition between the two communities, and the same was done for the liabilities.[3]

It was not to be so simple in Indiana.

Certainly the religious of Holy Cross in Indiana were delighted to see their Father Founder. Father Granger had gone to Detroit to meet him, but they missed each other. Father Moreau and his companion, Father Louis-Job Letourneau, a young American who had been studying in Rome, reached Notre Dame the morning of August 26; Father Granger came in the next day. Father Sorin had been preaching a retreat in Chicago and had been taken ill on the way home. He had stopped in LaPorte and came into Notre Dame the afternoon of the 26th, expecting that Father Moreau could not arrive until at least the next day.

The church bells were rung at Notre Dame upon the Visitor's

arrival; the Sisters at Saint Mary's heard them and guessed the reason. It was an exciting time. Father Moreau wrote:

> A large group was already crowding around me, and for a long time I could do nothing but give them my blessing and embrace them. The surprise of my arrival made the excitement all the more lively and widespread. We then went to the church, where I intoned the *Te Deum* and celebrated a Mass of Thanksgiving, at which everyone hastened to assist.[4]

There are two eyewitness accounts of Father Moreau's first appearance at Saint Mary's. They are very different. Father Moreau himself wrote his account on the ship on his way back to France about a month after the Visitation. Presumably the affair was fresh in his mind and the account is accurate.

> The Superior, who had been ill in LaPorte from the fatigue of preaching the Sisters' retreat in Chicago, arrived some hours later. I went with him and the other brethren to Saint Mary's, which is about as far from Notre-Dame-du-Lac as the Solitude of the Savior is from Notre-Dame-de-Sainte-Croix. We had scarcely gone half way when we saw the entire community of Sisters lined up in procession, with the boarding students in the lead, and after them the orphans carrying their banner and holding flowers in their hands. It was a touching scene when they all fell on their knees to receive the blessing of the poor pilgrim, and then intoned the *Magnificat*, which was followed by several French hymns. Then it was that tears betrayed my emotion! I marvelled at the work of God and blessed His Providence. On my return to Notre-Dame-du-Lac, where I had called a general meeting of the two communities, I proceeded to the installation of Reverend Father Sorin as Local Superior and Vicar of the Province.[5]

Mother Elizabeth, who was also present in person, remembers it differently. According to her memoirs, Father Moreau did not come to Saint Mary's that first day. Instead, Father Sorin sent word that they would all come by carriage the next day and remain for dinner. Mother Angela thereupon informed the cooks that a grand dinner would be required, including a ragout and wines. She then turned her attention to the Sisters, the pupils, the Children of Mary, the white dresses, the banners, the flowers, the music, covering every detail.

> Before starting, Mother Angela said the youngest children should be nearest the gate, and should scatter roses on the path where the Very Reverend Father, after alighting from the carriage, would walk toward the house. The choir and the pupils should begin the *Magnificat*, the community singing the alternate strophes. After, if there was time, to sing the *Ave Maris Stella* and *O Sanctissima* until they arrived in front of the Academy, where chairs would be placed for the guests, and the Procession to form in circles; then Miss Sweeney should read an address of welcome in French.[6]

Mother Elizabeth continues that the procession formed and waited an hour, with Mother Angela "once in a while [sending] Sisters outside to see if there was sign of a carriage turning into the road leading to the Academy." Nothing appeared but the bread wagon. The children were allowed to sit down on the grass.

Then a Sister near the front saw a stranger walking toward them through the Notre Dame woods.

> "I do not know what he is; he don't look like a Brother and yet he has no cape. There he is — has a hat under his arm and is walking slowly — yes, he is reading in a black book and never looks up — who can it be?" By this time he had closed the book . . . and coming to the stile sat down and looked uncertain. . . .
>
> Then Sister Emily . . . screamed out, "Father Rector!" and dashed toward the stile, followed pell mell by all the French Sisters and the Brothers. . . . In a moment all were on their knees for his blessing. Mother Angela whispered to Sister Emily to get the procession on their feet, and she would keep him surrounded by the Brothers and Sisters until all were in order. . . .
>
> He was too overcome to speak when all the old Brothers and Sisters surrounded him. . . . When the children knelt he was surprised, being so preoccupied he had not realized he had reached Saint Mary's precincts.
>
> But when the children began to strew flowers before him, he turned to Mother Angela shaking his head, and cried, "No, no! I am but a poor pilgrim — flowers only before the Blessed Sacrament."
>
> But here he was interrupted by the sound of carriage wheels stopping near the river bank, and Father Superior and all the clergy from Notre Dame came forward and knelt . . . for the Father Rector's blessing — to the astonishment of the pupils, who never dreamed anyone less than the Pope could possibly be above their

> Father Superior. . . . When all were seated . . . Father Superior stood and said, "I am going to tell you what a trick Father Rector played on us this morning," bending over toward the Father, telling him he intended to apologize for being late, and whisper[ing] something that seemed to cause merriment between them.[7]

Father Sorin explained that the community at Notre Dame had expected the founder to offer Mass just before breakfast.[8] When Father Moreau did not appear for breakfast, they went to his room, found it empty and the bed made, and after searching the grounds decided to try Saint Mary's and then if necessary to drag the lake.

Father Sorin then invited Father Moreau "and those who did not wish to smoke" into the academy parlor. There he asked Sister Elizabeth to play the piano. She inquired what she should play, and Father Sorin named his own favorite, the *Marsellaise*, and told her to play it with spirit. She speaks of herself in the third person.

> When she was through, the Very Reverend Father Rector came to the piano. Of course she stood, but, not understanding a word he said, was surprised at his long speech. [She] listened attentively, and when by the inflection of his voice she recognized the termination of a sentence, bowed in assent.[9]

Reporting a later conversation with Sister Emily, she moves to the first person.

> I asked Sister what Reverend Father said to me. She burst out laughing. "He was so astonished you played that piece. If you were in France, you would be put in a prison, and he really scolded. . . . He must think you very aimiable, for you bowed just in the place you were being so severely admonished, and looked so calm."[10]

The next day Father Moreau visited all the buildings, stables and sheds, the dairy, and the Brothers' house. "He saw we were poor enough." The Sisters were still without bedsteads, sleeping on pallets on the floor, and in most of the old buildings from Bertrand, seeing the light come through the cracks in the walls and roof, he knew that rain and snow could do the same.

Father Moreau's account of the Visitation says that he first completed the work at Notre Dame and then turned his entire attention to Saint Mary's. Mother Elizabeth's sounds as if he went back and forth every day.

Father Moreau praises "the spirit of faith, the winning simplicity, and the admirable docility" of the religious at Notre Dame, but says also:

> I felt as if some invisible force were working against me. I encountered a mysterious kind of resistance from this bitter enemy of all God's works. This resistance became the more painful when, eight days later, I began the Regular Visit of thc Community at Saint Mary's. There, as at Notre Dame, . . . there had been many cruel trials and much physical and moral suffering. None of this surprised me, however, when I beheld the marvels accomplished by zeal and religious devotedness in the midst of these age-old forests.[11]

Father Moreau was not, of course, mistaken in sensing a certain amount of resistance in Indiana. It was not to him personally; in his person he was as highly revered by his American daughters as by any elsewhere. This was demonstrated by their enthusiastic reception of him, and there was more to come. But an undercurrent of discomfort with the Visit existed, arising from three sources.

First, there was fear. The Reverend Father Rector had once tried to take Father Sorin away, and the very thought caused flutters of panic to the American Sisters. Second, a widening gap of incompatability was beginning to show. Things were not always done in America the way they were in France, and the American Sisters, who found out during the Visit that they were no longer members of the same congregation as the priests and Brothers, had no wish to be placed under a Rule and government that failed to understand and make allowances for the difference. Speed and haste, for example, are not necessarily the same thing, but the American preference for speedy dispatch was often seen in France as unthinking haste, which it was not. Practicality and efficiency were not prized in France as in America. The Americans spent more time traveling because they had greater distances to cover. Because teamwork between bishops and religious, men and women, religious superiors and subjects, was absolutely necessary in a frontier diocese, American women religious were much more likely to accept responsibility and voice their conclusions than their European counterparts: a legacy the Roman authorities are just becoming aware of at the end of the twentieth century. Also, a neat French system of accounting did not always fit into a place where the barter system was still in partial operation; within the next few years, one man would pay his daughter's tuition by putting windows into the new academy building at Saint Mary's.

Third, there was some division among the Indiana Sisters themselves. This was largely, but not entirely, along French-American lines, with the "American" group more than half Irish-born. But Sister Ascension, French born and bred, was strongly pro-American and was only now beginning to share her leadership with Sister Angela. And much of the opposition to the motherhouse had recently come from that very place. In 1856 Father Moreau had sent to Indiana "a colony of Sisters who could no longer get their living at Sainte-Croix."[12] Two or three of these turned out to be good acquisitions, notably Sister Ursula, younger sister of Sister Ascension, who had a long career as a general councillor and mistress of novices. Most of the others, according to the chronicle, were guilty of

> jealousy, indiscretion, levity, and especially the itching to talk of the miseries of Sainte-Croix, which they made contemptible, especially in the person of the Very Reverend Father Moreau, whom they represented as a man who wanted to do everything himself and who embroiled whatever he meddled with, who could keep no one near his person, and with whom it was enough to intimate to be dismissed from the Society. (Amongst other things they spoke of his temptation[13] as a proof of mental aberration in a very flippant way, rather joking about the effects than grieving for the cause.) Such were the dispositions of these . . . Sisters . . . until Father Sorin put them all in absolute silence for an indefinite period. . . . They changed all the sympathies and compassion for the Mother House in its distress into indifference and even disgust.[14]

The last statement may be too strong, but the fact is that while Father Moreau was doing his own evaluating, he was also being silently evaluated. The Sisters wanted peace and harmony with the motherhouse, but not at any price. Nevertheless, their genuine respect and pleasure at receiving his attention were to be expressed symbolically in a great celebration.

Meantime there was work to be done. Father Moreau says he appointed Mother Angela as provincial. Mother Elizabeth says an election was held and adds convincingly that four ballots were taken before the tie was broken between Sisters Angela and Ascension. Mother Ascension was then named "mother superior" or local superior, and Mother Elizabeth mistress of novices. All three were ceremonially installed after Mass the next morning. Then the steward from Notre Dame presented his account books and Father Moreau went into the matter of separation of temporalities. Says Mother Elizabeth:

> And then we learned that Rome would never approve the Rules of the Sisters under the existing union of the three branches. And by a special favor we were allowed by the Bishop of the Diocese to be under the guidance of the priests of Holy Cross as confessors. . . . And therefore the Sisters were to retain one third. . . . Then came the difficulty.[15]

Notre Dame needed the services of Sister cooks, laundresses, clotheskeepers, and infirmarians. Saint Mary's needed the priests as chaplains and the Brothers as gardeners and maintenance crew. The solution reached would never have satisfied a later generation — equations proclaiming that five Sisters equalled one priest, and three Sisters equalled one Brother. Even this did not meet the demand. "In a few years the college increased so rapidly [that] girls *(old ones)* were hired to work in the kitchen and laundry."[16]

Writing with the hindsight of many years, Mother Elizabeth found in this separation the re-founding of the American Sisters — perhaps the first of many.

> [They were] days of deep reformation and I might almost say the beginning of our community life. We had to make our living and do for ourselves in all temporal affairs. But for our spiritual guidance the Bishop of the diocese . . . still gave us the privilege of being under the priests appointed by Reverend Father Sorin. This was a favor few can understand, for the spirit of the Rule is the same. And those privileged to remain at home cannot be thankful enough, and only find the difference when sent to other places, where the clergy of other orders, or secular clergy, become their spiritual guides.[17]

On September 8 Mother Angela asked Father Moreau if he would bless a little island in the St. Joseph River that evening. A full moon would give plenty of light to see their way down the bluff. She then asked Father Sorin to bring as many priests and Brothers as could come from Notre Dame.

Sisters and girls had been working to make archways covered with flowers and illuminated by Japanese lanterns. These were placed at intervals all along the path leading to the river. Tin candle holders had been nailed to trees, as had brackets for religious pictures. Old Joseph and his helpers had raked piles of brushwood together for bonfires at suitable distances from the path. The rustic bridge to the island was covered with red, white, and blue bunting. An altar was erected under a great tree on the island, and decorated with candles and wild flowers.

At four in the afternoon Mother Angela sent a carriage to the sacristy at Notre Dame, and the Sister sacristan loaded in the surplices of all the priests. The Sisters at Notre Dame had an early supper and set off for Saint Mary's.

Mother Angela and her helpers kept the priests entertained inside or in front of the house until all was ready. Then just as it was growing dark, she invited them all into the academy parlor, where each was surprised to find his own surplice ready to be donned. Finally she led them through the house and opened the back door. The Sisters and girls were drawn up in a long procession, each one with a lighted candle. The candles twinkled on the trees, and the bonfires leapt on either side. The lighted arches showed the way down the bluff, and the altar on the island nearly a mile away blazed with candlelight; and, says Mother Elizabeth, "the river in the moonlight glimmered as a broad silver band enclosing the whole in St. Joseph's protecting arms."[18]

Father Moreau followed the procession in a sort of trance. "It took half an hour to reach the rustic bridge,"[19] and when they did, the procession halted and parted, and only the clergy passed over to the island. Father Sorin and Father Sheil, provincial from New Orleans, assisted at the blessing, and Father Moreau named the spot St. Angela's Island. Afterwards he tried to make a little speech, translated by Father Sheil, "who had a loud voice," but gave up, saying, "The American night birds sang so loud, it was impossible to make myself heard." Even years later, Mother Elizabeth was getting some enjoyment out of the memory:

> Father Sheil shouted . . . and explained [that] Father Rector had mistaken the katydids and tree frogs, who were too frightened at the unusual light to move. . . . Poor little things, they no doubt handed down to their posterity the wonderful unheard-of event of

> 1857. . . . It has often been a wonder . . . what Katy did? But that night revealed she was a scold, and she certainly proved it by out-talking the head of a community.[20]

It could be taken as the central metaphor of the whole relationship between Father Moreau and his American daughters. The scene had been prepared with reverence and love, and was filled with beauty and blessing. But it came down to the saintly founder, trying to get his message across from an island, at night, in a foreign language, against an insistent chorus of local voices. And when it was over, only one permanent thing was left, the name on the island. And that was Angela.

Both accounts seem to agree that the separation of temporalities had been accomplished. Actually, the principles to be followed had been laid down, but otherwise the process in Indiana was barely started. It would continue past the founder's lifetime, twenty years into Father Sorin's administration as superior general.

Unaccustomed to the distances in the United States, Father Moreau had left himself no time to visit New Orleans. He met with Father Sheil and with Sister Mary of the Passion, who had come north to consult him. On September 12 he and Father Sorin went to Chicago, where Father Moreau again imposed upon himself a killing schedule of High Mass, direction of all the religious, conferences, and Visitation of both the Sisters' and Brothers' schools. He then returned to Notre Dame, took leave of the religious in Indiana, and, accompanied by Father Sorin, took the train and arrived September 17 in Philadelphia.

This was the foundation which had replaced the one in New York. Father Moreau reviewed the place with his unfailing conscientiousness, but by then he was close to the limit of even his superhuman energy. Father Sorin, too, was too weary to go any farther. They parted at Philadelphia. Father Moreau and Brother Vincent, who had been elected a member of the general council, went on to New York, where they rested in a hotel for about six hours, and then boarded the *Arago* for the voyage back to France.

Father Moreau's work was not quite finished. On board the *Arago* he wrote a long circular letter. The first part described the visit to America. The second part convoked a general chapter of the Sisters to meet at the motherhouse August 10, 1860. This gave the Sisters nearly three years to prepare. The names of the chapter and council members for each vicariate were given.

For the vicariate of Notre Dame du Lac, the council of administration consisted of Mother Ascension and Sisters Alphonsus Rodriguez, Elizabeth, and Arsene. The provincial council consisted of Mother Angela, Mother Ascension, and Sister Emily. The provincial chapter added to these two groups Sisters Immaculate Conception (McIntyre), Liguori, Circumcision, and Ambrose (Corby). The letter continued:

> Beginning with the reception of this Circular Letter, the temporal government of the Sisters is and will remain entirely separate from that of the Salvatorists and Josephites. The same services, however, will be rendered by the Sisters as in the past, with no other remuneration than lodging and board. . . . In the case of the Sisters, dependence on the Bishops is absolute. . . .
>
> Sisters Superiors and Directresses should not be too easy in allowing their religious to correspond with those of other houses.[21]

Most of the American religious never saw their founder again.

16

They Do All the Governing, 1858–60

For the Sisters of the Holy Cross in Indiana, the two most important developments of 1858 were the promulgation of their new constitutions and the division of the diocese of Vincennes.

Long before the first Sisters achieved any canonical status, Father Moreau took up the task of writing a constitution for them. On March 25, 1843, he informed the little community at Le Mans that he had begun the work, in view of the fact that some Sisters would be leaving in a few weeks for America. "The Sisters designated for America would take with them this little book of Constitutions, which would be a safeguard and a guide. These Constitutions could eventually be submitted to the Bishop of Vincennes."[1] There is no evidence that the constitutions ever were so submitted, or even that the earliest Sisters actually brought constitutions with them. In fact, by the time the Sisters arrived, there was already some question about their relations with Bishop de la Hailandière.

By 1847, however, Father Moreau had produced a daunting tome of nearly four hundred pages, which mixed rules and constitutions together. It contains a preface enjoining the Sisters "most rigorously" to keep secret all that regards their congregation. An introduction follows, beginning with the admission that the gospel should form sufficient rule for any individual life, but stating that for a society further regulation is necessary. A "Preliminary Constitution" entitled "Nature, end and means of the Society of Holy Cross" gives the general plan of the whole tripartite congregation. There are seventy-two pages of "Rules and Constitutions common to the Association of Holy Cross"; this section is followed by its own Table of Contents and Index. The Preliminary Constitution begins, "The Association of Holy Cross is composed of three societies: that of the Priests of Holy Cross, that of the Brothers of St. Joseph, and that of the Sisters of Holy Cross or of Our Lady of Seven Dolors."[2]

The "Second Part" of the document, where the page numbers begin anew, is entitled "Rules and Constitutions peculiar to the Society of the Sisters of Holy Cross or of Our Lady of Seven Dolors." This second part is divided into three sections: Government, Conduct of the Sisters in general, and Rules peculiar to each kind of employment. Then follows another Table of Contents and Index. It is worth noting that the term "Marianite" does not yet appear.

It is unlikely that this unwieldy document was ever translated into English in its entirety. Father Moreau occasionally complained of the slowness with which the translating was being done. The letter from the *Arago*, the ship he took back to France in September 1857, says that he has appointed Sister Angela to make the English translation of the Rules, the Directory, and the first part of his book called *Pedagogy.*

The same letter also convokes the general chapter of the Sisters to meet in Le Mans in August 1860. Father Moreau had organized the Sisters into four provinces: France, Indiana, Canada, and Louisiana. The chapter would be composed of the provincial and one delegate from each province. In Indiana this would mean Angela and Ascension.

The problem of the separation of temporalities between the men's congregation and the Sisters had been addressed, but not solved, during Father Moreau's visit. It was a much more complicated matter in Indiana than anywhere else. "Father Founder," say the *Marianite Annals*, "did not judge the time opportune to propose a change, and so the community of temporal interests was to continue [in Indiana] between the Fathers and Brothers and the Sisters as long as the Superior would deem it expedient."[3] The interests of Notre Dame and Saint Mary's especially were bound up together at this time, and it was not to the advantage of one side or the other to force them apart or to set up a sort of fictional arrangement which would cloak or deny the reality.

In addition to property and finances, there were a number of other problems growing up between the Indiana Sisters' community and the French administration of the Marianites. They can be grouped under four general headings, though there is overlapping.

First there was the problem of accepting postulants, giving the habit, admitting to profession. The motherhouse allowed the local groups to do the first, but wanted some voice in the second, and strove to maintain full authority over the third. But the young American Sisters certainly did not go to France, and the councillors at the motherhouse never came to Indiana. The council in Indiana felt that they were competent to judge these candidates — they had lived with them, tested them, knew them. It was not that French authorities were likely to disregard the recommendations of the Indiana superiors — in fact, there is no record that they ever did so. It was simply that the Americans felt they ought to be able to make decisions, not recommendations. In point of fact they often did, and notified the French council when they got around to it. But this was irregular, as they were constantly reminded.

Part of the same problem was the matter of accepting, staffing, and closing foundations, usually parish schools. The American bishops wanted quick responses. A community that had to write to France about taking a new school and wait seven weeks for an answer would find the offer withdrawn and a quicker-acting community functioning on the site by the time the permission arrived. The American Sisters' community was growing rapidly and had the Sisters available to be sent out. They sent them, notifying France later. Sometimes the administration in France was notified of the closing of a house of whose opening they had not been informed.

This was partly a matter of where authority would eventually lie, and partly a matter of the second problem, communication, especially with its factors of time and distance. One place was too far from the other for a swift exchange, and a slow exchange is a poor exchange in these matters. And another difficulty in communication was growing daily — the matter of language. In 1859 the American community had 176 Sisters, of whom only 32, or 18 percent, spoke French as their first language.

The French are traditionally more tenacious than most in defending their need for their own language. It is an indispensable tool in maintaining the culture and, they used to claim, the faith. But the Sisters in Indiana were trying to be of service in a culture very different from the French, and Father Sorin had not found English any less useful than French in spreading the faith. Letters and documents from France, including the constitutions, had to be translated before they were accessible to 82 percent of the community.

Third, the cultural disparity resulted in a growing disparity of vision of what the congregation *ought to be*. Though Father Moreau had acknowledged that the Sisters might do some teaching outside of France, neither he nor his councillors were prepared for the fast spread of an active American apostolate of teaching. From a few orphan girls, deaf mutes, and Indian children in the early forties, the Sisters had progressed by 1859 to operating four flourishing academies (at Saint Mary's, Morris, Michigan City, and Baltimore), two orphanages (at Washington, D.C., and Baltimore), a manual labor school at Saint Mary's, and at least eight parochial schools as far apart as Philadelphia and Bourbonnais Grove, Illinois, besides their continuing service at Notre Dame. Furthermore the country was on the brink of the Civil War, which would carry the Sisters into a new apostolate of professional nursing. At the same time, as Connelly points out, "most of the Marianites in France continued to do domestic work," and "the general administration in France seems to have had a more contemplative understanding of religious life than did the American Sisters."[4] Or, as Bishop Luers would write somewhat later to the archbishop of Baltimore, referring to the Marianites:

> In France they are as yet without property, & number some 65 or 70 Sisters — who do the kitchen work for 4 Colleges & they have besides 1 or 2 small parochial schools with 2 Sisters in each. Yet, as you will perceive, besides doing all the cooking, washing, & mending for these 4 Colleges, they also do all the governing for the entire Congregation, wherever it is, France, Canada, & U.S.[5]

Connelly quotes this and adds in a footnote that there were "six houses in France comprising 53 Sisters, of whom 11 were teachers, 40 were engaged in domestic work, and 2 were novices."[6]

Finally, there was Sorin's absolute conviction that the only way to run the American houses was to have them all run from one central place, by people who understood the American scene. Notre Dame was that place, and, for the time being at least, Sorin was the chief of those people. He would have preferred to keep New Orleans under his jurisdiction because he believed that houses located in America should be thoroughly American, but its loss was the less difficult to concede since it was apparent that the New Orleans area would remain French-speaking long after the other scenes of Holy Cross labor in the United States had become completely English-speaking.

No congregational historian has missed this tendency in Sorin. And without exception they have treated it as a negative trait. The view of Sorin popularized by the Cattas has affected even the historians writing in the shadow of the golden dome. What never seems to be mentioned is that the Holy Cross religious, male and female, who lived under Sorin's authority *wanted* it that way. The whole Sisters' council panicked in 1852 when it looked as if he might be sent to Bengal. Every time he went to Europe there were pleas and prayers for his quick and safe return. When he was elected superior general in 1868, a flood of letters begged him not to make his headquarters in France but to return to those who needed him in America.

This is not to say that everyone on the American mission was blissfully happy. The small French minority consisted of two groups: those who had entered wholeheartedly into the American apostolate and never expected to do anything else, such as Sisters Ascension, Circumcision, and Arsene;[7] and those who were putting in their time out of sheer obedience as if serving a penal sentence and counting the days until they could return to France or at least to Canada. Among these were some whose letters complained of tyranny (though more on the part of their female than of their male superiors) and a certain number who were torn both ways, aware of owing respect and veneration to Father Moreau, but needing the freedom to get on with their work.

On September 22, 1857, Rome announced the formation of the diocese of Fort Wayne, Indiana, to be comprised of the forty-two counties in the northern half of the state. The new bishop, John Henry Luers, was consecrated January 10, 1858.

Bishop Luers was a priest of the diocese of Cincinnati, where he had already become acquainted with the Brothers of Holy Cross. He paid an early visit to Notre Dame after his consecration and seemed to be pleased with what he saw. Unfortunately, the amity was soon disturbed by contention arising over inadequate documents provided by the diocese of Vincennes to the new diocese of Fort Wayne, some of which documents dealt with the Notre Dame property. It was also charged by Bishop St. Palais of Vincennes that Father Sorin had paid too much attention to, among other things, the development of the Sisters. This at least may have had the merit of directing Bishop Luers' attention to the Sisters. By 1862, when Father Charles Moreau's visit forced everyone to take sides, Bishop Luers came down firmly in favor of autonomy for the Indiana Sisters.

The separation of the men's and women's congregations again necessitated new constitutions for the Sisters. Father Moreau wrote on January 22, 1858, that he was working on them. He worked speedily, for the new documents were sent out to all the houses in the congregation on April 13, under the imprimatur of Jean Jacques Nanquette, the new bishop of Le Mans. They were accompanied by a circular letter from the founder. He acknowledged that some were already complaining about the new constitutions.

> If I could have foreseen the rapid development of our Institute from its origin, I would then have been able to regulate and coordinate everything in advance; but were that so, Holy Cross would have been the result of human effort and not the work of Divine Providence.[8]

He assured the Sisters that he would revise "as experience will prove the need or utility."[9] The general chapter called for 1860 would pass on the document, adding the weight of its authority to his. Meanwhile the Sisters were to receive, study, and even memorize the constitutions, learning to follow the spirit as well as the letter.

The non-translation, or the slowness of the translation, became one of the points of contention between France and Indiana. It is not clear how many copies of the constitutions were received in Indiana, how many of the Sisters who did read French had the ability to translate such abstract material (Angela certainly, Ascension possibly, but these two were much occupied about other things); or indeed how many of the 172 Sisters could read well enough in any language to understand the books by which they were asked to live.[10] No doubt the priests of Holy Cross were asked for and gave conferences, but, under the best possible circumstances — and this is not a matter of good will or bad will but simply of personalities and viewpoints — the instructions given by Father Sorin and the Indiana priests would have differed greatly from those given by Father Moreau and the priests in France.

At any rate, the Sisters went ahead for over a year, living out what they perceived to be their obligations.

Mother Mary of the Seven Dolors visited Saint Mary's in 1860. It is unclear whether she came in the spring, the fall, or both.[11] She seems to have been welcomed more cordially by some than by others but to have met with no discourtesy or opposition. Father Sorin had tried hard to get her and Father Moreau to agree to have the chapter at Notre Dame, but that had proved impossible.

Mothers Angela and Ascension traveled at least from New York with Mother Seven Dolors and the other capitulants. Their policy was to make no waves. It was enough that Sorin had descended into grouchiness, having lost the location argument, and was declining to attend the men's chapter. The Sisters were going to keep quiet, say little, and await what would happen between Rome, their new bishop, and Father Sorin.

The Cattas say, "[A]ll difficulties were apparently smoothed out."[12] The operative word is "apparently." The 1858 Constitutions were "unanimously" approved by the chapter and sent to Rome. Among other things, the house at Sainte-Croix was (now, for the first time officially) declared to be the general house. The chapter decided to reopen the house in New York and make it dependent entirely on the motherhouse. The Sisters from Indiana did not object, verbally. The capitulants parted peacefully.

It was a false peace.

17

Autonomy without Separation, 1861–62

Two major problems had gone unresolved following the Founder's visit to Indiana in 1857. One was the extent to which Mother Mary of the Seven Dolors had authority over the Sisters in Indiana. When Father Moreau gave her the title of superior general, he recognized that the Sisters in Indiana were unlikely to accept her authority and advised her not to use the title in her few dealings with them until the chapter of 1860 had confirmed it.[1] That had now been done.

The second problem, the separation of temporalities, was more of a problem in Rome and Le Mans than in Indiana. The Holy See was refusing to approve the Sisters as a separate congregation until their financial matters were disentangled from those of the men. These were much more complicated in Indiana than elsewhere and seem not to have been a high priority anyway. The Indiana group could probably have moved faster than it did to clear things up, but it could not have moved as fast as the rest of the congregation wanted it to.

Father Moreau had agreed that Father Sorin alone would serve as superior of the Indiana Sisters until further orders. This arrangement was entirely satisfactory to the great majority of Sisters, but in writing to them May 8, 1861, Father Moreau managed to make it sound like a punishment.

> I have therefore found it necessary to charge your Father Superior to use all his authority as my representative, in order to reform these abuses by subduing unruly spirits and compelling all to observe the Rule, thus releasing your Mother General from all responsibility in this matter until further orders from me. Besides, I shall send a Visitor who will make a conscientious report on present conditions in this province, and after conferring with me, he will, with Father Sorin and the Ordinary, take the needed measures to bring about peace and order.[2]

The paragraph is an excellent example of the way in which Father Moreau forged ahead in all innocent serenity, doing what turned out to be all the wrong things for his relationship with the Indiana Sisters. He was dividing the authority for them three ways: among the Visitor, the superior on the spot, and the bishop. Each was assured that he had full authority — the bishop by ecclesiastical right and the other two by delegation from the founder. But fullness of authority for one group cannot reside in three people, and it would not happen that the Visitor would, "with Father Sorin and the Ordinary, take the needed measures to bring about peace and order," because Father Sorin and the Ordinary had radically different ideas from the Visitor as to what path would lead to peace and order.

Another event of enormous proportions was about to leave its mark on the Indiana Sisters. Seven southern states set up the Confederate States of America on February 8, 1861. On April 12 their army fired on Fort Sumter, South Carolina, and the American Civil War was on. Casualties mounted throughout the summer and early fall. The appeal of Governor Oliver P. Morton of Indiana for nurses reached Notre Dame the evening of October 21, and Father Sorin immediately brought it to the Sisters. Those at Saint Mary's volunteered almost unanimously. Assignments were hastily juggled, light packing was hastily done, and Mother Angela left the very next morning with five others for Cairo, Illinois.

The story of the Civil War will be told in its own place, but it must be kept in mind that for the next few years the whole community led a double life. More and more Sisters went into the battle zones, with altogether about eighty-five (of a total population of about two hundred) serving at one time or another, some for many months. The rest doubled up on the teaching, housekeeping, administrative, and formation duties at home, while trying to keep the war nurses supplied with what they needed. Meanwhile those with responsibility or a personal interest endured the strains of community politics, the whole autonomy question, and the effects of an ill-conceived and appallingly executed Visitation.

The Visitor was Father Charles Moreau, nephew of Father Basil, and the only member of the general council in Le Mans who was at all fluent in English. He arrived in New York December 31, 1861. Father Sorin expected him to come immediately to Notre Dame, as the official Visitation to a province usually begins and ends at provincial headquarters. But Father Charles stopped first at the re-foundation in New York, then went on to visit six schools in Philadelphia, then to Baltimore and Washington. By this time it was the middle of March 1862, and Father Charles decided to go to New Orleans; but finding his route blocked by war, he turned north instead and went to Canada.

Father Sorin, in his personal account of the Visitation, says that he was at first eager to meet with Father Charles. But the longer the Visitor delayed his arrival the more the enthusiasm at Notre Dame died down. Winter turned into spring and brought a further problem. A circular letter from Father Basil, dated March 26, 1862, would have reached Indiana around April 20. The first six paragraphs were an exhortation to union, then came the announcement of the Visitation (which had already been going on for three months when the letter was written), the provisions of which disturbed Sorin greatly:

> Take up with him everything which deals with your temporal interests, and present to him all the acts of your Councils and Chapters, in order that he may be able to furnish me with a conscientious report, and obtain my approval or that of my Council. This approval is essential especially for admission to profession, and until it is obtained all professions will be postponed, as well as the reception of Sacred Orders. In addition, as regards the Sisters, it will be necessary in every case without exception, and notwithstanding any concession made in this respect in the Vicariate of Indiana, to obtain previously the written consent of their Mother General. Without this consent of the Mother General I would never give my approval for perpetual vows, and thus the profession would be null and void.[3]

It had been agreed that the mother general would not extend her authority over the Indiana Sisters until further orders from Father Moreau. Here were the further orders. It was not too soon. It had been a year and a half since the chapter of 1860 had confirmed her title and authority. The matter had to be settled eventually, and with the Visitor on his rather roundabout way to Notre Dame, the time had come. The letter seems to have been timed to give Charles a chance to find his feet in America, with plenty of time left before he had to face Sorin.

Since the mother general and her council never denied profession to anyone recommended by the Indiana council, it is hard to see why this became one of the absolute sticking points on which Sorin would accept no compromise; but it did. Sorin claimed that this was the chief condition on which he undertook to serve as superior of the Indiana Sisters. This letter canceled the condition, he said, and therefore canceled his obedience regarding them. He would wait to discuss it with Father Charles, then resign if Charles made no change.

Sometime after the middle of June, Charles left Montreal and notified Sorin that he was re-entering the Indiana province. He made the Visit at Cincinnati, Columbus, Zanesville, and Toledo in Ohio, and then went to Fort Wayne, Indiana. Bishop Luers received him on July 7, accepted his credentials, and gave him full priestly faculties in the diocese. The bishop warned the Visitor that the subject of the mother general's place of residence would come up and that the financial matters would be difficult to untangle; but neither of them seems to have anticipated the extent of the resistance which Charles would partly find waiting and partly build for himself.

It was July 11 when Father Charles finally arrived. Knowing that he had been in the province for some time, Father Sorin and the Notre Dame staff had hoped he would be present for the Notre Dame "prize-givings" (commencement). His failure to arrive in time for this exercise was an additional cause of offense. "The disappointment was greatly felt," wrote Sorin, "and from that time the desire for his arrival soon changed to indifference."[4]

Father Charles arrived on a Saturday noon. Learning that Father Sorin was at Saint Mary's, he went there immediately, and both priests remained there for the rest of the day. Father Sorin informed him that he (Sorin) felt himself in an impossible situation regarding the Sisters, that he thought the arrangements in the latest circular were "obviously directed at him"[5] and that he planned to resign as superior of the Sisters. He also said that the mother provincial (Liguori) should be changed, at least away from Saint Mary's.

The next day, July 12, Mother Liguori gave Father Charles a list of the novices recommended for profession. Charles had a second copy of the list made and sent one to Father Basil in Le Mans and the other to Mother Seven Dolors in Canada.

This was exactly in accordance with Father Basil's orders, but it set off Sorin like a match to fuel. He announced his resignation, both to Charles and to the Sisters' council. Charles replied that he had no authority to accept the resignation. Two days later Sorin produced his "written resignation in proper form,"[6] a copy of the one he was sending that day to Le Mans. Charles took it and said nothing, and Sorin later claimed that silence gave consent.

Charles had moved his personal effects to Saint Mary's July 12. Sorin found this further cause for offense, later complaining that in the whole six weeks of the Visitation, Charles had spent only one night at Notre Dame; also that "during all this time he never so much as put a foot inside Father Granger's novitiate, which should have been one of the first things he visited."[7]

Father Charles decided to convene the provincial chapter on July 16, and to the usual capitulants he added the directresses of Notre Dame and of Morris, Illinois. Father Sorin protested that neither of these Sisters had been elected to the chapter and that their inclusion made the group too French. They were excluded. The chapter confirmed the obedience list, which would be made public at the end of retreat.

Father Charles met with the council almost daily. The matter of an academy in Cairo had been mentioned; they sent to Mother Angela, then in Cairo, for more information. Another day they discussed the new academy building at Saint Mary's (now Bertrand Hall). The present council knew little or nothing of the financial arrangements for it. Charles informed them that they had been given permission to spend $10,000 and had already spent $24,000. Taking no account of rising prices brought on by war, nor that a building cannot be left half-built when prices go up, he lectured the council as if they were children, telling them that a good religious would not spend fourteen cents without permission, much less $14,000, and that the building would certainly not be blessed. (This account is being written in a perfectly serviceable Bertrand Hall, which has served dozens of community purposes in its first 130 years.) The contrite council, which had not had the responsibility for the building, wrote "a letter of reparation for the faults committed against obedience" in building the academy. Another of Sorin's rockets went up. "If," he wrote, "there were such great blame attached to the building of this house, it was to Father Sorin and his council that he should have addressed himself and not to the Sisters, who should not have heard one word of this displeasure."[8]

By August 3 Mother Angela had not sent the information on the proposed academy in Cairo, and Sister Eusebia had not returned to Saint Mary's with the novices who were serving as war nurses and whose return Charles had ordered. Sorin, who had been in touch with the group concerned in the Cairo project, offered to write them saying that he was no longer the Sisters' superior and the plan would have to be discontinued. Charles asked Mother Liguori to take the letters to Cairo and if possible to find Sister Eusebia and her novices and head them toward home. The next day, however, it was decided that Sister Regis should go, and the following day that Charles himself would make the trip.

Among other things taken up by the council there was the case of young Sister Annunciata (McSheffrey) "whose health had been a cause of inconvenience to the community."[9] Charles and the council decided to send her home but never turned the decision into action. She became superior general in 1895.

While the meetings with the council were going on, Charles was apparently also preaching the Sisters' retreat. By the clearly dated evidence of the council minutes, Charles left for Cairo August 5 or 6 and was back by August 11. He had come back so quickly because Bishop Luers had arrived at Saint Mary's and wished to see him. It was Charles' tactical misfortune not to be on hand when the bishop arrived, thus giving Sorin plenty of time to discuss matters with Luers.

Charles reported to the council on August 12 that he had seen the Sisters in Cairo and Mound City engaged in their "noble work of charity,"[10] but he had not seen Mother Angela. She had left for Memphis, and he would have followed her there (and probably missed the telegram with the bishop's message) except that he had met the other Gillespie, her brother Father Neal, who told him that he thought Angela would go from Memphis back to Saint Mary's.

Father Charles also told the council that he had seen the bishop on the previous day. The bishop taxed him with having accepted Father Sorin's resignation, which Father Charles denied. The bishop also told Father Charles to make no important decisions regarding the Sisters without Sorin's consent and to leave the financial future of the Sisters in the hands of Mother Angela, who alone (with Sorin) understood it. Luers claimed that no set of constitutions had ever been presented for his approval, nor, as far as he knew, for that of any bishop of Vincennes; that whatever the Sisters did in France, in Indiana their teaching was to be directed at the leadership training of an American Catholic elite; and that his own plan was for them to gain "real autonomy without . . . actual and formal separation." It was clear that in the bishop's mind "real autonomy" was more important than the avoidance of formal separation.

It is still customary for the Sisters of the Holy Cross to renew their vows at the end of the annual retreat. At present this is done out loud during the closing liturgy. In 1862 it was done by having them all sign a written declaration. A few declined to sign. The statement read:

> In the Name of the Father and of the Son and of the Holy Ghost. Amen. We, Sister Marianites of Holy Cross, undersigned, renew before Almighty God, our perpetual vows of Poverty, Chastity, and Obedience, and, in the person of our Reverend Father Visitor, our engagements of inviolable fidelity to the Constitutions and Rules received from Very Reverend Father Basil Anthony Moreau, our venerated Founder and first Superior.
>
> Given at St. Mary of the Immaculate Conception, near Notre Dame du Lac, the twelfth day of the month of August 1862, on the feast of St. Claire, at the close of the annual Retreat.[11]

Much has been made of this declaration in some quarters, as if any further moves toward Indiana self-government constituted a particularly dreadful kind of treason. But the renewal of vows was an ordinary annual event, and since a Visitor was present that year, it was right that the renewal should be made into his hands. The Constitution and Rules were still under construction, as they have been reconstructed many times since, so to work and petition for certain changes in them was not a violation of the fidelity promised. The fact that practically all the Sisters signed the statement indicates that they saw it as consistent, some with their hopes for more control from the motherhouse, some with their hopes for less.

Bishop Luers wrote that he would be returning to Saint Mary's on August 27, and Father Charles, apparently deciding that another interview would be futile, went to Morris on August 25. Bishop Luers brought with him Father Julien Benoit, a French-speaking priest who helped the bishop interview each Sister. After two days of seeing the Sisters, the bishop announced that he would take the case to Rome; meanwhile the Sisters were to consider Father Sorin as their "sole superior." All Father Charles' faculties with regard to the Sisters were revoked.

A few days later, Father Basil Moreau wrote to Father Sorin that since Bishop Luers had entered the case, it would now have to be settled in Rome[12] but that meanwhile Sorin had no authority over the Sisters. But Sorin had resumed the authority on the command and with the approval of the bishop four or five weeks before the letter arrived.

On September 8 Bishop Luers wrote to Father Charles telling him to restrict the rest of his Visit to the priests and Brothers. With that understanding, Charles' faculties could be restored.

On the same date Bishop Luers wrote to Mother Liguori, provincial of Indiana, telling her that he was giving Father Sorin exclusive direction of the Sisters in the diocese of Fort Wayne. She would have to accept that arrangement if she were to continue as the Sisters' superior. A crisis of conscience was thus created for Mother Liguori. Sorin had been her spiritual director, but it did not seem to be a matter in which she could consult him. When Luers put the whole thing into a formal letter addressed to all the Sisters on September 19, the council sent for Charles to come from Morris and see the letter. He helped Mother Liguori to formulate the terms of her reply to the bishop: that she did not feel that her vow of obedience allowed her to recognize in Father Sorin any authority which was not delegated to him by Father Moreau. It had come to a choice between the authority of Father Moreau and the authority of Bishop Luers, each in a different way legitimately claiming to be backed by the authority of Rome. Mother Liguori chose Father Moreau. This made it impossible for her to remain in Bishop Luers' diocese, and she left for Canada.

Father Moreau wrote to Bishop Luers reminding him that the first thing Rome wanted done was the separation of finances. He also disagreed with the bishop's view that the Rules were still developing.

> [A]nything in the ordinances of Your Lordship which would be opposed to these Rules would have no more binding force for [the Sisters] than for myself. You can forbid the Visitor or myself any spiritual or temporal contact with the Sisters, once the financial question has been settled. But they would then remain free to leave your diocese to rejoin their companions elsewhere.[13]

The word *rejoin* suggests a basic flaw in Father Moreau's perception of his Sisters in Indiana. Ninety percent of them had entered from the United States, mostly the midwestern states. They had no "companions elsewhere" to "rejoin." There would be no general exodus from Indiana even if the bishop made them a diocesan community, which he was not attempting to do. The American Midwest was the site of their mission (soon to be extended to further boundaries), and, then as now, the mission came first.

A very few Sisters did leave with Mother Liguori. Who they were and why they went will be among the subjects for the next chapter, for it is time to consider the personalities involved in this struggle.

18

Good and Bad and Very Bad, 1862–63

Father Sorin would not have taken kindly to the problems of the visit of 1862 under any circumstances, but his difficulties were multiplied by the absence of his two faithful lieutenants. Mother Angela had gone to war within hours of the first call for nurses. She was moving about setting up hospitals just behind the battle areas, so that the people at Saint Mary's were not always sure where she was. Sister Ascension was serving as superior in Philadelphia.

Both of these long-time allies of Father Sorin were widely respected in the community and had considerable influence among the Sisters. Had one or both of them been on hand when Father Charles arrived, the whole Visitation might have been different (meaning either that they might have soothed the developing hostility between Sorin and Charles, or alternately, might have left Charles nowhere at all to stand). As it was, the government at Saint Mary's was in the hands of the provincial appointed by the last chapter in France, Mother Liguori, and her (at the time) devoted American councillor, Mother Elizabeth.

Sister Liguori (Chrétien) had come to the United States in 1853 as a clotheskeeper and dressmaker. She was part of the delegation to New Orleans in 1854 and seems to have given less offense than anyone else. She and Sister Augusta had been the first to move in 1855 with the Manual Labor School from Mishawaka to the Rush property, which became Saint Mary's. She then went to the Manual Labor School in Philadelphia as assistant superior until 1857 and served as superior of St. Paul's School in that city until 1860, when she was appointed to be provincial superior in Indiana. At the time of this appointment she was thirty years old.

Like Mother Angela, she had responded quickly to the need for nurses in the Civil War. Exactly one week after the call came to Saint Mary's, Mother Liguori left with Sisters Bartholomew (Darnell) and Angeline (Blake) for the Jefferson Barracks in St. Louis. This hospital, however, remained open for only six weeks after their arrival. The other two Sisters were then assigned elsewhere, and Mother Liguori returned to her provincial duties at Saint Mary's.

The elections (or appointments) which took place in 1857 during Father Basil Moreau's visit had resulted in Mother Angela being named provincial and Mother Ascension mother superior at Saint Mary's. In this year Sister Liguori was changed from one Philadelphia assignment to another. Two years later, still in Philadelphia, Sister Liguori wrote to Mother Seven Dolors:

> It seems to me absolutely necessary that Mother Angela be withdrawn from administration as soon as possible and that this administration depend on only one Superior, who would be in agreement with the Provincial Superior.[1]

The letter is in French, and the words "Provincial Superior" are masculine. It appears that from her post in Philadelphia, Sister Liguori was detecting some disagreement between Sorin and Angela serious enough to call for Angela's removal from office. This view is not supported in any of the extant documents. The letter continues even more surprisingly.

> The future of our Province is in great danger unless they give us a First Superior whom God has favored with supernatural gifts which enable her to fulfill her office. The one we have [now] has [only] the title; and you know that our Very Reverend Father General has removed for *personal reasons* (those are his own words) many things which ought to be her responsibility to give them to the administration of Mother Ascension; [and] that she cannot do it because the failure of the other one to bestir herself prevents it.[2]

Much correspondence has been lost since those early days, some of which might have thrown light on this paragraph. If by "First Superior" is meant Angela (and it clearly does not mean Ascension), there are some unusual accusations in it. Sister Liguori was free to hold the opinion that Angela was deficient in supernatural gifts, though it does not seem to have been a widespread opinion. It may have seemed to someone in Philadelphia that Angela merely held a title. But though Angela has been variously accused of favoritism, jealousy, short-sightedness, elitism, stubbornness, secretiveness, deceitfulness, and at least as many other faults as there were Sisters who found something to be discontented about, never anywhere else has she been accused of failing to bestir herself. Quite the opposite.

With her appointment as provincial, Sister Liguori left Philadelphia, where she was replaced by Sister Ascension, and came to Saint Mary's. The government there was still operating under a clumsy two-council system. As appointed by the chapter in France, the original members of the provincial council were Mother Liguori, with Sisters Ursula,[3] Edward, Angela, and Emily, in that rank. Angela was serving as prefect of studies, which meant chiefly directress of the academy. The local council consisted of Mother Elizabeth as mother superior, with Sisters Arsene, Ambrose, Cherubim, and Francis de Paul. From the time these appointments took effect until the arrival of Father Charles, the council minutes were signed by Sister Arsene as secretary, and by Father Sorin when he presided and Mother Elizabeth when he did not. They were, therefore, minutes of the local council, which actually governed Saint Mary's.

After Father Charles' arrival, he signed the minutes, followed by Mother Liguori with Sisters Eugenie, Edward, Emily, and Elizabeth. These were the meetings of the provincial council. Sister Ursula had been replaced by Sister Eugenie as assistant provincial. Sister Regis was signing as secretary, Sister Arsene having gone as superior to Morris. Mother Seven Dolors had removed Sister Francis de Paul from the council upon discovering that Sister Francis de Paul could neither read nor write.

At Saint Mary's, Mother Liguori had returned to the practice of having Father Sorin as her spiritual director, placing herself under his guidance with French enthusiasm.

> My conscience as all else is and ever shall be open to you — as far as you will allow me. No, nothing do I wish to hide from my most venerated Father and superior; good and bad and very bad are all the same to his charity.[4]

Of one problem at Saint Mary's, she says, "If you could possibly come it would make the matter much easyer [*sic*], *plus facile*. I have something too that I would like to ask you."[5]

This sounds somewhat like Sister Mary of the Five Wounds, some years before, protesting her soul's need for guidance while seeking reasons to be in the director's personal presence. Three and a half weeks later Liguori wrote a letter, mostly in English, as she knew he preferred; but the heart of it is in French and shows considerable psychological insight.

> It seems to me that some women cannot, without great danger and difficulties, be governed by a [male] superior because of the tendency of our sex toward a natural love, so subtly dangerous, for men. . . . [O]bedience mixes with a desire to please, to be esteemed, even to be loved, which leads us away from the pure spirit of faith. . . . On this and the above I have had much struggle and temptations, and they may come again.[6]

This is fairly plain talk. We do not have Sorin's reply to it, but he must have indicated that he preferred not to get into these depths, for the very next day she tried to take some of it back. "[Y]our own little daughter from home, who so confidently loves you as her Father! Why then do you so easily mistake my inmost feelings toward you?"[7]

A month later, just before the call for nurses came, he must have been considering sending her on a long, if temporary, assignment elsewhere. She knew he just wanted her out from under his feet. "As to my going to Washington . . . it would be a good opportunity to have me out of the way. [But] . . . to the eyes of the community it would have a very bad effect."[8] She would have no problem with simply being demoted. "Do not fear to proclaim my demotion openly, and please remember that *I need no other offices*." She suggested that Sister Ursula (Salou), originally named her first assistant, could replace her.

He must have reprimanded her at this point, for she wrote October 18 that she wanted to reveal her soul to him, but his "turning in disgust" from her "poor soul . . . has trampled down all my courage. . . . I dare no longer go to you. I love you so much, and if it were possible venerate you more. But — in another way than I did before." She concludes with a prayer (addressed in form, at least, to God, not to Sorin) to be relieved of all responsibility so that she could "have the courage to live on, to weep and do penance for my sins."

We do not know whether Sorin responded to this, but the next day she made one last try.

> [I]ndeed you know [your poor child]. Better than she knows herself. May you see how much, how exceedingly great, how indispensable

> to her is your fatherly care. *Trust me as your own* on all occasions . . . and let me concentrate in yourself alone all that my heart and soul require . . . you cannot be indifferent to the truest sentiments of your own daughter . . . because I feel the certainty of being yours without limits, I feel what a miserable *own* I am.[9]

Fortunately, the call for nurses came two days later, and in less than a week she was on her way to Missouri.

She returned before Christmas. Aside from the rather ordinary business visible through council minutes, there is no way of knowing how she occupied herself. By spring of 1862 the relationship with Sorin seems to be even more strained. In a letter of apology for an unnamed offense in May, she seems again to be approaching the breaking point. She speaks of

> the needs of a withered heart — of which its past breaks the heart . . . the strange penance of being made the Mother and example at the head of a community, from which I ought to have been ignominiously removed — to be in daily contact with a priest who is distressed by the mere sight of me, and whose well-deserved expressions of sorrow, of scorn, of fear for the future and of weakened confidence for the present supply every hour of my life with sacrifices . . . does not all this explain to you, my Father, the timidity of your poor child? When above all her office forces her to act as if she had always been what you had the right to expect.[10]

It is quite understandable, then, that when Charles arrived one of the first recommendations urged upon him by Sorin was that Mother Provincial needed a change of scene. Instead, Charles' presence brought a different kind of change to Mother Liguori. Her rather hysterical dependence on Sorin disappeared, now that there was someone else from whom she could borrow strength. In the conflict over whether the two directresses (Notre Dame and Morris) could join the meetings of the two councils, Liguori supported Charles for including them. Sorin apparently rebuked her for it quite strongly. She wrote him a letter — her favorite refuge — letting him see her own hurt at his attitude. ("It would have been better for me not to know how deeply you despised me.")[11] But she said she had been convinced by Father Charles' pointing out the applicable place in the Constitutions, and his assurance that the procedure had worked well in Canada. Then the directee turned director and urged obedience on Sorin, ending with the wise conclusion, "Eternity will be long enough for everybody's rights."

At the same time she was transferring her letter-writing to Charles. She wrote on August 2, apologizing for visiting him after night prayer and deploring the quality of religious life at Saint Mary's. Again, she is upset, switching languages in mid-sentence three times. She complains of having heard a report that Mother Angela had written a letter to Rome and that "the intrigue of Mother Ascension" (who was apparently still in Philadelphia) had rendered life in the community "insupportable for many and not very religious for most." She now saw that, for whatever reasons, she herself had failed in effectiveness as a major superior. "Oh my Father, please consider before God . . . if it would not be better for me to get away from here." Six days later the bishop faced her with the choice that resulted in her departure for Canada and France.

We need to see Mother Liguori, not only through her own eyes, but through the eyes of some of the Sisters of the time. But first we need to examine the character of her strongest (for a while) supporter, Mother Elizabeth. This is one of the strangest women in community history, the childhood friend of Mother Angela, convert, music teacher, widow who brought her mother and her two small children to Bertrand with her, then arranged for her mother to bring up the children when she entered the community. Her skill on the piano and her docility when he scolded her for playing the *Marseillaise* (scolding of which she did not understand a word) impressed Father Basil Moreau, who appointed her mistress of novices, local superior at Saint Mary's, and finally American provincial, an appointment which never went into effect. A mercurial, enthusiastic, changeable creature, Mother Elizabeth was at first profoundly attached to her old friend Angela, then passionately devoted to Mother Liguori and the pro-French party, then somewhat more quietly returned to the support of Angela, Sorin, and the separatists.

Her correspondence begins in October 1862 after Mother Liguori had left Indiana. It is almost always addressed to "My Very Honored Mother" and refers to Mother Liguori in the third person, so that the Mother addressed would be Mother Mary of the Seven Dolors. This must have caused a translation problem, one knowing only English and the other only French, especially in view of Elizabeth's excitability, which frequently led her into incoherence. Her letters are full of underlined words, dashes, and double exclamation points. She seems to have had a cloak-and-dagger mentality in which she took it as her mission to outsmart all the multifarious schemes with which she saw herself surrounded. Her letters read like a nineteenth-century spy drama.

October 10, 1862: "You would never believe how I am watched." November 1: "If it was found I communicated with Canada I do not know *what* would *be the consequence*. . . . I am certain they will never let me go without trouble." February 16, 1863: "I am doubly watched and suspected about letters." About two letters which she had written to Father Basil Moreau and forwarded through Canada, "I hope they are on the ocean *if not all is lost*."

The whole correspondence was, in fact, a clandestine one. She sent and received letters through a Mr. Toll in Niles, whose daughter was a boarder at the academy. She occasionally had her own mother mail letters for her in South Bend, but always with the injunction to her correspondent that the return letter must go through Mr. Toll. That there were return letters is indicated by her occasionally thanking her correspondent for them — none are extant. Once she wrote that Sister Cherubim wanted Mother Seven Dolors' permission to steal some stamps. When the permission did not come, Sister Cherubim stole the stamps anyway and Elizabeth asked that she be pardoned. Another time Sister Ambrose found an academy girl mailing one of Elizabeth's letters, and the girl said she was mailing the letter for her mother. Elizabeth rationalized, "This she said because she looks on me as her mother."[12]

The smallness of the minority to which she belonged worried Elizabeth while it made her feel heroic. In her first letter to Canada she wrote, "All are turned but four."[13] She identified three— Sisters Cherubim, Xavier, and Emily, with the fourth either herself or a novice, Sister Macrina, whom she describes as "*tormented*" (emphasis hers). This leads her to the reflection, "Sometimes I think I am wrong when all think otherwise?" Two weeks later she laments, "Alas! The number is small that would remain faithful."[14] By December 8 Sister Xavier has managed to leave for Canada, and Sister Emily has other concerns, so "Sisters Cherubim and Macrina are alone faithful."

By December 14 she is weakening. "If all is arranged . . . and peace restored, I am willing to stay, *but*, if not — I will write to you my whole trouble, and reasons — *then* do with me what you wish. . . . There is nobody . . . who can speak French that I can trust [for correspondence purposes, apparently]. They all feel contrary — all the Fathers also."[15] On New Year's Eve she muses, "Father Provincial is very kind to me," but he confines his remarks to professional matters, in her case music.

By mid-February 1863 she had recovered the spirit and vocabulary of the heroine of a bad espionage novel. When one Sister addressed a rather cryptic remark to her, "She did not know how perfectly I understood her meaning." She has two more loyalists — "Sisters Crucifix[ion] and Archangel are firm." Sister Crucifixion had been a community problem ever since Sister Five Wounds had struggled with her in Kentucky, and she was now the oldest living member of the congregation. Sister Archangel has left only a statistical record of her existence, besides this mention.

The year or so after Mother Liguori's departure appears to have been a great time for writing letters. There were as many viewpoints as there were Sisters (a characteristic which has remained true of the Sisters of the Holy Cross), most, but not all, on the side of American autonomy. Sister Eleanor (Kelly), who taught at Saint Mary's Academy, wrote to Sorin December 8, 1862, urging him to speak up in his own defense. "I fear that unless the hand of God stops Mother Liguori she will ruin the community."[16] She accused Mother Liguori and most of her councillors of failing "almost daily" to appear for community prayers, and Mother Liguori of cutting herself off from the community once the Visitation began, and spending too much time in Father Charles' room. "I was very much surprised one night to hear her coming from there between eleven and twelve at night. I do not mean to insinuate that there was anything wrong, but found [it] rather irreligious in persons bound to give good example." She declares that Liguori and Elizabeth both know that they can never hold office again in "our establishments."

But by St. Patrick's Day 1863 Sister Eleanor is writing, apparently to Mother Seven Dolors, to ask to be removed from the Indiana province. "If Very Rev. Father General gets any authority beg him never to sanction Sister Angela or any of her followers as superiors. . . . They are Sisters Eusebia, Edward, Ambrose, and many others. . . ." Poor Eleanor had thus put herself on the bad side of both groups of authority. In the end, she remained with Indiana. Her record shows that she was changed twelve times in twenty-two years, suggesting that she was either very adaptable or just the opposite.

Father Basil Moreau wrote a letter of great importance on January 29, 1863; it was probably received in Indiana in early March. Because of its importance in the history of the congregation, it seems best to quote it in its entirety.

> Our Lady of Holy Cross, Mans
> Jan. 29, 1863
>
> My dear daughters in J.C.,
>
> If you have not received an answer to your kind wishes of the New Year any sooner, it is because I was waiting to know the result of the regular visit in our houses in America, to inform you of it, in order to give you a correct idea of the moral state of your Society on the foreign missions, but seeing that Rev. Father Charles is detained at Notre Dame or elsewhere in Indiana by difficulties always springing up to determine one telling of it, saying first, that inasmuch as your establishments in France, in Canada, New York, in New Orleans and in Bengal console me by their devotedness, obedience, and attachment to the Mother House, and regularity, those of Indiana, afflict one by acts, which I am certain shall pain you as much as myself.
>
> Know then, as I am compelled to say the sad truth that after having brought all sorts of difficulties in the way of the Visitor from the beginning of his visit, the Sisters of St. Mary's of the Im. Conception, with some from the other houses of the Province, have written to the Ordinary of the Diocese that the Visit which was hardly commenced had brought trouble in the establishment, that they had only received from France, unfit subjects, — without regard for the devotedness of Mary of the Cenacle, and M. of the Savior, who do not deserve such an outrage, —that they had lived 20 years without rules — as if they did not have them since the commencement, with the repeated command of having them translated in English, which being done at last were not distributed, that the Visits from France had never produced any good — as if they had forgotten the many thanks they had returned to me for the advantages they had derived from *mine, etc., etc.* In a word they ask not to be visited, as if they had not complained that the Visit was not

terminated. I pass over many other calumnies with which it is useless to entertain you, to say that the Visit shall be continued, — that I love to hope this scandal will cease, and to recommend to you to pray for it. I command all the Sisters of Indiana who still acknowledge me for their superior to inform me of it without delay, and I tell the others beforehand that if they do not re-enter under obedience at the receipt of this letter they shall cease to reside at Notre Dame at the end of February next, and an order shall be given to prevent our religious there to render them any service, moreover they shall not have any share before God in the temporal goods, but will only receive dowry or a part of it; they will make arrangements with those who have directed them in their ways, and shall at once leave the marks of their profession.

And the present Circular shall be sent to all the Houses in the Congregation, in French and in English, either directly or through the Visitor who will modify it or see to its execution according to his own wisdom.

Given at Our Lady of Holy Cross, Mans,
the day, month, and year as above.

Moreau

P.S. Whoever has taken part in the acts mentioned above have trampled under foot the sacred engagement of their profession, in what regards the dependence on the Mother House, and all those who for the time being shall correspond with anyone else than the ordinary, the General Superioress, and myself or the Visitor, until the conclusion of the Visit will be considered as separated from the Society.[17]

One wonders, as one often does in the case of Father Moreau, where he got his information (see New Orleans chapters, among others). No such letter from the Sisters to the bishop is extant. There is no record of the Sisters' having written to Bishop Luers between July 1862, when Father Charles arrived in Indiana, and January 1863, when Father Moreau made these charges. It is true that both Father Sorin and Father Charles were in communication with the bishop. It is also true that the bishop came to Saint Mary's and spoke to the council, the chapter, some individuals, and possibly the community as a whole. As to the various charges which they are supposed to have made:

"[T]hat the Visit . . . had brought trouble in the establishment . . ." True.

"[T]hat they had only received from France unfit subjects . . ." This is quite true as regards most of the more recent ones, the 1856 group who had come to Indiana because they "could not get their living at Sainte-Croix,"[18] and whose comments on the motherhouse showed such bad dispositions that Father Sorin had put them all into absolute silence (not that persons of this stripe were likely to obey such an injunction). And even that group contained Sister Ursula (Salou), Mother Ascension's blood sister and a future councillor. Of the two hundred Sisters in the congregation in 1863, forty-three had been in Indiana with Sister Bethlehem, seventeen had lived under Mother Cenacle, and fifty-five had lived under Mother Savior. These French Sisters were all much loved and admired, and the number who had known one or more of them would have been enough to keep any others from making such a rash statement as the one quoted above, certainly to keep them from making it in the name of the community.

"[T]hat they had lived 20 years without Rules . . ." They had certainly been asking for almost twenty years for modification of the Rules to suit their mission, if that is what is meant; they had not addressed these requests to the bishop.

"[T]hat the Visits from France had never produced any good . . ." It seems simply not credible that the Sisters would have said that to the bishop or anyone else. Sister Immaculate Conception's visit got mixed reviews from the memoir-writers of later years, and Father Moreau's own early announcement that Rome had separated the Sisters from the rest of the congregation had caused a shock. But on the whole they seem to have been grateful for all the visits until Father Charles upset and confused them by clashing, not only with Sorin, but with their bishop.

"[T]hey ask not to be visited . . ." This was an idea the bishop had on his own, requiring no prompting from the Sisters. Charles was told he could finish the Visitation if he confined himself to the men.

In short, all of this seems to be less a document from the Sisters to the bishop which Father Moreau is quoting than a report from Charles to Father Basil. The trouble with this solution is that Charles sent two reports to Father Basil shortly after he arrived in

Indiana, one on July 16 and one on July 24, and then no more for the rest of 1862. So the question remains, where did Father Basil get the information he put into his document of January 1863? Much of it seems unlikely — was it also partly imaginary? It was not, at any rate, what it gives an impression of being — a paraphrase of an actual single document from the Sisters in Indiana to their bishop, of which Father Basil had somehow obtained a copy.

On March 13, 1863, Sister Incarnation wrote to Father Moreau in response to his request that all the Sisters in Indiana who still regarded him as their legitimate superior write and tell him so. Sister Cherubim added a two-line note and her signature. There is no way of telling how many of these letters there may have been, certainly a good many. Most of the Sisters in Indiana would not have understood the problem in terms of legitimacy of superiorship. For them it was a matter of adjusting the Constitutions to life in Indiana, of electing their own major superiors, of deciding on professions and the acceptance of missions.

Sister Caroline (O'Leary) did not write such a letter. She was an angry woman when she wrote to Father Moreau on St. Patrick's Day, if indeed she wrote the letter to which her name is signed. The date may have helped her to the gift of self-expression; she was a housekeeper, not a teacher. Her letter was long, defensive, and eloquent. It bears certain resemblances to the Overton letters (see below) and is presented as a sample of this type of letter, with no guarantee as to its authenticity.

> I now comply with your wishes in acknowledging the receipt of your circular which has indeed grieved me and shocked the heart of every religious who heard it; by the false accusations brought against us in regard to the Visitor. If indeed he came as a Visitor; he did not act the part of Visitor here, but *only that* of a *Superior.*
>
> . . . I was completely surprised to learn from the circular that you had been listening to such accusations without ever inquiring . . . as to their truth. . . . I am led to think your experience has not yet taught you the character of a woman not guided by the dictates of religion or any sense of human justice. When her pride is tuched [*sic*] and ambition opposed, when she sees her vicious projects detected and she is thrown into confusion — think you that if she has not adheared [*sic*] to truth and justice at first — she would do so after? . . . I do not blame superiors for listening to such peo-

ple . . . but I do condemn them for not listening to the reasons of one as well as the complaints of the other.

. . . [W]e could all clearly see to whom you alluded as having guided the Sisters of Ind. in the late proceedings of which you accuse them. It could have been no other than our most holy, edifying, most venerated Superior Father Sorin. . . . [H]ow in conscience [could you] listen to *any*one who dare say anything now against him who has been so truly devoted to you, who has labored so zealously in the community for the last twenty years and who has proved *Such* a *true*, *efficient* benefactor . . . and . . . one of the *first* to *sacrifice himself* in assisting *you* in the grate [*sic*] work begun! Without him what think you your community would have been here? What is it elsewhere? a mere nothing. If then the three branches have flourished here almost miraculously, . . . to whom under God is it owing? To Father Sorin alone. . . . And yet . . . at the instigation of a few . . . members who have never done anything for the community except to scandalize it, you intend . . . removing him from authority. . . . Before God, Very Revd. Father, I think it is the most imprudent and detrimental step you could take. . . . You even accused him of abusing the Sisters' confidence and prevented him from hearing our confessions. I could not describe my feelings . . . when I brought a Sister who had been confined to . . . bed . . . the last two months to confession and she had to come back without it. . . . [O]nly for him you would have no Sisters here whose confidence could be abused. No accusation was ever more calculated to arouse all [our] feelings of justice . . . than this *most unjust* one.[19]

All this is only from the first half of the letter. The defense of Sorin goes on, with a statement that they know Father General has been misinformed and that not he, but the informers, are to blame. She does not want to know who all of them are, but "I know the four or five among whom it originated." She urges the superior general to consult only his children's good, and she ends by putting him on probation. "If we find that you do this . . . we shall ever as now love and esteem you as our holy founder and Beloved Father no matter how we may be situated as to temporals."

Another whole group of letters came from the Sisters in Morris.[20] Charles stayed with them only a few days but made a very favorable impression. Sister Francis Assisium was the chief correspondent, but it is hard to know to whom she was writing — perhaps to several different persons. Her letters proclaim her loyalty and that of all the Sisters in Morris to the motherhouse in France, though the Sisters do not envision living anywhere but in the United States.[21] They formalized this position by a letter to their own bishop in Chicago with copies to the Archbishops of Baltimore and Philadelphia and the Bishop of Fort Wayne.

> Rt. Rev. Bishop,
>
> The Sisters of Holy Cross residing in the diocese of Chicago learning lately that Your Lordship was under the impression we wished to be separated from our Mother House in France hasten to inform you that such is not the case.
>
> By our Rules and Constitutions we are already placed under the control of the bishops who are pleased to admit us to their dioceses. We do not feel the least incommoded by being governed from France since it is on the same plan as the Sisters of Charity. We wish always to remain united to the M. House. Therefore we humbly beg Your Lordship not to facilitate by your influence such a proceeding as would tend to separate us from our holy Founder, whose wise regulations for our welfare & spiritual advantage have been appreciated even by the Holy Father himself who gave him charge over us.
>
> Most humbly and respec. etc. etc. asking your benediction,[22]

None of the five Sisters who signed this letter cast their lot with the motherhouse when the actual separation occurred. Two of them, Sisters Arsene and Francis Assisium, were among the general council members in 1869 who voted unanimously to accept the decree of autonomy. Bishop James Duggan of Chicago expressed surprise at the contents of the letter and urged that it be sent on to the other bishops, "though he expressed a full concurrence that they would effect the separation."[23]

There are three more mystery letters, the existence of which must be acknowledged lest a later researcher conclude that there was an attempt to hide something. All three are written in the same hand.[24] All are dated from the Overton Hospital in Memphis, Tennessee, where the Sisters were doing war nursing. All three are addressed to Father Basil Moreau. The longest one is dated March 24, 1863, and signed Sister Mary Augusta. The other two are dated March 27, 1863, and signed Sister M. Helen and Sister Flavia.

The letters are so strange as to be highly suspect. The author is (or authors are) under the impression that Father Moreau is trying to remove Father Sorin from a position of authority in Indiana and also trying to have Mother Angela "expelled" from the congregation. It is true that Father Moreau forbade Father Sorin to hear the Sisters' confessions, and that this brought about considerable distress at Saint Mary's. It is also true that Father Moreau's letter of September 27, 1862, had negated any orders of Father Sorin's which conflicted with those of Father Charles and declared any Sister who obeyed Father Sorin rather than Father Charles to be in formal disobedience to the superior general. But by the time that letter arrived, Bishop Luers had taken charge, rendering the communication largely ineffective. There is no evidence anywhere of Father Moreau's ever having moved against Mother Angela in any way.

The letters also contain accusations of Mother Liguori remaining in Father Charles' room until late at night, keeping liquor in her room and sharing it with Sister Eugenie and other cronies, staying up so late at night that she was unable to rise in the morning, attending Mass only on Sundays and seldom receiving the Eucharist, practically never showing up at community exercises, and of being "dissipated and altogether disedifying in serious matters." At the same time there are passionate defenses of Sorin and Angela, which show great loyalty and devotion to the American leaders but a certain shakiness on some of the facts.

But the most damning feature of the Overton letters is the shrill, almost hysterical tone they take toward Father Moreau — impertinence raised to screaming defiance. While other letters of the period from Sisters to priests are liberally sprinkled with "Reverend Fathers" and "Most Reverend Fathers," the writer of these letters does not bother with any form of courtesy, even toward the superior general. He is addressed as "you," sometimes underlined, and is blamed for all the troubles of Indiana. The writer predicts ruin for the Indiana community unless he withdraws his minions and leaves Indiana to elect its own superiors.

There may have been a few Sisters who would have written to Father Moreau in that vein, but Mother (then Sister) Augusta was not one of them. Because of her years of service as mother superior and superior general, plenty of her correspondence is available for comparison. The style, the structure, and the tone of the Overton letters are all alien to hers, yet the signature strongly resembles hers. Did she sign what someone else had written? She was not a woman to sign anything without reading it carefully; and it is unlikely that, having read this, she would have put her name to it. If her name was forged, were the other two forged as well? Sisters Helen and Flavia have left us no other signatures to compare.

At any rate, one may ask whether these letters or that of Sister Caroline ever reached Father Moreau. It is questionable whether they were ever posted, though they may be copies of letters that were (and that may account for the similarity of handwriting). If they reached France, were they translated? Father Charles Moreau was Father Basil's chief translator. The likelihood is low that Father Basil ever saw any of them, but he was acutely aware that the stresses between Indiana and the motherhouse were growing too strong to be contained.

19

Overflowing with Patients, 1861–65

The message from Governor Oliver P. Morton of Indiana, which the Sisters at Saint Mary's heard from Father Sorin the evening of October 21, 1861, was one of the four or five most decisive influences on the Sisters of the Holy Cross. On that October Monday they were a community dedicated to the teaching of small children and young ladies and to the performance of domestic duties in their own establishments and in some of those of the Holy Cross men. On Tuesday they had embarked on their new ministry of caring for the sick, the wounded, the dying.

After a night spent in light packing and probably lighter sleeping, with part of the night required to arrange for replacing themselves in academy duties, six Sisters left for Cairo, Illinois. They were headed by Mother Angela and included Sisters Adele (Moran), Anna (Dorsey), Mary Magdelene (Kiernan), Veronica (Scholl) and Winifred (McGinn).

They reached Cairo on October 24, and within a few days Mother Angela had had an interview with General Grant, who was not yet in charge of Union operations. He told her that the Army wanted the Sisters to take charge of the hospital in Mound City, Illinois, when it was ready and in the meantime there was much to be done at the regimental hospital in Paducah, Kentucky. While Mother Angela's group was taking hold at Paducah, Mother Liguori left Saint Mary's for St. Louis, accompanied by Sisters Angeline (Blake), Francis de Paul (Sullivan), Fidelis (Lawler), Augustine (Flanagan), and Callista (Pointen).

Early in December Mother Angela was told that it was time for her to go to Mound City. She went with a secular companion, looked at the hospital, and telegraphed to Saint Mary's for more Sisters. Sisters Patrick (McGookin) and Athanasius (O'Neill) were sent on the sixth. In this same week the Sisters in St. Louis finished their work there when the hospital was moved. Mother Liguori returned to Saint Mary's and the other Sisters reported to Mound City on December 9.

Sisters Patrick and Athanasius, the first recruits to Mound City, found Mother Angela cooking meat for her patients. They had already been waylaid by a Dr. Burke of the military hospital in Cairo, who had begged them to come to his hospital. They informed Mother Angela, who replied crisply that Dr. Burke had earlier been offered the services of the Sisters and had refused them, and would now have to "repent at his leisure"[1] and wait his turn.

The hospital at Mound City was a "large block of twenty-four unfinished warehouses," according to the recollections of Sister M. Ferdinand. Because their original purpose had been merely storage, they were roughly built, with the floor boards rather widely spaced in some places. The beds were furnished with black blankets of such poor quality that the black dye came off on both patients and nurses. Before the arrival of the Sisters, the ambulatory patients waited on the others, and the food was sent in from military kitchens, the same fare supplied to the men in the field.

The Sisters made changes as fast as they could. Sister Ferdinand (Bruggerman) recalled:

> Mother Angela . . . soon had a neat little kitchen, well supplied by the Quartermaster with rice, eggs, milk, chicken, etc., where light and palatable dishes were prepared. . . . In my ward, too, there was an immense stove, and I made so much toast at that stove that my eyes were injured by the heat. Later, we were furnished with better blankets, in fact good stores of every kind.

The problem of the floorboard spacing was not as easily solved as that of the blankets and food. Sister Francis de Sales recalls what that could lead to.

> [On a] February day in 1862, soon after the battle of Fort Donelson, . . . Mother Angela was assisting the Chief Surgeon on the lower floor. He was performing a difficult operation, the exact accuracy of which would determine the life of the soldier. His head and that of Mother Angela were bent over the poor boy. Suddenly from the ceiling a heavy red drop fell upon the white coif of Mother Angela, who . . . did not move. Another, and still another, drop after drop came till a little stream was flowing. At last, the final stitch had been taken, and the two heads . . . rose simultaneously. Not till then did the doctor know that a stream of blood, trickling through

> the open chinks of the upper floor, had fallen steadily upon the devoted head of Mother Angela, who now stood before the Surgeon with her head and face and shoulders bathed in the blood of some unknown soldier.

A soldier who had been a cabinet maker or woodcarver in civilian life made a tabernacle for the little chapel which the Sisters installed at Mound City, and some of the Catholic patients pooled their money and bought a chalice. Mother Angela wrote to Admiral Samuel P. Lee[2] on the gunboat *Blackhawk* asking for a pass for a chaplain. The admiral sent the pass immediately marked "Good till rescinded" — which it never was. Good ecumenical relations also existed with the non-Catholic chaplains. Sister Anthony (Mannix) characterizes the "government chaplain, a Mr. Merrill" as "truly a good man," and says that a Reverend Mr. Taylor and his wife often came to the Louisville hospital, bringing eggs, milk, and fresh bread for the patients.

Mother Angela met the next group of recruits in Chicago, intending to take them to Mound City. They arrived at Cairo at three o'clock on the morning of Sunday, December 15, and by the time they had found a hotel it was time to go to Mass at St. Patrick's. The housekeeper at the parish showed them the way to the hospital, then known as the Bulletin. Apparently Mother Angela's conscience was bothering her for having turned down Dr. Burke's plea for nurses. She ended by leaving Sisters Augusta (Anderson), Paula (Casey), and Isidore (Conlin) in Cairo, and taking only Sister Ferdinand (Bruggerman) with her to Mound City. Sister (later Mother) Augusta remembered their rather horrifying introduction to hospital work.

> Although we were tired and sick for want of sleep, there was no rest for us. We pinned up our habits, got brooms and buckets of water, and washed the blood-stained walls and scrubbed the floors. Dr. Burke sent some men to carry away the legs, arms, and other pieces of human bodies that were lying around. We had no beds that night, but we slept as soundly as if we had feathers under us. The hospital was full of sick and wounded, but after some days we succeeded in getting it comparatively clean.

According to Sister Anthony, there were similar problems in Louisville, where another group went that same December. The ladies of the city had been trying to take care of the hospital.

> [B]ut in spite of their kind hearts and willing hands, the work was too much for their inexperience, and the hospital was, in many respects, in a deplorable condition. They were not accustomed to nursing, nor to managing so large an establishment; nor had they the service at hand to which many of them had been used all their lives. Consequently, the hospital was in an unclean and unwholesome condition and the feeding of the patients was far from what it should be.

The Sisters also found prejudice in Louisville against their religion and their habit, but their dedication and skill soon overcame that attitude among their patients, if not among the women of the city.

In February 1862 the five Sisters of the Holy Cross in Paducah left the task there to their devoted co-workers, the Sisters of Charity of Nazareth, and came to Mound City. They were needed to attend to the survivors of the battle of Fort Henry and Fort Donelson. This battle had taken place in the worst kind of winter weather, with the elements doing as much damage as enemy artillery. Mary Livermore was a renowned nurse and nursing organizer of the Civil War who describes what she saw after that battle.

> They had no tents; they were obliged to bivouac in the line of battle, lying on their arms. All through the long winter night both armies were pelted by the driving and pitiless snow and rain. Many of the soldiers were frozen to death before morning. [Only] a few of the wounded could be removed from the field while the fight lasted. There they lay, some two or three nights and days, uncared for, many freezing to death. Hundreds who fell in the beginning of the battle, when the ground was soft and muddy, were frozen into the earth, and it was necessary to cut them out of the ground, and in this deplorable plight they were taken to the extemporized and unready hospitals. Their removal was horrible torture; for there were few ambulances, and the wagons and carts impressed into the service were of the rudest construction, and generally lacked springs. In these the poor fellows were jolted and pitched down the precipitous heights, where they had lain for two and three days and nights, encased in bloody and frozen uniforms.[3]

Sister Augustine estimated that the number in the hospital went up to 1,400 at this time. "It was nothing but dressing wounds from morning to night." And at night the Sisters gave up their beds and slept on the floor.

Sister Fidelis fell ill in Mound City in early April 1862. The Sisters had recently made new curtains for the warehouse-become-hospital (how they managed that with all their other duties only they and God will ever know) and the doctor who attended Sister Fidelis told her how much better the building looked, even from the outside. Sister Fidelis informed him that she had never seen the building from the outside. "It was late in the evening when I came," she said, "and so dark that I could not see what it looked like." The doctor was amazed and edified that she had never set foot out of the building in all the months of her duties there.

While Sister Fidelis lay ill, flood waters rose in the Ohio River and threatened the hospital to such a degree that it was necessary to begin evacuating the patients. Many were sent up to the Jefferson Barracks in St. Louis, which had been left empty the preceding fall. This was apparently accomplished by sending them overland to a place on the Mississippi above the flood, and by water from there north to St. Louis. Sister's condition made it impossible to move her. Sister Paula writes:

> I was with her when she died. She was conscious to the last. She told me that if she should have a change while I was with her, to be sure to press her crucifix to her lips so that she might kiss it. In a short time I noticed a great change. She looked at me and said, "Now!" I pressed the crucifix to her lips, repeating some aspirations, and in a few moments, without any struggle, her pure soul took its flight to the throne of God. This was April 18, 1862. As her lifeless body lay on her cot, the water rose rapidly as high as the legs of the cot. A soldier brought her coffin in a skiff, and we placed her body in it. It was then rowed through the woods to the railroad station, to meet the train for Chicago en route for Saint Mary's.

The following July Sister Elise (O'Brien), a second-year novice, also died. Records disagree as to whether her place of death was Mound City or Cairo, and there is no narrative to tell us why she died or who was present.

Regardless of age, the soldiers were "boys" to the Sisters. The Sisters did more than nurse and feed them; sometimes they had to save them from the consequences of their own acts. Sister Anthony, for instance, one day smelled smoke as she walked past the

Mound City baggage room, "where the kitchen boys slept." The kitchen boys were convalescent soldiers able to do a few chores. Sister pushed open the door and found the floor of the room on fire. Sister Anthony called another Sister and together they sloshed out the fire. Apparently the baggage room made a cold dormitory, and its occupants had built a fire in a grate during the night. Later some coals fell out of the grate to the floor and started the blaze.

> Had we reported them the poor fellows would have been dealt with in military fashion [wrote Sister Anthony]; but they were good boys, still weak from their wounds and only able for kitchen duty; so we said nothing to the officers or ward-master and no one but ourselves was any the wiser.

She found another endearing trait in them.

> There was the utmost good feeling between our men in hospital; Federals and Confederates discussed their battles as amicably as if they had been fighting side to side instead of face to face. . . .
>
> They were so careful not to offend us by swearing or bad language. We knew it went on when we were not present, because sometimes it was impossible not to overhear it. . . . [Once] there had been considerable swearing among a lot of men in a certain ward and the Sister in charge had scolded them well. At last, worn out with her duties, she was taken sick and was obliged to absent herself for a few days. Then the men missed her and began to . . . wish for her return. "She'll never come back," said one of the offenders sadly; "it was our swearing made her sick and I know she'll never come back."

The largest number of sick and wounded poured into the hospital after the battle of Shiloh, or Pittsburg Landing, in April 1862. But the most horribly wounded came in from the battle of Fort Pillow. Sister Anthony remembered how the blood soaked through the bandages, how "dressing applied to a wound at one spot would come through at another, or even a stimulant administered before a wound was dressed would flow from the orifice made by a bullet." One victim from that battle was a young woman, both of whose legs had been shot off. She died without their learning who she was or why she had been caught in the battle.

Among the most heroic nursing was that done on board the

Red Rover, the first United States hospital ship. This vessel had been built in 1859 at Cape Girardeau, Missouri, as a commercial side-wheel river steamer; it was purchased by the Confederate States as a barracks ship for the floating battery *New Orleans*. In May 1862 it was captured by the Union gunboat *Mound City* and taken to St. Louis to be fitted out as a floating summer hospital for the Western Flotilla. Dr. George H. Bixby of Boston was named senior medical officer.

The *Red Rover* reported for duty at Cairo on June 10, 1862, and the next day took on board her first patient, a cholera victim.

A week later the gunboat *Mound City* participated in the attack on Fort Charles, Arkansas, on the White River. A Confederate shell exploded the boilers of the *Mound City* and many men were scalded. These, along with those wounded in other ways, were brought to Memphis, and the *Red Rover* was sent to bring some of them to Cairo. Mother Angela apparently witnessed their arrival, for it was at that time that she volunteered the nursing services of her Sisters to the ship. The offer was accepted, but legal matters and the continuing renovation of the ship postponed its being carried into effect.

In September the prize court of the state of Illinois, which had jurisdiction over the captured vessel, sold it to the Union Navy, and it underwent winter fitting. It was finally commissioned in the United States Navy on December 26, 1862. The Sisters had come aboard two days earlier. From the Navy's official account:

> On Christmas Eve 1862 Sister M. Veronica (C. Moran), Sister M. Adela (M. Reilly)[4] and Sister M. Callista (E. Pointan) came on board the *Red Rover*, having transferred from the Army Hospital at Mound City for duty which would see the first two mentioned Sisters tending the sick on the hospital ship for the duration of the Civil War. On 9 February 1863 they were joined by Sister M. John of the Cross (C. McLaughlin) carried on reports as Sister St. John who served as a nurse on *Red Rover* until 30 September 1863. Sister M. Callista left the hospital ship on 2 March 1863 but again reported on board for duty on 28 January 1865. Female negro nurses working under direction of the Sisters on board the *Red Rover* were Alice Kennedy and Sarah Kinno. Those who later served were Ellen Campbell, Betsy Young, and Dennis Downs. These women may truly be said to be the pioneers or forerunners of the United States

> Navy Nurse Corps as they were the first female nurses carried on board a hospital ship.[5]

The Sisters were thus with the *Red Rover* when she moved out in January 1863 down to the mouth of the Yazoo and back to the mouth of the White. She was standing by as a hospital and supply ship when the fleet took Fort Hindman, Arkansas, and received wounded from the *Signal* and the *New Era*. She was fired on while trying to moor below Napoleon, Louisiana, on January 21, "two shots striking her and entering the hospital."[6] She returned the fire with "musketry" and "moved four miles farther to spend the night."[7]

In February Admiral David E. Porter notified General Grant that the Navy needed a hospital at Memphis, and the Commercial Hotel in Memphis was converted to hospital use over the next several months. It was renamed Hospital Pinckney in honor of an outstanding fleet surgeon. Sister St. John left the *Red Rover* in September 1863 to take charge of nursing in the new hospital. The *Red Rover* returned to the mouth of the Yazoo for double duty and more.

> [S]he often ran thirty miles up the river to procure eggs, chickens, milk and such from Harrison's Plantation. . . . Her crew . . . packed fresh beef in ice, built cattle corrals on shore . . . ; buried the dead, took on board stores and provisions; and off-loaded to ships of the Squadron medical supplies, provisions and stores.[8]

The *Red Rover* landed just above Vicksburg on April 16, 1863, and was there while the two sides dueled for possession of the town and its batteries. She returned to Memphis April 23 "overflowing with patients." The wounded were removed and the *Red Rover* returned at once to the battle scene, the Sisters never leaving the ship. Vicksburg fell on July 4, thus opening the entire river to Union traffic, and this time the *Red Rover* went all the way down to New Orleans, taking medical supplies to two gunboats, the *Carondolet* and the *Louisville*. Finally she went all the way back to Memphis, where she was tied up for inspection and assessment from August 15 to October 17. During this time only twenty-one new patients were admitted and the total number once went as low as three, so it is possible that the Sisters got some rest and some may have been able to leave the ship; Sister Adele categorically states that she never did. Extensive repairs were necessary in the Mound City Navy Yard, and the ship was out of action until April 11, 1864, though she seems to have continued to admit patients for much of this time.

The minor but extremely bloody battle of Fort Pillow began April 12, 1864. The fort was another strategic river defense. When the outnumbered Union garrison refused to surrender, the Confederate attackers overran the fort, killing 231 men, seriously wounding abut 100 more, and capturing 226. The *Red Rover* and the *Platte Valley* were sent to pick up those who could still be medically assisted.

> An agreement was reached to allow the Union Army to remove their wounded and bury their dead the morning of 13 April 1864. . . . Those who could walk were brought down the Bluffs, supported on either side by a rebel soldier. Other Union soldiers were sent in from Confederate camps after *Platte Valley* departed.[9]

The *Red Rover*, following *Platte Valley*, took on the remainder of the sick and wounded and slipped downriver to Memphis, putting the patients into the care of the military hospitals. These men were particularly difficult to treat because so many of the wounds had been received at close quarters. Doctors and visitors commented on the devotion of the Sisters to these patients, black and white — about half the defenders of Fort Pillow were former slaves.

By May 1864 the Mississippi Squadron numbered about a hundred ships, divided into ten naval districts, each assigned to a different part of the river. The *Red Rover* was not assigned to any district but continued to ply between Cairo and New Orleans, offloading supplies to other ships and taking on wounded. On her last voyage upriver she tied up in Mound City, December 11, 1864, and did not leave that spot. *Red Rover*'s last eleven patients were transferred to the steamer *Grampus* November 17, 1865. During her career she admitted about twenty-five hundred patients, of whom nearly four hundred were southerners, and of whom 90 percent recovered. "Her last record of those employed in her medical department is dated 30 April 1865. Sister M. Veronica and Sister Adele were still on board and it is presumed they remained to her last day of service."[10] She was sold at public auction November 29, 1865, for $4,500.

20

A Taste of Our Hospital Tea, 1861–65

One story of the Civil War begins on the Mississippi River and ends in the Memphis Hospital.

> On 17 June 1862 the Federal gunboat *Mound City*. . . took part in the attack on the White River which resulted in the capture of the Confederate Forts at St. Charles, Arkansas. During the action a shell from the Rebel batteries penetrated the port casement of the *Mound City*, killed three men in its flight; and exploded her steam drum. Eight men were scalded to death and 43 were either drowned or shot after leaping overboard. The total casualties were 135 out of a total of 175 on board the gunboat. Many of these men were admitted to the Army hospital at Memphis, Tennessee.[1]

Among those admitted to the hospital were a Captain Kelty, commanding officer of the *Mound City,* and a Colonel Fry, whom Mother Angela's account calls "a commander of the fort." Captain Kelty had been both scalded and shot, as had several of his men; Colonel Fry had broken both arms and one leg, among other injuries. Kelty was a popular officer; it was he who had originally captured the *Red Rover* from the Confederates and had it outfitted as a hospital ship. The doctor saw no hope of his recovery, and as word of this expectation spread through the hospital, an ugly spirit developed toward Colonel Fry, who was believed to have given the order to fire on the scalded men.

Sister Josephine (Reilly) was tending her patients in a second-floor ward at the front of the hospital when a number of men entered and began removing the patients — all but Colonel Fry. Outside the hospital some of the "soldiers detailed to guard the hospital, and gunboat men" were building a scaffold and mounting it with loaded guns. They announced that they were going to kill Colonel Fry as soon as they heard that Captain Kelty had died. A doctor appeared, took the key of the ward from Sister Josephine, and gave it to Dutch Johnny, an embittered convalescent who declared his intention of killing five Confederates in revenge for the deaths of his five brothers.

Sister Josephine, expelled from her workplace, went to Mother Angela. Together they presented themselves to the surgeon general of the hospital, demanding that he see to it that no murder be done. The doctor replied that he was sorry but the situation was out of his control, and the commanding officer of the guard unit was away from the hospital.

"Then," said Mother Angela, "I must call my twenty-seven Sisters from the sick; we will leave the hospital and walk down to Cairo" (three miles).

After further expostulation, the doctor obtained the key and gave it to Mother Angela. She and Sister Josephine hastened to the assistance of Colonel Fry. Sister Josephine had closed the window and lowered the shades before she left the room, but Dutch Johnny had opened both. Poor Colonel Fry "could see the faces and hear the voices of the soldiers and gunboat men, shouting every few minutes for him to be ready to die, for they would shoot him as soon as they heard of Captain Kelty's death."[2]

The men at the window called to the Sisters to leave, even threatened them, to no purpose; the Sisters remained, praying at the side of the Confederate officer, for the rest of the day and all of the night. That night Father Walsh[3] came from Cairo to bring the Last Sacraments to Captain Kelty. They had the effect they sometimes have; next morning Captain Kelty seemed much better, and the doctors soon pronounced him out of danger. The watchers on the scaffold jumped down, fired a few blank cartridges into the air, and dispersed.

Furthest removed geographically from the other military hospitals was St. Aloysius Hospital in Washington, D.C. The people of St. Aloysius parish had built a new church and opened it in 1859, two years before the war. When the churches of the city began to be used as emergency hospitals, the people of St. Aloysius were torn between the desire to be patriotically useful and the hope that they could preserve their nice new church from the hard usage it would necessarily get as an army hospital. The government was offering lumber to cover the floor of the church as some means of protection. The Jesuit pastor, the Reverend Bernardine Wiget, suggested that with that much lumber his parishioners could erect three separate hospital buildings. The plan was accepted and the work done in eight days.

Sisters Theodore (Kearns) and Rose (McDermott) arrived for

the opening of the hospital, October 7, 1862. Parish records say that 450 soldiers were admitted on the first day,[4] all wounded at the September 17 battle of Antietam, "the bloodiest day of the war."[5] Three weeks after the battle, wounded were still pouring into Washington by road and down the Potomac. Over nine thousand men were wounded *on each side*, so that nearly twenty thousand wounded had to be cared for somewhere. Right at the beginning of its history, little St. Aloysius Hospital was packed to the doors, and the two Sisters with their secular companions must have been run off their feet. Into this melée of haste, blood, pain, amputations, constant emergency, and death came the cool figure of Father Charles Moreau. One wonders if he saw what was in front of him when the evidence he left is merely a schedule for the regulating of the Sisters' day.

He ordered that the Sisters were to obtain a watch, until they could get a clock. They were to stop whatever they were doing every morning at half past ten, in order to do their spiritual reading together. At dinner they were to read the New Testament, excerpts from their Rules, and "some edifying works" (one eating and one reading, apparently), and after supper the *Following of Christ*. Supper was to be at half past seven, followed by forty-five minutes of recreation, the recitation of the beads, night prayer, and the reading of the subject of the next day's meditation. They were to edify those around them by their "modesty, silence, and punctual accomplishment of their religious practices."[6]

It may be doubted that the Sisters found it possible to spend even one day under such an ideal horarium, even when they got a little more help. Sister Alice (Flannery) arrived on New Year's Day 1863 and Sister Agnes (Nevelles) came August 21, 1863. Her service was short, for the hospital closed at the end of October, having functioned for only one year and having treated over thirteen hundred patients.

By this time all the Holy Cross war nurses were professed Sisters. Novices had been allowed to volunteer and had gone into the hospitals, some of them proving very valuable. But Father Charles found their service unsuitable and irregular, and ordered them all back to Saint Mary's. At first there was some difficulty in locating Mother Eusebia, who was in charge of all of them, but she was finally found either at Cairo or Mound City, with her seven novices distributed between those two places. She lost no time in obeying the summons home, no doubt a valuable lesson in obedience to her charges. "The message came late in the afternoon, and the next train would leave Cairo at two o'clock the next morning. Mother M. Eusebia told the novices to be ready to leave on this train."[7]

They should have been warned by the inauspicious beginning of the journey. The mule-driver who usually picked up passengers and baggage for the trains came to report that his mules had run away, and the Sisters in Mound City would have to walk to Cairo. They started at midnight, trying to follow the tracks in the darkness, each one carrying some of the supper she had not yet had time to eat. Though they sent two of the more energetic novices ahead to hold the train, its engineers merely slowed down, saw no one on the platform, and resumed speed. The Sisters sat disconsolately in the empty station until sunrise, when two more of them took over reconnaissance duty and encountered a farmer, who said his wife could give them breakfast in an hour. Sister Paula commented years later in her memoirs, "That was a very long hour."

They spent the day picking blackberries until two in the afternoon, when the next train arrived. In spite of the blackberries, they were hungry again. When the train made a six o'clock stop so the passengers could buy supper, Mother Eusebia sent another pair to see what they could get with her remaining cash — two dollars. They found with sickening disappointment that only regular meals were served, and two dollars would never cover meals for eight. They settled themselves resignedly in the now otherwise empty coach, four on each side of the aisle, two facing two.

Was someone praying for a miracle? In it walked — a Union officer followed by two waiters, each carrying a heavily laden tray, one tray for each group of Sisters. The officer kept the waiters on the train until the next station so the Sisters would not have to hurry their meal, then sent the men back with the trays and dishes.

They reached Chicago at eight o'clock the next morning, left at five in the afternoon for Niles, and arrived there at ten that night. There was no way to reach Saint Mary's at that hour, so they took off their caps and slept on the floor of the Niles station until two the next morning, when two ladies disembarked from an arriving train, talking loudly. The Sisters resumed their headgear and sat up for the rest of the night. They were able to get carriages about six o'clock in the morning, and finally arrived at Saint Mary's about eight, utterly exhausted. It is recorded that they received a warm welcome, despite the fact that the annual retreat was in progress. They certainly deserved at least that.

Saint Mary's Academy had such a good reputation by this time that southern parents continued to send their daughters to the school in northern Indiana. The presence of these girls sometimes created situations which required careful handling, especially after Mother Angela's cousin, Ellen Ewing Sherman,[8] moved her family to South Bend during the war and put her daughter Minnie in Saint Mary's. Minnie's father was General William Tecumseh Sherman, who in early February 1864 assumed command of the Army of the Tennessee and three months later would begin the invasion of Georgia.

The best-remembered outburst took place on Washington's Birthday, 1864. Our source is a letter dated February 14, 1901, signed "K. Kelly" and addressed to a Sister unnamed but surely Sister Emerentiana, who was working mightily in those days to compile and organize Holy Cross history. "K. Kelly" was not a witness to the incident. She says she got the first part of the story from "Mother Emily," who would be Sister Emily (Rivard), and the last part from alumna Julia McMahon Cannon.

Minnie Sherman, according to the account, had been "a model" student until her mother took her to visit General Sherman's camp. The young soldiers paid the general's daughter endless attention, "and it seemed to have turned her head, for . . . she seemed to think on her return that [as] her father ruled the Army, she should rule the school."

A celebration was planned for Washington's Birthday, but Mother Angela, home from the war herself on business, forbade any wearing of partisan colors. Minnie, however, had pinned a "rosette or flag" to her dress, and so arrayed met a southern girl in the hall. The southerner snatched off the decoration and stomped on it. Apparently nothing more happened for about an hour. Then:

> A carriage drove up at furious speed. Hardly waiting for the horses to stop, Mrs. Sherman jumped out, rushed into the recreation room, pinned a fresh one on Minnie, and wanted to know why her daughter could not wear the flag her father offered his life for! . . . This seems to have emboldened the other northerners to bring out their colors and flags, and to make a larger one for the evening's

> entertainment, which they did. But the others soon heard of it and wanted it given up. Words soon led to blows, and almost in an instant the whole school with few exceptions were engaged in pitched battle.

Sister Emily's recollections end there. The writer of the letter takes the rest of the story from Julia McMahon Cannon, an academy student at the time, losing her coherence as the excitement grows.

> The girls divided into two parts with flashing eyes and burning cheeks meant business and the poor Sister in charge, whose name I never heard, stood pale with the bell in her hand but no one paid any attention. . . . hair was being torn out in handfuls faces were scratched and bleeding and it only seemed to be growing more desperate when "Young ladies!" in Mother Angela's voice brought them to their senses and she at once asked for an explanation. . . . She told them to bring all flags and rosettes to her which was done, but the southern girls said the flag that caused the trouble had not been given up. Being refused again . . . the northerners were kept in. They . . . gave the flag to Katie Putnam. . . . [S]he got out of the window, slid down the porch, ran over to the ladies' house and gave the flag to Mrs. Sherman, who was there. She took it with a smile and handed it to Tommy,[9] then a little boy, telling him to "guard the Flag." He took it with an air of reverence, but Katie has it now, she says it is a poor homemade affair but quite a relic.

The community archives are filled with stories of the Sisters' Civil War service — edifying, touching, amusing, inspiring, and sometimes all at once. We will conclude with one more glimpse of Mother Angela at work, realizing that no matter how much we tell, the whole story can never be told. The account is taken from the *Freeman's Journal* of March 26, 1887, written by Eliza Allen Starr,[10] and quoted in Mother Eleanore's *On the King's Highway.*

> During the early days of the war and the hospital service, we all know how inadequate were the supplies for the sick and the wounded; how meager the equipment for the hospital nurses. . . . At this time the Commissary Board sent a visitor to the camp and hospital where Mother M. Angela and her Sisters were stationed. . . .

[T]he . . . visitor . . . was duly escorted to the hospital, which excited his warmest approbation for its order, neatness, comfort of every sort; but as he was bowing himself out from the presence of Mother M. Angela and her band of Sisters, she said to him, "But, Mr. —, you must allow us to show you some hospitality. Pardon our lack of silver and porcelain, but take a cup of hospital tea!" "Thank you, thank you, Mother Angela, but I have taken dinner already with the officers and need nothing." "Allow me to insist." And before another excuse could be urged, a Sister appeared with a snow-white napkin and the tin cup and spoon of the hospital and — the anything but fragrant beverage of hospital tea. "Sugar, Sister," said Mother M. Angela, and before the visitor could wave off this fresh specimen of hospital luxury, Mother M. Angela had dumped into the tin cup what resembled the scrapings of the molasses barrel. . . . Being a gentleman . . . he drank the cup of tea, well stirred, to its dregs, without a grimace, bowing as he handed the empty tin cup to the Sister, while Mother M. Angela rubbed her little hands with unmistakable glee . . . as she said, "I knew, Mr. —, you would wish a taste of our hospital tea."

The Commissary Visitor vowed in his heart as he turned from the hospital door, that the next train on his arrival home should take, as he said in his letter to Mother M. Angela, such stores to her own and to every hospital under his charge, as a Christian man could accept without shame from the hand of any hospital nurse in the land.

21

Change Is Unanimously Requested, 1862–65

When Mother Liguori left for Canada, the superiorship at Saint Mary's seems to have been divided several ways. The Sisters were accustomed to Mother Angela's direction, but at this time she was only appearing occasionally, being much more concerned with her military hospital work. Sister Ascension was back from Philadelphia and serving as superior of the community at Notre Dame. Sister Elizabeth was the highest-ranking council member, but her views put her in a decided minority. Somehow the community proceeded on its usual ways.

Father Moreau wrote to Mother Seven Dolors that the Sisters in Indiana were "doing the devil's work," though he thought that this was "unintentional."[1]

During the winter of 1862–63, Father Moreau composed a letter to Pius IX, together with a request for the approbation of the Sisters' Constitutions. It gives no hint that there is any disagreement about the Constitutions in the ranks of the Sisters. Much of the good work claimed for the Sisters was being done by those in Indiana; some of this is visible in the letter and some is not. He wrote:

> [T]heir Society continues to prosper; it now numbers three hundred and sixteen professed members and fifty-five novices. Moreover, they have thirty-four houses dispersed throughout twelve dioceses in France, America, and East Bengal. In France there are two in the diocese of Le Mans, two in Versailles; one in St. Brieuc; and one in Paris; in America, five in the diocese of Montreal; one in Chicago; six in Fort Wayne; one in New York; three in Philadelphia; two in New Orleans; two in Baltimore where, including those of Alton and Louisville, the Sisters direct five military hospitals; lastly, one in our Apostolic Vicariate of East Bengal. Everywhere, they obtain abundant graces of sanctification, particularly in the military hospitals where, since the beginning of the Civil War, they have baptized over three hundred non-Catholics.[2]

It will be seen that when he wanted to assure the Roman authorities that the Sisters were doing very well, Father Moreau needed the Indiana figures. Counting the military hospitals as "houses," Indiana had seventeen of his thirty-three houses (not thirty-four, unless one was omitted from the letter). They also had 145, or 46 percent, of those 316 professed Sisters. Father Moreau apparently did not have a complete list of the novices, as the Indiana figures for the winter of 1862–63 show fifty-nine novices, though he lists only fifty-five worldwide.

The complete letter to Rome was included with a circular letter dated February 17, 1863, and addressed to all the Sisters. The image of Satan-in-Indiana stalks through the letter.

> After all that the enemy of good has done to develop the cockle of disunion sown by him among your Sisters of the Indiana Vicariate, it is important to destroy it to the very roots by opposing to this spirit of discord that of union which can be strengthened only by religious obedience.

There is no openness to the possibility that the Sisters in Indiana might have a case that ought to be examined. There is no suggestion in the letter to Rome that half the community is uncomfortable with the Constitutions now being submitted. Whatever is not the work of the motherhouse is the work of the devil.

> This union did exist everywhere until certain of your companions in Indiana chose to ignore the authority of your Mother General and my own, in the person of the Visitor.

This "insubordination" is attributed to the failure to translate and observe the Constitutions. It should be pointed out that no Sister — not one — was ever "insubordinate" to Father Charles Moreau. The Sisters were dismayed and confused by the disagreement between Father Charles and Father Sorin, and when the bishop stepped in and settled it, the majority of them considered it settled. A contest between a foreign-speaking superior on another continent and a bishop in your community room is no contest at all.

> Be this as it may, my dear Sisters, I wish to forget what has unfortunately happened at Sainte Marie du Lac, and to remember only the good being done there, through the zeal and courage of its

> Founder, and advise you as to the means of preventing a recurrence of these attempts of the devil.

Why the sudden compliment to Father Sorin? The letter starts out as a rebuke for the Indiana attitude to Father Charles, quotes the entire letter to Rome, returns to the theme of unity under the Constitutions, and then includes the above paragraph. The next paragraph states that the Sisters owe "the greatest veneration and religious obedience" to their bishops, but they should also be "submissive and sincerely attached to your Mother General, not to mention what you owe me as the instrument . . . of the foundation of your Society, until such time as the Sovereign Pontiff deigns to accept my resignation" (which had been offered September 24, 1862). But the writer goes on, "Remember also that we have no jurisdiction over you except inasmuch as it may please the Ordinaries to grant it to us." He tells the Sisters that they have the right to leave the dioceses of any bishops who try to separate them from the motherhouse. He states that one article of the new Constitutions provides for the motherhouse to be permanently in France. He declared recent professions at Saint Mary's, if any, invalid.

Finally he convokes a general chapter to meet in Philadelphia March 27, 1863. He names Mother Elizabeth provincial of Indiana and summons her to the chapter, with Sister Eugenie, who had gone to Canada with Mother Liguori five months before, as the other Indiana representative. Father Sorin is to have "temporal jurisdiction" over the Sisters in Indiana but is not to serve as their confessor. The council at Saint Mary's, reorganized after the departure of Mother Liguori and her first assistant, is declared dissolved and its acts annulled.

The letter apparently was delivered to Father Granger, who was named to assist Father Charles in presiding at the Philadelphia chapter. He found it alarming. Its stated purpose was to "decide whether the profession in question is to be accepted, or whether these Sisters are to remain under the exclusive dependence of the Ordinary." Eight Sisters had made profession September 12, 1862. If the chapter decided not to validate the profession, they would become diocesan religious, not a part of Holy Cross. If the chapter accepted them, they were to remake their vows into the hands of Father Charles, after having had their religious obligations, including those to the motherhouse, explained to them. No other agenda was provided for the chapter, though it was free to take up any other matters which it might find pertinent.

Father Granger may or may not have known that Mother Elizabeth was one of the few whose sympathies lay at that time with France, but he certainly saw the one obvious thing — she would be the only non-French-speaking person at the chapter. The other Sister named to represent Indiana was already in Canada with Mother Liguori. In other words, the views of the very great majority in the Indiana community were not to be represented at all, and the new Indiana provincial would not understand the language of the chapter.

Father Granger took his perplexity to Bishop Luers, who had an abrupt solution. Neither Father Granger nor Sister Elizabeth would attend the chapter. Sister Elizabeth was not even to be informed that she had been summoned. Nor did the bishop recognize her appointment as provincial, which never went into effect. The bishop's statement was, "The question is no longer between the Sisters, but between me and the motherhouse."[3]

The chapter was postponed to April 9, 1863. On April 8 a letter arrived from Father Granger stating that

> His Lordship . . . forbade me to communicate the letters and telegrams received, stating that he intended to refer the matter to Rome, and that while awaiting an answer, he considered the capitulary acts null and void.[4]

The chapter produced only two acts. One was a declaration that the American problem needed to be laid before Father Basil Moreau immediately and in person, by representatives of the three provinces. Therefore Mother Seven Dolors (Canada), Sister Alphonsus Rodriguez (Louisiana), and Sister Eugenie (Indiana) were proceeding at once to France. The second was a document thanking the Founder for the graces of the Visitation.

> Father Visitor has given touching evidence of a disinterestedness, conciliation, charity and devotedness for which we are unable sufficiently to thank him. . . .
>
> We strongly protest against all the acts originating from a condemnable insubordination. Only the spirit of evil could have contrived the inventions and calumnies which had such dire results.[5]

Meanwhile, nothing of all this was known in Indiana, where a decision had been reached to try once more to make their problem clear to Father Moreau. Mother Angela left her military duties and sailed with Mother Ascension for France, leaving March 4. They would have arrived in France about the time the chapter was supposed to be convening. Father Moreau's surprise at their appearance may have accounted for their gruff reception; he at first declined to see them at all. He declared that he had not sent for them, and they therefore had no permission to be in France. Later he glanced at their documents but gave them no serious perusal. This was regrettable, for the Indiana Sisters had, for the first time as far as we know, condensed and codified their requests into four points:

1. All superiors, local or provincial, to be chosen by the provincial chapter, not by the motherhouse.

2. Novices to be admitted to profession on the sole authority of the province.

3. Provincial administration to have the authority to found and close houses, in cooperation with the bishops.

4. Freedom of financial administration — surplus to remain in the province and financial report, but not money, sent to motherhouse once a year.

When the attempt at presentation failed, Angela sent the document on to Rome.

Father Moreau seemed to think that Ascension's fault in questioning his judgment was worse than Angela's, possibly because Ascension was French. He sent Angela home with permission to stop in Paris and see her brother, Father Neal Gillespie, then teaching theology there. Of Ascension, Sister Emerentiana says:

> Mother Ascension, being a French subject, was kept in penance by the authorities there. . . .
>
> Later, Father Sorin in some way sent money to Mother Ascension, who effected her escape and in due time arrived in Philadelphia, where her religious garb awaited her. She arrived at Saint Mary's sometime in September.[6]

The question of a superior was definitely settled at the annual chapter held July 12, 1863, at which Bishop Luers presided. Mother Angela was named superior at Saint Mary's. Sister Edward

(Murphy) became mistress of novices and Sister Ambrose (Corby) stewardess. The same petitions which the Sisters had tried to present in the spring were sent to Father Moreau in the name of the chapter. There is no record of any reply.

By this time the bishops of Le Mans, Fort Wayne, Montreal and New Orleans were all corresponding with Rome concerning the Marianites. Cardinal Alexandro Barnabo, prefect of the Sacred Congregation of the Propaganda, wrote to Bishop Luers to tell him to call a chapter of all the North American groups. There was no question in anybody's mind that the chapter was meeting on the authority of Rome, not merely of Bishop Luers.

Bishop Ignace Bourget of Montreal wrote to Mother Seven Dolors, "I have told Sister Mary of St. Leocadie to go to the chapter at Notre Dame du Lac, because the chapter has been convoked by the authority of the Holy See and we must obey, but that nothing of any consequence will come from it."[7]

And Father Moreau wrote to Mother Alphonsus Rodriguez in New Orleans, "I learn with satisfaction . . . that you are going to the Provincial Chapter. This was . . . your duty . . . because of the invitation which you have received from the delegate of His Eminence the Cardinal Prefect of the Propaganda."[8]

The chapter was called for March of 1865, to meet at Saint Mary's. The Civil War was just coming to a close, and many southern soldiers were streaming back to their homes and farms without waiting for the final act. How the Sisters from New Orleans ever made the journey north is one of the great undocumented mysteries of the congregation, but they not only arrived, they arrived early.

The method of representation in this chapter differed from that previously provided for. Constitution 13 read: "[The Provincial Chapter] is composed of the Provincial and the superiors of every house in the province or their delegates." Since only large, substantial houses had "superiors" (the others had "directresses"), this would have made for a chapter of six to ten persons.

Bishop Luers, correctly or not, understood as his mandate the examination of the 1860–63 Constitutions — Constitutions which had been sitting in Rome for two years waiting for someone to take a look at them. For this he needed a larger group for discussion, especially since he knew that some dissatisfaction existed. So he arranged proportional representation, one delegate for every twenty Sisters. Much has been made of the fact that this gave the Indiana Sisters a majority. In that regard it should be remembered that in 1863 a chapter had been called (but not held) in which Indiana would have had only one delegate, who could not understand the language of the other capitulants; and in 1867 a general chapter was held in which Indiana, with half the entire population of the Sisters, was again limited to one delegate.

In his statement taking full responsibility for the chapter's procedures, Luers may have been anticipating trouble.

> His Lordship declares that he wishes to follow, as much as possible, the Rules and Constitutions relating to the present reunion, but that if any deviations from them are made, any member should not for that reason regard the proceedings of the chapter as null. His Lordship moreover adds that these Rules and Constitutions are not approved, and that Reverend Father Moreau, the Founder, made in them, up to the present time, the changes which he deemed necessary, and that even if they were approved, under the present circumstances, His Lordship is authorized to make the changes he considers requisite, and that no one need have any scruples of conscience on the subject, since, as Apostolic Delegate, His Lordship has full powers.[9]

In the second session he had some further advice.

> His Eminence the Cardinal [Barnabo] desires that the Society of the Sisters should follow as much as possible the government adopted by religious orders in general, and that in consequence the three Provinces in America should form but one.[10]

Accepting this, the Sisters voted for a provincial. If the Indiana Sisters had wanted to dominate the chapter, they could have elected one of their own on the first ballot. But after three ballots no candidate had achieved a majority, and the capitulants agreed that a plurality on the fourth ballot would suffice. Sister Alphonsus Rodriguez of New Orleans was thereupon elected. They then went on to the elections for local offices. Then:

> The President makes known that the Holy See has decreed that there shall be but one novitiate in America for the Fathers and Brothers of Holy Cross, and that the desire of His Eminence the Cardinal is that the Marianites should as much as possible conform to this rule.[11]

The Sisters were left to think this over for a day and were not nearly so docile in accepting it. The Louisianans cited climate, the Canadians language, both the expense of travel. Father Sorin, called upon, naturally supported the bishop. More discussion. Finally a vote was taken and resulted in a ten to seven vote in favor of the single novitiate. The minutes do not say whether the vote was by secret ballot; since there were ten Indiana votes and seven others, it has been generally (and perhaps erroneously) theorized that the votes fell that way.

The rest of the chapter's work consisted of a close look at the Constitutions and the adoption of whatever amendments were deemed necessary. Of the 138 articles, the chapter made changes in twenty-nine, or about one in five. Eight of these were stated to be unanimously requested. Most of them seem to have been of minor importance, except the change in Article 9, which had required that all surpluses be remitted to the motherhouse every year. The chapter asked instead that surpluses be allowed to remain in each locality and that whenever necessary the motherhouse issue assessments, which should be liberally responded to.

The change which caused the greatest outcry, however, was in Article 2. The minutes of the chapter say:

> The members of the Congregation will bear the name Sisters of Holy Cross, and everything will be suppressed which establishes a difference between the teaching Sisters and the housekeeping Sisters. The change in this article is unanimously requested.

It is not clear whether the unanimous request covered the whole article or merely the second clause,[12] but the name change met with great indignation.

Bishop Bourget had been about right when he said that nothing important would come out of the chapter. Mother Alphonsus Rodriguez, the new provincial, wrote quite accurately to Mother Seven Dolors, "We have touched up the Constitutions."[13] But it was not the idea of *what* had been done that raised the alarm, but that anything was done. Mother Alphonsus was told that she had been lacking in respect and veneration for the founder, had been acting boldly, had caused suffering; that the conduct of the Marianites in America was hardly believable, etc.[14]

The Sisters from Canada and Louisiana wrote, once the chapter was over, to Rome, begging for a restoration of their local novitiates. Mother Seven Dolors wrote to Rome asking that the Constitutions be speedily approved in their original, not their amended, form. The year 1865 played itself out in general uneasiness and dissatisfaction with the whole situation.

22

The Secret Votes Being Taken . . . , 1866–69

Father Basil Moreau's resignation as superior general of Holy Cross, which had been offered September 24, 1862,[1] November 29, 1865,[2] May 27, 1866,[3] and apparently at other times as well, was accepted by Pope Pius IX on June 14, 1866. Father Pierre Chappé was appointed vicar general to govern the men of Holy Cross until their next general chapter.

On September 30, 1866, Propaganda Fide approved the Marianite Constitutions for an experimental period of ten years. This action nullified, not only the amendments made by the chapter of 1865, but every other act of that chapter, including the election of Mother Alphonsus Rodriguez. The three provinces of Canada, Indiana, and Louisiana were re-established, each with its own novitiate. The Marianites were ordered to hold another general chapter in New York, presided over by Archbishop John McCloskey, in June 1867. They were told to elect a new superior general, who would live in America until Rome gave her permission to live in France or elsewhere.

Four Sisters came from Le Mans for the chapter, and the three American provinces were each told to send the provincial and one delegate. Following the deposition of Mother Alphonsus Rodriguez, the general administration had returned the title of provincial of Indiana to Mother Liguori, who had not been in Indiana for five years. Mother Angela received seventy-two of the eighty-six votes cast for the delegate. At least she would be able to follow the discussions in French.

Even knowing that they could not hope for their case to be heard, the Sisters again wrote out their requests with 132 signatures, and Angela presented them at the chapter. Archbishop McCloskey informed the chapter that it did not have the power to grant the changes sought, nor to give the alternate permission, which was for the Indiana Sisters to live independently of the motherhouse for an experimental period of ten years. The chapter appointed a committee of four to determine whether the new Constitutions could be satisfactorily lived in America. The four were Mother Mary of the Seven Dolors, who had spent fourteen years in Canada; Mother Liguori, who had lived nine years in Indiana; Sister Immaculate Conception, who had come as Visitor in 1854 and remained about a year and a half, filling in occasionally as local superior in Indiana houses; and Sister Mary of the Holy Cross, delegate from Louisiana. None of them, of course, really represented the almost unanimous Indiana viewpoint.

These members prepared a statement reporting that:

> We, members of the commission named . . . to examine the question of dispensations asked . . . by the Sisters of the Indiana Province . . . declare that all the Articles of our Constitutions have appeared to us to be practicable and in perfect accordance with the needs of our Community. . . . In consequence . . . we protest with all our might against any request for dispensations. . . . Should, which God forbid, our very dear Sisters of the Indiana Province persist in their refusal to keep within these bonds, we wish them to be no longer considered as belonging to the Congregation of the Marianites of Holy Cross.[4]

The report was accepted by the chapter with only one dissenting vote — Angela's, obviously. But she must have secretly felt a great relief. She and her Indiana colleagues had grown more certain over the years that separation was the only answer, and now the chapter had gone on record as taking the same position. Now Rome need not hesitate for fear of offending anyone. The Indiana requests had been mailed to Rome as early as June 3, four days before the chapter opened. Now it was just a matter of how soon Rome would act.

For it was never a case of whether the Constitutions were suitable to "America." "America" was too big a place to subscribe entirely to one life-style. What was suitable for French enclaves in Canada and Louisiana had turned out to be not at all suitable for a mostly Irish-German community in the United States' Midwest. The suitability was to come into question again in less than ten years, when the Sisters in Canada began asking for the same modifications which Indiana had requested, plus a few others; and since the motherhouse had learned nothing from the struggle with

Indiana, the Canadians also eventually asked for and were granted complete autonomy.

Expecting a refusal from the chapter, the Indiana Sisters had given a copy of their petition with the 132 signatures to Bishop Luers, and he had sent it on to Rome with a letter of his own. He seems to have been particularly irritated by the re-appearance of Mother Liguori with the title which she had surrendered on choosing to leave his diocese five years before.

> When I have examined the Constitutions to satisfy myself as to the degree to which they correspond to the needs of the Sisters here, if a referral to Rome seems necessary, I shall declare the acts of the next chapter in New York null and void for the Sisters in my jurisdiction, until I can present my case in Rome regarding this affair. This measure appears to me the more necessary in that this Province, that is to say half the congregation and more, will actually have only one representative in the chapter. Mother Liguori, with whom I have had a number of difficulties from the beginning, who has calumniated me, and who has never offered since a word or a line of excuse, comes to the chapter as Provincial of Indiana; it can really be said that these women have lost all reason, prudence, and common sense.[5]

Obedient to the Holy See, the chapter elected Mother Mary of Egypt as their new superior general but sent a petition asking that Mother Seven Dolors be allowed to resume the office. To this Mother Mary of Egypt immediately added her own request to resign, in the same letter in which she informed Cardinal Barnabo of her election. Propaganda had also ruled that the new superior should remain in "America" for an unspecified time, but Mother Mary of Egypt declined to go until Rome had definitely refused her request to resign. When told by Cardinal Barnabo that she should not have left New York after the chapter, she replied that she had not been a member of the chapter and had not been out of France for eight years.[6]

The year of 1868 was apparently a quiet one. Some reports say that by this time the Indiana community was not accepting any correspondence from France. This kind of statement can neither be proved nor disproved.

Sister Emerentiana says that, as separation came closer, "several" Sisters were concerned that they would no longer be living under the vows as they had originally made them, especially a vow not to separate from the motherhouse, and that "these Sisters" went to Canada during 1868. She names, however, only two, Sisters Annunciation (Hopkins) and de Chantal (or Jeanne de Chantal) (Hale). Both had received the habit in New York and Sister de Chantal had never been to Saint Mary's. Sister Annunciation "regretted the step she had taken, and begged to be readmitted. Her request was granted, but as a penance she was obliged to return to the novitiate, where she attended all the exercises, though she wore her heart and cord."[7]

During the spring of 1869, the right hand of the Sacred Congregation of the Propaganda appears not to have known what the left hand was doing. One committee was preparing a document approving Mother Mary of Egypt's resignation and reinstating Mother Seven Dolors but ordering her to live in Indiana. Another committee was preparing the decree of autonomy of the Sisters of the Holy Cross.

The first document was dated April 30 and reached Mother Seven Dolors in May. She wearily repeated to the Sacred Congregation that the time for reconciliation was over and she would not even attempt it. The decree of autonomy was ratified by Pius IX on July 11, just ten weeks and two days after Mother Seven Dolors' return to office.

The last act in Indiana was in two scenes, both of them almost unbelievably low-key. The annual chapter was held as usual in July. The minutes of the first session say:

> The members having been informed that the Rt. Rev. Bishop of Fort-Wayne had requested the V. Rev. Father General [now Sorin] . . . to write a set of Constitutions for the use of the Sisters belonging to this Province, this had been done and already examined by the Council, but it now remained to be examined and voted by the Chapter. Therefore it was necessary to know if the members preferred to be reunited with France, or to form a Comty. by themselves by the adoption of said Constitutions. The secret votes being taken the separation was unanimously agreed upon.[8]

The chapter then proceeded, at the same session, to such matters as adding two Sisters to the Notre Dame kitchen and approving the services of a lay teacher in LaPorte, Indiana.

The names of the Sisters who formed this historic chapter deserve a close look. They were Sisters Angela, Charles, Ascension, Emily, Eusebia, Ursula, Ambrose, Francis, Circumcision, and Arsene. Of Sisters Angela and Ascension we have already heard much. Sisters Charles (Flynn) and Francis (also called Assisi or Assissium) were blood sisters from Ireland, and Sister Ursula was a blood sister of Sister Ascension. Sisters Circumcision and Ascension were by far the seniors in service, having come from France in 1844 and 1845 respectively. Thus, those who cast the final vote for separation consisted of one Canadian, Sister Eusebia (McIntosh: she who had brought the novices home from war); two Irish; two Americans, Sister Ambrose (Corby) and Sister Angela; one French-speaking American, Sister Emily (Rivard) from the French community of Bourbonnais Grove, Illinois; and four French from France. Sisters Francis and Arsene had been in Morris in 1862 and had written burning letters of undying fidelity to the motherhouse following Charles Moreau's visit there; but their views had altered in the meantime.

On August 27, 1869, there is another entry in the Council Book:

> [T]he Most Rev. Archbishop of Cincinnati [John Baptist Purcell], having received from the Holy Father the appointment of Apostolic Visitor, being at St. Mary's to discharge the duties of his office, called the members of the council and asked their opinion as to the propriety of having an election take place immediately. The Council being unanimous in their opinion that it should be postponed till next retreat, accordingly His Grace consented to it and confirmed the present administration under the titles given in the new Constitutions — M. M. Angela, Superior; M. M. Charles and Eusebia, Assistants; M. M. Ascension Mistress of Novices; M. M. Emily Stewardess.

Purcell had been given powers of superior general by Rome. Like Luers, he delegated these to Sorin under the title of ecclesiastical superior.[9] The Sisters continued to refer to and address Sorin as "Father General," the same title used by the Holy Cross men.

The letter announcing the separation arrived in France on August 1. Mother Seven Dolors sent out a letter the next day. She took the position that Rome had done the French community a great favor by severing this troublesome branch, which would now experience a well-deserved retribution for its evil ways.

> I hasten to make known to you the supreme decision by which the Holy See has deigned to put an end to the discord so long stirred up in our Congregation by our Sisters of the Indiana Province.
>
> We had hoped that our beloved Pontiff would be spared the sorrow of this extreme measure, he to whom our Community owes the honor, so little merited, and already discarded by those who had wearied the Holy See with their petitions and their protestations of obedience to the new Constitutions, whose delay served as a pretext for an anticipated separation.
>
> Nevertheless, hardly had the General Chapter . . . been convoked in New York for June 15, 1867, when already the Sisters of the Indiana Province had addressed to Rome complaints and new petitions against these holy Constitutions with which they were not yet familiar, and against the Acts of a General Chapter which had not yet assembled. . . .
>
> . . . His Holiness, . . . deigning to take into paternal consideration the long sufferance of our Congregation which was exhausting itself in an unequal struggle with a Province determined to become independent, ordered the execution of the resolution . . . to separate the Sisters of the Indiana Province. . . .
>
> [W]e must grieve over the Sisters who have neither considered nor desired the final consequence of that which may have been done in their name but unknown to them and contrary to the vow of obedience. But the practical lesson for us as the act of God's justice on an entire branch of our religious family . . . is one of humility . . .
>
> "The Congregation is not in need of a multitude of subjects, but it is in need of subjects who want to become saints. . . ." [Quotation from St. Philip Neri] It is preferable to have a few good subjects, rather than a great many who are proud and turbulent. . . . God does not reign in hearts devoid of Christian humility, fraternal charity and peace. . . . I fear more when we fail to respond to God's grace, than when we are harassed by persecution from men and demons. . . . If we do not act according to God's will, we may expect chastisements instead of protection.
>
> [T]he Most eminent Fathers granted the petition . . . to main-

> tain our Mother House in France . . . where it is now organized, despite the powers of darkness. . . . [10]

Although the Indiana Sisters have never known it, this was the note on which their relationship with their French superior general ended. Not only had Mother Seven Dolors steadfastly refused over the years to understand or even hear about their problems. In her closing volley she accused them of not being familiar with the 1863 Constitutions, which they had gone over word by word and inch by inch at the chapter of 1865 with representatives of the other North American groups, and of acting against a chapter which had not yet assembled, when it was more clear than it needed to be that the chapter would hear nothing of their presentation (which was exactly what happened). The fact that she apparently believed it when she said that the Indiana Sisters "neither considered nor desired" what was being done shows how little she ever understood the situation.

The Indiana Sisters are "the multitude of subjects" but not the ones who "want to become saints." They are the "proud and turbulent" ones, in whose hearts "God does not reign." They have "failed to respond to God's grace"; they have not acted "according to God's will."

The letter, of course, was not sent to Indiana. Not knowing they had anything to respond to, the Sisters of the Holy Cross did not respond.

23

A Province Yet Not a Province, 1870–79

This chronicle cannot conclude at this, its natural ending point, because the volume called *Superior Generals,* part of the centenary publications of 1941, really begins the history of the Sisters of the Holy Cross with Mother Augusta's election as superior general in 1889. (An entire separate volume is devoted to Mother Angela.) Some work on the twenty years between 1869 and 1889 is presented, but the chronology and conclusions of those authors must be briefly looked at again in the light of fuller information gained since then.

Whatever announcement was sent to the Sisters regarding the 1869 separation has not survived. The only reference to the change in status for the rest of that year was a letter from Cardinal Barnabo to the council saying that Sisters Good Shepherd and John Evangelist wished to return to Indiana from Canada. The vote of the council was split,[1] but apparently an agreement was reached, as both are buried at Saint Mary's. Otherwise life took a prosaic path, with "a washing machine"[2] (whatever that may have been in 1869) being purchased in August, and permission refused for a "sewing machine" in December.[3] It was easier to make decisions because they had dispensed with the two-council system.

Mother Augusta was elected stewardess at the annual chapter of 1872. This was also the year when the Propaganda asked Father Sorin if the Sisters could renew their mission in Bengal. There was no one to send at the time, but it started Sorin thinking; in 1889 he sent ten sisters from Notre Dame to renew the ministry which had been discontinued in 1876.

Bishop Luers died, gratefully remembered by the Sisters, June 29, 1871. His successor, the Right Reverend Joseph Dwenger, C.Pp.S., was installed as bishop of Fort Wayne, April 14, 1872.

Lourdes Hall, a major building project then known as "the academy wing," was planned and mostly built in 1871, with completion in the spring of 1872.

Early in 1872 Father Sorin sprang a new idea which was to

mean benefits for Notre Dame, a considerable population increase for the Sisters, and endless trouble for the newly autonomous community. Since the Sisters were giving their efforts more and more to teaching, constantly upgrading their standards of education, they tended to attract postulants who were interested in a religious life of teaching and study. Each year the labor pool of sacristans, cooks, housekeepers, laundresses and infirmarians fell a little lower, and some of these had to be retained at Saint Mary's. Notre Dame found it necessary to hire women to fill the void. Father Sorin did not like the quality of their service, he regretted having to pay their wages, even at the appalling wage scales of the day, and he claimed to fear that they were a source of temptation to his young men, though they can hardly have been high on beauty and charm. (Ecclesiastical regulations required that they be over forty, which was old in those days, and either married or widowed.) If Saint Mary's couldn't supply him with Sisters for these duties, he proposed to set up a novitiate and supply them himself.

His plan was to have Sisters enter at Notre Dame and remain there. He first envisioned a whole new community, and in writing to Archbishop Purcell in Cincinnati on February 10, 1872, he asked if he could give the new group "the cap and collar of your Sisters of Charity." He also asked the archbishop to obtain for him a copy of the Rule of those Sisters. In a circular sent to parish priests he asked them to direct subjects to this new novitiate, promising that these Sisters would live under an "easy rule," words which he capitalized in the printed form. In the circular, he calls the proposed group "the coadjutor Sisters of the Holy Cross."

He presented this plan to the council at the February 14 meeting. The Sisters' reaction was shock and dismay. This certainly sounded as if Father Sorin, whom they regarded as their founder, was now about to found another group separate from them.

They coped very well. Over the spring, in meetings for which no minutes exist, they hammered out an alternate plan, which they presented in writing on June 14. The question was not whether there should be a "manual labor" novitiate at Notre Dame; obviously there was going to be one. Archbishop Purcell had declared himself "delighted" with it.[4] The problem was to keep the new group within the congregation.

They offered to supply all the Sisters needed "for the laundries, kitchens, clothes-rooms and infirmaries" not only of Notre

Dame, but of all "the other houses of education of our Rev. Fathers in America." This they would do from the end of the next retreat — that is, in about a month. Thereafter they would send Sisters to Notre Dame at the end of their first year of novitiate. The second year of novitiate would be made at Notre Dame, under "a professed of St. Mary's." This superior could then propose the names to the council at Saint Mary's for profession, but the ceremony of profession could take place at Notre Dame, "these subjects at no future time to return to St. Mary's, and as an indemnity for their support in sickness or old age, Notre Dame to receive all dowries, etc., brought to the community by said subjects." If this depleted Saint Mary's, they would get their own hired help.

Father Sorin accepted the Sisters' plan with modifications. The new novitiate opened when Mother Ascension and all housekeeping postulants moved to Notre Dame February 28, 1873.

Saint Mary's Academy took its first steps toward becoming a college in 1870 by accepting two postgraduate students, Emma Kirwan (later Mother M. Aquina, superior general 1919–1925) and Alice Carmedy. Students could remain one or two years after the completion of the academy work, taking courses they had not had time for previously. No special courses seem to have been designed for them.

Mother Angela and Sister Ferdinand went to Europe in 1873, and brought back "a goodly number of postulants."[5] Some of these were probably for the Notre Dame novitiate, the status of which remained unclear.

> Some questions were asked as to the standing of the community in regard to Notre Dame. Rev. Father said in explanation that the Sisters formed one community to be administered as a Province, yet it is not a Province.[6]

It was not a province because only Rome can erect a province, and, even with Archbishop Purcell's "delighted" approval, Sorin was being very cautious about mentioning his second novitiate in Rome.

History was made all unknowingly on September 22, 1874, when Sister Leonie Paradis accepted an obedience to take charge of the housekeeping Sisters at the little mission of St. Joseph's University in Memramcook, New Brunswick. Sister (later Mother) Leonie had been born and professed in Canada, but had asked permission to come to Indiana in September 1870.[7] The story of her life has been told elsewhere[8] and is outside our scope, but she was the first and so far only daughter of Holy Cross to be beatified by the universal Church. She found her true life's work through this obedience. Sorin had been her spiritual director for some years.

Connections with the outside world improved when the Michigan Central Railroad put a station house and ticket office "supposedly," says Mother Eleanor, "at Notre Dame but really on what are now our grounds."[9] Another connection was opened when the council voted on September 18, 1879, to have "a telephone between here and Notre Dame."

In June 1878 the council first considered building a real infirmary. The community was just beginning to notice the effects of the ageing process. It had been thirty-seven years since the foundation. The oldest member, Sister Providence (Daget) was seventy-two; she died the following year. The vote in June was split; in July, the affirmative decision was taken but not acted on.

The congregation was expanding its mission fields in Texas, Utah, Maryland, Pennsylvania, and Indiana. Twelve missions which played an important part of community history were opened during the 1870s.

Mother Angela returned from another trip to Europe in 1877 with permission to establish the Archconfraternity of Perpetual Adoration and Work for Poor Churches. In appreciation of the work the Sisters had done and were doing at Notre Dame, Father Sorin gave "all the Sisters, living and deceased, and their relations . . . a share . . . in the daily Mass to be said until the end of time at Notre Dame for all the benefactors of the University."[10]

The seventies had an exciting ending. At eleven o'clock in the morning of April 23, 1879, a group of minims (small boys) at Notre Dame saw flames coming from the roof of the main building. The spot, six storeys above the ground, was virtually unreachable, and in spite of heroic efforts of priests, professors, students, workers, and bystanders, the whole building was soon burning furiously. Everyone did what was possible to save what was saveable. Father Hope says, "[A] Sister, passing through a rear door, had not gone more than ten feet when the rear porch collapsed."[11] Anna McAllister thinks that this was Mother Angela;[12] it was more likely one of the Sisters who lived at Notre Dame. (McAllister also thinks the fire was at night.)[13]

Sorin was in Montreal on his way to Europe at the time of the fire. He hurried back to Notre Dame, surveyed the ruins of nearly forty years' work, called all the other sad spectators together in the church, and announced that they would rebuild in time for school to open in September and that he would bless the new cornerstone May 1.

Mother Angela sent a circular letter to the Sisters commanding, not requesting, each of them to raise twenty dollars toward the restoration of the main building at Notre Dame. Gifts poured in from friends, alumni, merchants, other educators, benefactors of all ages, places of residence, and economic levels. The Saint Mary's Academy alumnae officers began collecting funds to put a bigger statue on a bigger dome. The new building opened on time in September, not complete, but usable.

By 1880 the separation was eleven years in the background. Feelings that had run high had settled down. Almost none of the group who had vowed undying fidelity to the motherhouse had actually gone to join it.[14] No French and almost no Canadians had come to Indiana.

Mother Elizabeth, one of the most vocal supporters of Mother Liguori, had been given other things to think about, more by God than by the congregation. Her son, Edward Lilly, had been ordained a priest of Holy Cross in 1872 amid such general rejoicings as would cause one to wonder whether Father Sorin and Mother Angela had ever learned of Mother Elizabeth's clandestine correspondence after Mother Liguori's departure. Father Sorin wrote to a Sister on a distant mission:

> The new Bishop of Fort Wayne [Dwenger] took dinner at St. Mary's with 2 doz. priests, Sisters & ladies in honor of our new Father Lilly, who was ordained priest at Notre Dame this morning. Of course, Grandmother has become younger by 25 years & seems to be the very embodiment of happiness. The Mother & the Sister follow suit; they are all a most joyful little family. May they enjoy long the realization of their pious happiness.[15]

Only Mother Elizabeth herself had a fairly long future that day. Father Edward died December 30, 1879, it was said from the effects of his exertions in the clean-up after the great fire; his obituary card says only that his illness (apparently tuberculosis) was "long and painful."

His sister, Edith Lilly, had entered Holy Cross in 1870 and became Sister Cecilia. She made her profession three months after her brother's ordination, and outlived him by six years, dying in 1885. As the eighties opened she was already struggling with poor health, and her grandmother, Harriet Redman, was dying. One of the first decisions of the council in the year 1880 was to allow Mrs. Redman to be buried in the habit of Holy Cross. Sister Elizabeth lived on to 1901. In her later years she began a highly laudatory and excruciatingly detailed life of Mother Angela, which ends abruptly with the "hospital tea" episode of the Civil War. One would never guess from reading it that there had ever been a breath of disagreement between her and Angela.

24
Priceless Spirit, 1880–93

"Another hook to be put on the Seven Dolor beads," say the council minutes for November 25, 1880. This meant that the chaplet worn at the side would not dangle with the crucifix so close to the floor. In small ways, the set of the cap, the cut of the collar, the arrangement of the beads, the Sisters of the Holy Cross were moving away from the Marianites.

More significantly, they were building their own version of the Constitutions and Rules. The first set of Constitutions, that of 1870, was patterned after the Marianites' and frequently follows theirs word for word. The Indiana document contains twenty-two separate constitutions, based on the Marianites' twenty-eight. It describes the nature and end of the congregation; its relationship to the Holy See, diocesan ordinaries, and other ecclesiastics; the duties of its officers, superiors, and directresses; the vows, profession, and dismissal. Indiana combined the offices of stewardess and treasurer and did not need the constitution on provincial superiors. It also dropped the constitutions on foundations, works proper to the congregation, furniture, rank and precedence, sickness, death and suffrages, and obligation of the constitutions (most of these were reinserted later).

Indiana made some interesting additions. Sorin wrote a constitution on the ecclesiastical superior — himself, in fact. It requested the Holy See to allow the Sisters to elect their own ecclesiastical superior every six years; this never came about, and Sorin continued to be appointed by the bishop. The qualifications he puts down are both ideal and a rather unblushing self-portrait:

> an Ecclesiastic who by age, personal merit, and irreproachability of character, will seem best fitted to watch over the interests, both spiritual and temporal, of the Congregation, and to preside over its councils, to inspire all its members with confidence, so that in all difficulties and trials inseparable from such a momentous undertaking, among so many obstacles and dangers, the new-born Religious family may find in him the wisdom and devotedness of a father.[1]

They also added a rather horrifying constitution called "State of Souls," in which each Sister was given an individual numerical rating, culled from reports of superiors, directresses, and visitors on "health, regularity, obedience, efficiency, temper, devotedness, and success."[2] Moreover, "at the close of the general retreat some of the most unsatisfactory reports should be read in public to the community, for a warning to all."

Both of these constitutions were dropped from the next edition. The one that remained was the new one on the scholasticate, or the study program of the young Sisters. This changed substantially as the Constitutions were rewritten, twice more before 1900 and four times since.

The Rules of 1871 are the first to contain the remarkably beautiful Preface, so well loved by the community for over a hundred years, and still existing, though in a greatly shortened form, at the beginning of the Constitution of 1982. For a large part of the twentieth century the Sisters of the Holy Cross have been under the impression that Father Moreau had written that Preface. He did not; it was written by Father Sorin. It makes its first appearance after the separation, and neither the Marianites nor the Holy Cross Sisters of Canada have ever had it.

The Preface requires the Rules to be "received and studied and acted upon with a special disposition," and then asks:

> And what is this precious disposition? Is it the consciousness of having brought to the Community a fortune, an accomplished education, a rare talent, or some extra personal advantage?
>
> None of these; it is something far more precious, while it is within the reach of all. *It is the spirit of faith* — of that faith without which "it is impossible to please God." It is that mysterious disposition which reveals to the eyes and to the heart of a religious the adorable Will of God, and makes every line of her Rules a source of contentment and merit; it is that holy spirit of faith which transforms the exercises, the duties and labors of a religious life into so many manifestations of the love of the Divine Spouse to His chosen one; it is that priceless spirit of faith which ennobles every act of an humble and devoted Sister, whose continual attention to God's presence, and fervent prayers, save the house where she lives, while by it she becomes an object of edification to all, and of admiration to the angels above. The spirit of faith sustains her in the hour of fa-

tigue, of trial, of affliction, of sickness; for in the light of faith, the tribulations of this life bear no comparison, in her estimation, with the degree of glory awaiting her in eternity.

The first rules cover admission, novitiate, the scheduling and performance of duties, prayer and penance, the vows, virtues, and discipline. The second volume, which followed in 1877 and eventually became Part II of the Rules, deals with such matters as chapters, elections, administration, finances, and the fulfilling of various offices. The first, especially in dealing with prayer and the virtues, is almost a book of poetry. The two were combined, with slight changes, in the Rule of 1895, from which the Rule of 1933 was taken, again with only minor modifications, except in the rule on the scholasticate. After Vatican II the congregation existed from chapter to chapter on experimental decrees until the approval of the *Constitution and Statutes* of 1982.

The chapter of elections in 1882 decided it was time for Mother Angela to share the burdens of office with someone else. They chose Sister Augusta as mother superior. Angela was named mistress of novices, but before she could enter upon the office it was decided that Mother Lucretia, who had been elected second assistant, should go temporarily to the growing academy in Salt Lake City and that Angela should replace her as directress of studies at the academy while she was gone. The temporary arrangement lasted a year and a half.

This shifting of council members after they had been elected and before their terms had expired was not unusual. In 1875 the council had replaced Mother Augusta, then serving as stewardess, with Mother Colette, so that Augusta would be free to open a new mission in Salt Lake City.

This she did, with Sister M. Raymond (Sullivan), in response to an appeal from Father (later Bishop) Lawrence Scanlon. The opening of their academy in 1875 was followed the same year by the arrival of Sisters Holy Cross (Walsh) and Bartholomew (Darnell), who opened the first Catholic hospital in the enormous Utah territory. Sister Augusta continued as superior of the academy until 1878. She spent three of the next four years consolidating her school experience in three well-established academies of the Midwest (Logansport, Michigan City, and Morris). The other year was spent in an effort to establish a tuberculosis sanatorium in Germantown, Pennsylvania, but this was given up after a year. Thus, by the time she became mother superior she had experience in schools, both new and continuing, both academic and manual training; in hospitals, both military and civilian; and in administrative service to the congregation. She was an ideal leader for the new community age which was shaping up.

But she carried one almost insurmountable handicap into office. Sorin could not adjust to Angela's replacement by anyone and was not prepared to be very helpful to her successor. This needs to be looked at.

Sorin had always been authoritarian and was getting crotchety as he grew older. In 1882 he was sixty-eight, which was old for those days. (Even as late as 1920, life expectancy for white American males was only 53.6 years.)[3] He would live eleven more years. Up until 1889 he was the Sisters' superior general, and Mother Augusta was the mother superior. After that, for the rest of his life and beyond it, she was the superior general.

His preference was for women of ability, education, background, and culture. At the beginning of his Indiana missionary life, all those years ago in Vincennes, the cousinly tie between the Brothers of St. Joseph and the Sisters of Providence had led to his acquaintance with Mother Theodore. He admired her greatly and after leaving Vincennes continued to correspond with her.

He probably thought he had found his ideal helpmeet in Mother Cenacle, who brought to Indiana all the qualities he wanted in the woman who should lead the Sisters, but she died after less than two years of service. He was devastated by her death (see chapter 4). He asked Mother Theodore to provide a superior for his orphaned Sisters, but though she personally made the hard journey north on a superogatory visit of consolation, she could remain only a short time and had no other Sister to spare.

He seems to have been more reluctant to warm up to Mother Savior, the next French superior in Bertrand. She had all the qualities he wanted but one great flaw with them — she looked forward to the day when she could return to France. This disqualified her as his ideal.

At last came Angela. He told her the hour he met her, "You are the one we have been praying for for so long." She not only had ability, background, education, and culture, she had magnificent political connections. And she came to him untarnished by anyone else's system of religious training, for him to mold. Even when he sent her to France for her novitiate, it was not to the motherhouse, where she might have been touched by the lingering remains of Jansenism; besides, his own relationship to Sainte-Croix was rather touchy at the time (see chapter 9). When she completed her training in Caen and came to the motherhouse to make her vows, he was there too, ready to escort her away as soon as the vows were made, back to their common mission.

They worked together as a perfect team for the next thirty years, and he was not always an easy man to work for or with. He saw the grand design; she supplied the details. He was the architect, she the contractor. It was not always just a matter of the Sisters' schools. He thought a Catholic family magazine was needed; she edited the *Ave Maria*. He was dissatisfied with the readers provided in the Catholic schools; she wrote the whole Sadlier series. He was heartbroken at the death of his beloved colleague, Father Cointet, in the cholera epidemic of 1854; she, who had barely known Father Cointet, wrote his biography, almost in terms of the life of a saint. And when she was collecting funds for a church at Saint Mary's which would also be the center of an archconfraternity for devotion to Our Lady of the Sacred Heart and she learned from another priest that Sorin had similar plans, she turned over all the funds to Notre Dame, saying that after all it was a better place for such a center.

She was almost exactly ten years younger than he (both were born in February), and he was disconcerted when her health showed signs of failing before she reached sixty. We do not know the nature of her problem — in several of her letters after 1875 she speaks of a pain or "gathering" in her head, and her recurring times of illness were characterized by fever. The fever or other causes may have affected her mental powers during the days the illnesses lasted, but when she recovered, she recovered both physically and mentally. *Superior Generals,*[4] following a shaky source, makes much of her supposed mental weakness, especially in the matter of papers.

> Important community documents had been lost, misplaced, or removed from the archives at Saint Mary's, and could not be accounted for. Records that should have been in the courthouse at South Bend could not be located. They were thought to be at Notre

> Dame. In her impaired physical [note: even this source does not say "mental"] condition, Mother Angela could not account for these things.[5]

Angela's illness was actually upon her at the time of (or shortly before) the chapter of 1882, which may have brought about the election of a different superior. The missing documents were readily located.

> They had all been put by Father Sorin into the archives at Notre Dame. It became Mother Augusta's duty to procure them. As she was properly authorized to do so, Father Sorin returned them all.[6]

Probably Sorin and Angela had agreed that the documents would be better housed at Notre Dame, which was already collecting the archives of as many American dioceses as would send them there. There is less in the matter than meets the eye.

In 1875–76 Mother Angela had gone to Europe rather reluctantly. She returned with postulants, teachers of lace making, and various artifacts, but she had not felt very well during the whole trip. In January 1877 she was seriously ill with "fever," but six months later she was visiting Sister Augusta's new missions in Utah Territory, and six months after that she was in Washington, D.C. In the spring of 1880, at the request of the council, she spent time in Austin and Clarksville, Texas. The chapter of 1882 has been discussed. In 1884 she was in New York on business, and looked in on the presidential campaign of her first cousin, James G[illespie] Blaine. That December she took over the novitiate. By April 1886 (eleven months before her death) she was back in Utah dealing with railroad officials over the establishment of a railroad hospital. She went from there to make the foundation of Holy Rosary Academy in Woodland, California, then crossed the continent to Baltimore, where, among other things, she attended the enthronement of Archbishop Gibbons as cardinal, and had an interview with him on the subject of the approbation of the Constitutions. She then went to Columbus, Ohio, where she and her companion, with no other help, tackled the jobs of nursing and cleaning in the new hospital, sleeping on the floor the first night. She was planning to return from there to Woodland, but the need for help in Columbus detained her until chapter time in July. The chapter elected her second assistant.

Failing in health she may or may not have been (the above account certainly does not suggest serious impairment), but her letters from Ogden and Columbus are eminently clear, crisp, and businesslike, not the maunderings of a woman whose mental powers are failing. But this takes us ahead of the story.

Clearly Angela was what would be called today a hard act to follow. And Augusta had the duty of following her, even while Angela was still alive.

One of Sorin's first expectations of Mother Augusta was that she would be as willing to travel on community business as Angela had been. There is no evidence in her letters that she raised any objections, though the account in *Superior Generals* suggests that she did. It is true that she wrote from Salt Lake City to ask whether she should expect to remain there, or whether she would be coming back to Saint Mary's, explaining that her next actions would depend upon the answer. When Sorin and the council delayed the decision, she asked again, strongly recommending Mother Colette for the Salt Lake post. And the arrival of Mother Colette in our narrative brings up the whole Mother Colette/Sister Cyril story.

Sister Madeleva (Wolff) was one of the most outstanding Catholic writers of the first half of the twentieth century, a leading educator, and president of Saint Mary's College from 1934 to 1961. She was commissioned to write the chapter on Mother Augusta for *Superior Generals*. There is a letter in the archives from Sister Cyril (Books),[7] saying that she is glad to know that Sister Madeleva has undertaken this task. Sister Cyril then offered a manuscript narrative of an account which she says Mother Colette (Cunnea) "gave [she does not say whether orally or in writing] on her deathbed."

Sister Cyril was gifted with extremely skillful hands and a mechanical turn of mind, and is best remembered in the congregation as the inventor of the fluting machine. Until she sat down under obedience to work out a new device, the Sisters' white victoria lawn caps were pressed into shape with tongs like curling irons, in which the heat could not be maintained at a constant level, and which usually resulted in blistered fingers for the operator. Sister Cyril, working with the Aerothrust Engine Company of LaPorte, designed a machine controlled by a foot pedal. Even temperatures were maintained first by a "stove," later by electricity.

But Sister Cyril's formal schooling had been brief and rudimentary. Her handwriting is sprawling and childish, she spells badly, and she has no knowledge of punctuation or hyphenation. An unlikely choice for an amanuensis.

The papers in the set consist of four kinds: twenty-two pages of six-by-nine-inch convent stationery, written on one side in pencil, containing the first half of the story in Sister Cyril's handwriting; two sheets of the same stationery in another handwriting, written on both sides in pencil and dealing with later affairs; four sheets of the same stationery in single-spaced typing, which is a transcript of Sister Cyril's manuscript with some changes in the wording; thirty-five pages (eighteen sheets, the last one only partially used) on school copybook paper, neatly written in still another hand, with further changes to improve the literary style. From this material has been fashioned a story which has been accepted in the congregation as literal fact, and which must now be re-examined.

First, neither Sister Augusta nor any other young Sister "walked back and forth between Bertrand and Notre Dame to wash and clean and cook for the university."[8] The Sisters who did those things lived at the university, and some washing was brought by horse-drawn cart to Bertrand. The only recorded walk was Sister Basil (Coffee)'s with a schoolgirl when Bertrand one day ran out of both food and money (see chapter 3).

Second, when Father Sorin first mentioned his second-novitiate idea to the chapter of 1872 (not 1873), *Superior Generals* says, "Eleven members agreed to it,"[9] as if the rest of the chapter withheld their agreement. Eleven was the total membership of that chapter.

Third, following the Colette/Cyril document, *Superior Generals* says of the chapter of 1882, "This was the first chapter presided over by a bishop. . . . By a unanimous vote Mother Augusta was elected superior."[10] Bishop Borgess of Detroit presided over the 1870 chapter of elections, the first after separation. Bishop Joseph Dwenger of Fort Wayne himself presided at the second chapter of elections in 1876. There is no question about this; the signatures of the bishops are in the chapter books. Mother Colette was a member of the chapter of 1876. Either her memory failed, she deliberately distorted the facts, or Sister Cyril got the story wrong. The vote was not unanimous; Mother Augusta got twenty-two votes out of thirty-two.[11]

Fourth, no evidence can be found for the account of Mother Augusta taking Mother Angela to LaPorte and caring for her in her last illness. Until the beginning of 1887, Mother Angela was, as noted above, criss-crossing the country on community business. After that Mother Augusta was presiding at council meetings every week and could hardly have been commuting from LaPorte. Mother Angela became ill at the beginning of the year and was cared for at Saint Mary's until her death the first week in March. McAllister says that Father Richard Shortis, a classmate of Mother Angela's deceased brother, Father Neal Gillespie, visited her daily,[12] which he could not have done had she been in LaPorte.[13]

The manuscript next mentions the "missing" documents, which have been dealt with above.

The next part of the narration in *Superior Generals* concerns the supposed ordering about by Father Sorin of Mother Augusta on long travels to get her out of the way. In fact, the mother superior was expected to travel and to make foundations. During the eighties she made one trip to Salt Lake City, staying a little more than two months. She was present at Saint Mary's for the council meeting of May 3, 1885, went to Salt Lake City, and was present again at Saint Mary's July 21. She also made one trip to Texas and was gone from January 1886 until early June. She kept writing back to the council saying she did not want to leave until she could bring Sister Mildred, the superior, who was very ill. Sister Mildred was finally deemed able to travel at the end of May, but died after her arrival at Saint Mary's.

Superior Generals:

> Finally in desperation at her persistent exile, Mother Augusta sent a letter of protest to Father Sorin. He replied advising her to send in her resignation to the bishop. This she did July 24, 1884.[14]

In the paragraph before the one just quoted, the author of *Superior Generals* has correctly placed the travels to Salt Lake City and Texas as "between 1885 and 1889." But 1884 comes *before* those dates. One does not resign in protest of something which has not yet happened. In fact, *there was no resignation* but only the offer of an offer. Travel, at least Mother Augusta's travel, had nothing to do with it. The activities of a person not mentioned in the Colette/Cyril scenario had everything to do with it.

Sister M. Claudine (Maginnis) had been superior at St. Joseph's Academy in South Bend and a member of the chapters of 1870, '71, '72, '76, and '79. In 1884, giving her poor health as a reason, she asked to visit her brother's farm in New York state. The permission was given, with a time limit. When she had not returned at the conclusion of the time, Mother Augusta summoned her to come back to Saint Mary's immediately. She did not reply. After another lapse of time, Augusta sent for her again. No reply.[15]

In late June 1884 Bishop Dwenger received a letter dated June 24 from the Reverend J. J. Hamel, pastor of St. Mary's church, Olean, New York, stating that

> Sister Claudine . . . is for the last four weeks in my mission stopping at a hotel and collecting indirectly. . . . She has a little book, a May devotion, printed at Notre Dame. And she goes to all the public works to have people subscribe. . . . In three weeks she has not been to [Mass or Communion]. . . . Last week the pastor at Bradford denounced her from the Altar by order of his Bishop of Erie. This I will do too if she remains any longer. . . .

Bishop Dwenger sent the letter to Father Sorin (it should be remembered that at this time Sorin was still the Sisters' highest superior) demanding a full explanation, and Sorin sent the letter on to Augusta. She wrote the bishop June 30, admitting giving Sister Claudine permission to visit her brother. Mother Angela, questioned with the rest of the council, said she had sent a few May devotion books to Claudine, who had written for them saying she could "dispose of them among her friends." Neither Mother Augusta nor Mother Angela knew anything about collecting or subscribing. Sister Claudine had been telegraphed to return to Saint Mary's at once.

Bishop Dwenger wrote Augusta on July 5:

> This case has revealed to me a laxity, a worldliness in your practice that has absolutely astonished and pained me. The idea of a Sister, living away for months . . . is a perfect horror to me. I reserve to myself . . . the decision in her case.

She replied the next day that part of Sister Claudine's delay had been caused by "storms of great severity." She stated her principles for allowing a Sister to visit relatives, and then bravely (or foolhardily) asked permission for another Sister to visit at home, the permission having been already approved by the council. The letter, a long one for her, ends, "And I wish to say further, if I am in any way obnoxious to you, and you wish me to resign, let me know."

The bishop replied July 9 (this was all done by correspondence; at no time did the bishop come to Saint Mary's) that the other Sister could go if her father had need of her, but not if the need was on her side; sick Sisters should stay in their convents. He went on, "I cannot properly answer the other question you propose as my words might be misconstrued." He wrote to Father Sorin on July 11, "She asked me whether she should resign. She did not offer her resignation nor did she say plainly what she would do. To this . . . I had to decline to answer."

Sister Claudine returned to Saint Mary's before the end of July, and Mother Augusta sent her to Fort Wayne to explain herself to the bishop — escorted by Mother Colette.[16] In other words, Mother Colette knew all about Sister Claudine, but either Claudine was never mentioned in Colette's narrative, or she was edited out by Sister Cyril. The rest of the story, with the bishop upbraiding Augusta before the whole council, Colette intervening to report personally "the whole state of affairs" to the bishop, and the bishop then publicly rebuking Father Sorin for his "petty persecution" of Augusta by sending her running about the country, is pure fiction. Colette, as a council member, *knew* the bishop never came to Saint Mary's. But either she or Sister Cyril has assigned to Colette the starring role as the one who set the bishop straight.[17]

The statement that "Father Sorin remained away from Saint Mary's for some time after this,"[18] is not borne out by the fact that he continued to sign the council minutes with the same regularity as before.

On the morning of March 4, 1887, he made one of his frequent visits to Mother Angela, now an infirmary patient, and found her no better and no worse than she had been for weeks. So he was astounded when someone brought him news of her death a few hours later. He was as hard hit as he had been by the death of Mother Cenacle all those years ago in Bertrand, but he was older now and less resilient. It took him a month to compose a circular letter to the Sisters. He did write at once, however, to Bishop Pierre Dufal, his immediate predecessor as superior general, then serving as procurator general for Holy Cross in Rome.

> Since my arrival in the New World forty-six years ago, I do not remember having suffered as I am suffering from the great loss that we have just felt in the unexpected . . . death of Mother Angela. She was buried this morning at Saint Mary's by the Bishop of Cleveland,[19] who spoke admirably of her rare merits and great success to the many friends who came from all parts to express their veneration for the illustrious and humble deceased. . . . The universal impression that this unexpected death is making surprised even me and opens my eyes to the greatness of the trial that is afflicting me. I can no longer rest; I do not know what can happen to me next.[20]

He goes on to suggest to Bishop Dufal that the slowness of the progress of approbation of the Constitutions had something to do with Angela's death. This appears to be merely a stick to beat the bishop with, as Sorin lashed out in his grief at any object. In her obituary notice he had said that he agreed with the doctor, who ascribed her death to heart failure brought on by the death of her young artist friend, Sister Lioba, "whose funeral procession passed under her window four hours before."[21] One cause seems as unlikely as the other.

Sister Emerentiana's large *Chronicle* contains twenty-one pages of printed tributes to Mother Angela from the Notre Dame *Scholastic* and other publications.

Superior Generals, following Sister Cyril, also suggests that there was something shady about the chapters of 1888 and 1889. The actual sequence of events was this.

The chapter of affairs for 1888 was concluded on August 10, but the members could not proceed to the chapter of elections because of the absence of the bishop, who was delayed by a meeting of the diocesan school board.[22] He arrived on August 14, called the chapter together, and

> requested them to inform him in writing if they wished the election to take place now, or postpone it on account of the season being so far advanced. On Thursday August 14 the Rt. Rev. Bishop assembled the members again and announced to them that it was the unanimous wish to postpone the Chapter of Elections for one year, which he approved.[23]

The approbation of 1869 had been for ten years. The year of 1879 had slipped by with no request for renewal, leaving the Sisters in a canonical limbo, a fact to which no one seems to have adverted at the time. Sorin's letter to Bishop Dufal at Angela's death suggests that it was one of the projects Dufal was working on in Rome. Sorin may not have pushed it very hard in order not to raise too many questions about the Notre Dame novitiate.

Bishop Dwenger went into the matter with more determination than Bishop Dufal. On March 26, 1889, he wrote to Sorin that he had just received the seven-year approbation from Rome and would come in person to bring "the Decree, the Letter, and Constitutions." He did this in April, then came back "early in vacation, one Sunday after Vespers"[24] to give the Sisters an explanatory conference. The conference dealt with the Sisters' obligations, and Sister Emerentiana's summary says nothing about the bishop's difficulties in securing the approbation, nor is there any mention of these in the chapter minutes of 1889.

The new Constitutions completed the separation of the Sisters from the priests of Holy Cross. At the election presided over by Bishop Dwenger, Mother Augusta was elected (on the third ballot) and became superior general in her own right. The Sisters seem to have invited Father Sorin, as a courtesy, to sign the minutes of the first council meeting after the election. After that his signature does not appear. They continued to refer to him as "Father General."

Contrary to popular understanding, the approbation was not contingent upon closing the Notre Dame novitiate. That came the following year. The records of the professed convent at Notre Dame say, under July 5, 1890:

> After visiting St. Mary's the Bishop came here, had all the Sisters, even the postulants, assembled in the chapel, and read to them the Cardinal's [Giovanni Cardinal Simeoni's] letter, which recommended the withdrawal of the Sisters from this mission, or placing it on a proper business basis with regard to the Mother House. Ninety days were allowed to fulfill this work.
>
> . . . the Propaganda had decided there should be but one novitiate for the order . . . the Bishop said very emphatically, "There must be unity or disbandment." He also took care to remark that the Sisters who had been professed at Notre Dame need not be dis-

> turbed; their professions were valid. This was a very important decision as the doubt was the cause of much trouble.
>
> After the annual retreat of 1890, a contract was drawn up by mutual consent of the members of the councils . . . fixing an annual salary of $6500 for the services of 105 Sisters at Notre Dame. . . .
>
> The Novitiate at Notre Dame was then closed and the novices sent to St. Mary's to commence their novitiate on the twenty-ninth of August. . . .
>
> The Scholastics followed in bands, as many as could be spared. They had to make one full year's novitiate at St. Mary's before making their profession. Several of these Sisters had the Habit for six or seven years at Notre Dame.
>
> Some of these Sisters were returned to Notre Dame, others were sent to distant missions. God reward good Bishop Dwenger for all his labor and anxiety about this matter.

The document includes the names of the four novices and six postulants who began their canonical year at Saint Mary's. Though the Notre Dame group is generally remembered as heavily German, seven of these ten were Irish.

Father Sorin was getting noticeably older. In 1888 both campuses and uncounted organizations had celebrated his golden jubilee in truly royal splendor. The Sisters worked till midnight the night before and were up by three in the morning, attended Mass at four, "and from that [time] until late in the afternoon they never rested."[25] Father Sorin offered a low Mass at nine o'clock, and the Solemn Pontifical High Mass was offered by Cardinal Gibbons. The homily by Archbishop Ireland is still quoted in Holy Cross circles.

In 1891 Father Sorin went to Europe and the Holy Land. He continued to write inspiring circular letters, but he was tiring. In July 1893 his almost-lifelong colleague, Father Granger, died. Sorin wept at the news. "Mon cher Alexis! Who next?"[26] He was next.

He was not well when school opened that September. He was unable to attend his own feastday celebration on October 13. Priests, Brothers, Sisters, and students kept up constant prayer for him. Mother Augusta and Mother Genevieve seldom left him during the last two days, and Mother Ascension neither ate nor slept. On the morning of October 31,

> At a quarter to ten he slowly opened his eyes and gazed at the religious kneeling around him. It was the only farewell he could make. Then, gently closing his eyes, he expired without the slightest movement or struggle.[27]

He had been given to the Sisters by Bishop Luers as their "living Rule." Now the living rule was a closed book. But he had left them his vision, his determination, his "priceless spirit" of faith. Mother Augusta and her Sisters faced the coming century with hope and without fear, in the strength of the gifts bequeathed them by Edward Sorin, Angela Gillespie, and Basil Moreau.

NOTES

1. THESE FORTUNATE SHORES

1. Charles Lemarié, C.S.C., *De la Mayenne à l'Indiana: Le Père Edouard Sorin (1814–1893)* (Angers: Université Catholique de l'Ouest, 1978), 24. This excerpt trans. Sister M. Georgia (Costin), C.S.C.

2. Basil Anthony Moreau, *Circular Letters*, trans. Edward L. Heston, C.S.C. (no publication data) Nov. 8, 1835, I: 6.

3. Lemarié, 27.

4. Edward Sorin, C.S.C., *Chronicles of Notre Dame du Lac* (Notre Dame, Ind.: University of Notre Dame Press, 1992), 31. Trans. John M. Toohey, C.S.C., ed. James T. Connelly, C.S.C. Hereafter *N.D. Chronicles.*

5. Dec. 5, 1842. The letter is quoted in its entirety in Father Moreau's Circular Letter no. 17. This part of the letter appears on p. 6, vol. I of the English version.

2. AN ASSOCIATION OF PIOUS PERSONS

1. Etienne Catta and Tony Catta, *Mother Mary of the Seven Dolors and the Early Origins of the Marianites of Holy Cross (1818–1900)* (Milwaukee: Bruce Press, 1959), 26. Hereafter *MMSD.*

2. *MMSD*, 26.

3. Ibid., 29.

4. Ibid., 61.

5. Quoted in Sister M. Eleanore (Brosnahan), C.S.C., *On the King's Highway* (New York: D. Appleton, 1931), 117. Hereafter Brosnahan.

6. *MMSD*, 63.

7. Brosnahan, 120.

8. *N.D. Chronicles*, 38. Connelly's footnote on the same page identifies him as Brother John Cronin, who was born in England, joined the community at St. Peter's, and left before profession.

9. *MMSD*, 63.

10. Brosnahan, 120.

11. Ibid., 123.

12. Ibid., 124.

13. *Annals of the Congregation of the Marianite Sisters of Holy Cross 1841–1941* (Le Mans: 1947), 21. Hereafter *Marianite Annals.*

14. Ibid.
15. Ibid., 130.
16. *Marianite Annals*, 22.

3. WILD ROSES AND SWEETBRIAR

1. Brosnahan, 134.
2. Sister Mary of St. Elizabeth (Lilly), C.S.C., unpublished recollections, II: 203. Hereafter Lilly.
3. Ibid.
4. Sister Mary Emerentiana (Nowlan), C.S.C., unpublished Chronicles, I: 31. Hereafter Nowlan.
5. Ibid., 30–31.
6. *Marianite Annals*, 24.
7. *Catholic Miscellany*, February 1846. Quoted in Nowlan I: 39.
8. Sister Mary of the Compassion (Gleeson), C.S.C., unpublished recollections, 22. Hereafter Gleeson.
9. Brosnahan, 144.
10. Ibid.
11. Ibid., 145.
12. Gleeson, 21.
13. Council Minutes, Feb. 23, 1846. Hereafter CM.
14. Ibid.
15. CM, Mar. 9, 1846.
16. CM, Mar. 16, 1846.
17. CM, May 18, 1846.
18. Gleeson, 23–24.
19. Her name appears as witness of the reception into the Canadian community of Blessed Léonie Paradis.
20. Gleeson, 23–24.
21. *Marianite Annals*, 24–25.
22. Brosnahan, 149.
23. Etienne Catta and Tony Catta, *Basil Anthony Mary Moreau*, 2 vols. (Milwaukee: Bruce, 1955), I: 525 ff. Hereafter Catta.
24. Sister Five Wounds to Sorin, 1848 (no other date). Box, Sister Five Wounds (Paillet) letters to Father Sorin. Trans. SMGC. All the quoted letters of Sister Five Wounds are from this source. Originals in Indiana Province Archives, Notre Dame.
25. Brosnahan, 150.
26. Nowlan I: 28.
27. Letter from Sorin to Moreau, Nov. 9, 1847, quoted in Brosnahan, 150. Original in Holy Cross Archives, Rome.
28. Nowlan I: 48.

29. Sorin, as in note 27.
30. Gleeson, 29.
31. Ibid.

4. AS EDIFYING AS CARTHUSIANS

1. *N.D. Chronicles*, 77. This translation (from Brosnahan, 153–54) differs slightly from Toohey's.

2. Canon law required that each house of a congregation or order be officially visited by a major superior on a regular basis. These Visits (distinguished in this text from ordinary social visits by capitalization) were usually annual. The results of the Visits formed part of a congregation's annual report to Rome.

3. Sister Mary Borromeo Brown, S.P., *History of the Sisters of Providence of Saint Mary-of-the-Woods*, vol. I (New York: Benziger Brothers, 1949), 755.

4. Ibid.

5. Sisters of Providence, Book of Important Events I: 1840–1880, 94. Sisters of Providence Archives, Saint Mary-of-the-Woods, Indiana.

6. Blessed Marie Léonie (Paradis) was a Canadian who entered the Marianites in Canada. The year following Indiana's autonomy, she transferred to the Indiana community (see chap. 23).

7. Catta I: 930.

8. Drouelle to Moreau, Nov. 1, 1848, quoted in Catta I: 931.

9. Ibid.

10. Sister St. Francis Xavier to Sorin, May 10, 1847, quoted in Brown, 754.

11. *Centenary Chronicles of the Sisters of the Holy Cross*, vol. IV.

12. Sister Five Wounds to Sorin, Apr. 10, 1848.

13. *Marianite Annals*, 26.

14. Ibid.

15. Sister Five Wounds to Sorin, Letter no. 22. Undated, but contents indicate that it was written shortly before leaving Lebanon.

16. Letter no. 24.

17. *MMSD*, 94.

5. MAINTAIN YOUR INDEPENDENCE

1. Catta I: 434.
2. Brown, 253.
3. Ibid., 404.
4. Ibid., 232–33.
5. Ibid., 446.

6. *S.v.* "Bouvier" by P. Disser.
7. Catta I: 82.
8. Brown, 474–75.
9. Catta I: 496.
10. Ibid., 499.
11. Ibid., 511.

6. I SAW A MAN!

1. Gleeson, 37.
2. CM June 20, 1850.
3. Big Book of Accounts, 98.
4. *Journal and Letters of Mother Theodore Guérin,* ed. Sister Mary Theodosia Mug (Saint Mary-of-the-Woods, Ind.: Providence Press, 1937), 35. Quoted in Brown, 69.
5. Brown, 65.
6. *Journal* as in note 4, quoted in Brown, 66.
7. Quoted in Brosnahan, 156.
8. Ibid., 161.
9. Ibid., 162.
10. Ibid., 163.
11. CM Nov. 19, 1851.
12. Catta I: 969, n. 46.
13. Brown, 146.
14. Sister M. Euphrosine (Pepin), C.S.C., unpublished recollections, 14. Hereafter Pepin.
15. Ibid., 5.
16. Ibid., 5–6.
17. Ibid., 7.
18. Ibid., 8.
19. Ibid., 9.
20. Ibid.
21. Ibid., 12.
22. Ibid., 13.
23. Ibid.
24. Ibid., 17–18.
25. Ibid., 19–20.
26. Ibid., 21.
27. Ibid., 22.
28. Ibid., 24.
29. Ibid., 27.
30. Ibid., 28.
31. Nowlan I: 79.

32. Pepin, 29.
33. Ibid., 32.
34. Ibid., 34.

7. HERE WILL I DWELL

1. Sorin to Archbishop Purcell, quoted in Catta I: 953.

2. This translation (by SMGC) differs from Heston's quoted in Catta, that the Sisters "would stop at nothing in order to obtain the revocation" of the order, and better reflects the tone of the original, alarmed and pleading, rather than defiant. Box, Separation from France, envelope, Sisters' Council to Father Moreau, Oct. 7, 1852, contains a xerox copy of Sister Ascension's original letter and a typescript of it (both originals in Holy Cross Archives, Rome) and this translation.

3. Moreau to Sisters' Council, quoted in Catta I: 958.

4. Gilbert Français, C.S.C., *Circular Letters* (Notre Dame: 1913), letter of Oct. 3, 1900, 176–77.

5. James T. Connelly, C.S.C., "Charism: Origin and History," in *Fruits of the Tree*, I: 110–11.

6. Quoted by Lemarié, 14.

7. Ibid.

8. Ibid.

9. Quoted in Catta II: 909.

10. Ibid.

8. THIS QUESTION OF FINAL SEPARATION

1. Catta I: 978.

2. Details of this rather lengthy process may be found in Catta I: 952–83 and II: 3–25.

3. *N.D. Chronicles*, 110.

4. Father Granger feared that a seminarian who drank too much would "renew the scenes which Father Gouesse gave us in the past," Sept. 1, 1852; and Cointet says that, among other things, Gouesse is too much in the company of young ladies, Dec. 1, 1852. Original letters in Holy Cross General Archives, Rome; copies in Province Archives, Notre Dame.

5. Some German communities, such as the Franciscan Sisters of the Sacred Heart (present motherhouse in Mokena, Ill.,) and the Sisters of St. Francis of the Holy Family (Dubuque, Iowa) were ordered by Bismarck to disband and chose to leave the country instead. Entire congregations emigrated. The Sisters of the Congregation of the Humility of Mary left France as a congregation when the bishop of Nancy in 1864 re-

fused to let them carry out their chosen ministries to the poor. The Congregation of Divine Providence (San Antonio, Tex.) separated from their French roots in 1886, securing Roman approval in 1912. The Congregation of the Incarnate Word and Blessed Sacrament founded missions in Texas and Mexico from 1850 on, many of which became autonomous houses; the original motherhouse in Lyons has since voluntarily placed itself under the jurisdiction of one of the Mexican houses. By various routes and means European communities were becoming American ones.

6. Years later, with the autonomy of the Sisters pending, Father Sorin asked Bishop Dwenger of Fort Wayne for assurance that he and his successors as superiors general of the men of Holy Cross would always remain the canonical superiors of the Sisters. Dwenger replied, "Rome does not intend to disturb your position, yet they will not make your successor or the father provincial in office 'ex officio' the canonical superior of the Sisters for all future," Sept. 14, 1888. In Mother Augusta box, envelope Letters of Augusta and Dwenger: 1883–1894.

7. From Kentucky, May 27, 1849: "I told you of my desire to see you, before going to another mission. I have in fact many reasons for this desire. . . ." Undated, before leaving Kentucky: "some among us . . . are desirous of returning to Notre Dame du Lac, and . . . will be cruelly disappointed to receive an order to go so far away, without first having been able to make their little representation to you, which naturally is freely permitted." Also before leaving Kentucky: "It is very necessary and very important that we come to Notre Dame du Lac to make a little retreat before being sent anywhere. There we will see you. . . ." From New Orleans: "To tell you how I long to see you would be difficult. . . . Remember how I was asking you to let me return to Notre Dame. . . ." She finally gave up on this and switched her plea to one that he would come, first to New Orleans and then to New York.

9. THE ONE I HAVE BEEN PRAYING FOR

1. See Anna Shannon McAllister, *Flame in the Wilderness* (Paterson, N.J.: St. Anthony Guild Press, 1944), 1ff. See also Brosnahan, 165–66.

2. Neal Gillespie to Eliza Gillespie, Feb. 19, 1853, quoted in McAllister, 67.

3. Lilly III: 221.

4. Brosnahan 169, quoting Lilly.

5. McAllister, 96.

6. Pepin, 37.

7. Catta I: 118.

8. Lilly III: 251–52.

9. Ibid.

10. According to the Cattas, the progress of the assignment was as follows (page numbers are from vol. I of the two-volume English version): Granger was asked in June if he were "ready to be a member" of the mission and to accept "whatever obedience I shall deem it advisable before God to give you." He refused (839); the Cattas do not give the reason but Connelly says it was to remain in formation work. (See chap. 7.) Cointet was considered but not actually asked or assigned, apparently in view of what New Orleans had done to his health. Sorin refused (895 et passim). Verité was named superior but understood not to be in line for a bishopric (895). Verité and Baroux formed a kind of superior team until November 1855, when one bishop died and another was transferred, and Holy Cross was required to supply a bishop (17). Champeau refused in order "to devote himself" to "teaching, for which he had been prepared" (918). Verité was proposed and reacted with "embarrassment and terror" (921). The Cattas remark: "Le Mans found itself in a very embarrassing position, especially since some of its most outstanding religious had refused the proposed appointment" (923). Dufal was proposed July 16, 1859, when the see had been vacant for nearly four years. He accepted and was consecrated.

11. Records differ about this; some say Dec. 15.

12. It is not clear how this was reconciled with the fact that the Sisters were sent into other dioceses to make proper canonical vows (see chap. 5, above). Sister Emily had made some preliminary vows at Notre Dame. At this time in the congregation's history, only one profession was necessary. Bishop Bouvier, who had objected to the Marianites' vows, did not die for almost exactly another year — Dec. 26, 1854.

13. Pepin, 38–39.

14. Brosnahan, 172.

15. Ibid., 188.

16. Ibid., 189. Although the account is printed as if it were a direct quotation, it is actually a greatly shortened paraphrase of Mother Elizabeth's highly detailed personal account (Lilly II: 372–73).

17. Gleeson, 40.

18. Ibid., 41.

10. THE MARSH BETWEEN THE LAKES

1. Lilly III: 452.

2. Nowlan I: 126.

3. *N.D. Chronicles*, 129–30.

4. Ibid., 131.

5. Ibid., 134.

6. Ibid., 177.

7. Pepin, 42.

8. Nowlan I: 48.

9. *N.D. Chronicles*, 133.

10. Ibid., 137.

11. Ibid., 138.

12. Lilly III: 400. All the following material on the closing of Bertrand is taken from this part of Mother Elizabeth's account.

13. Nowlan I: 140.

14. Ibid., 133.

15. A more detailed account of this transaction can be found in *N.D. Chronicles*, 143–44.

16. Lilly III: 413.

17. Ibid., 414.

18. Ibid., 141–15.

11. COMING TO CERTAIN DEATH

1. Preface to the 1870 edition of the Sisters' Rule.

2. *MMSD*, 153.

3. *Marianite Annals*, 44.

4. Sister Five Wounds to Sorin, May 27, 1849.

5. Sister Five Wounds to Sorin, Aug. 6, 1849.

6. Sister Five Wounds to Sorin, Jan. 21, 1850.

7. Catta I: 935.

8. She was thought to have left religious life in 1856 and opened an agency for the placing of domestic servants. (Letter from Sister Georgette Sauriol, Saint-Laurent, to Sister M. Georgia [Costin], Feb. 16, 1989.) She turns up, however, with Mother Léonie's Little Sisters of the Holy Family in 1877. Mother Léonie writes to Sorin March 9, "The religious exercises are held regularly and all attend regularly except Sister Mary of the Five Wounds, whose health has not been good for some time." (Trans. SMGC) Sister Five Wounds would have been sixty-one years old at this time. The French original of this letter is in the archives of the motherhouse of the Little Sisters of the Holy Family, Sherbrooke, Quebec.

9. Between their emotions and their limited educations, the Sisters sometimes had trouble with coherence. The "it"s in the last two sentences may mean that Sister M. of the Angels was assigned by Sorin to help with the infirmary, that Gouesse added to her duties, and that anyway everyone, Mary of the Angels included, thought Sister Nativity was a better infirmarian.

10. Sister M. of the Angels to Sorin, Apr. 21, 1850. In Sister Five Wounds box.

11. Sister Five Wounds to Sorin, May 4, 1850.

12. Idem.

13. Catta I: 935.

14. Ibid., 939.

15. Ibid., 940.

16. Ibid., 943.

17. See Connelly, "Charism: Origins and History," in *Fruits of the Tree* I: 111.

18. Sister M. of the Angels to Sorin, Apr. 21, 1850.

19. Catta I: 938.

20. Ibid., 939.

21. *N.D. Chronicles*, 94.

22. Catta I: 940.

23. Sister Five Wounds to Sorin, Apr. 17, 1851.

24. Rev. Napoleon Perché, as a young priest, became involved in Father Moreau's controversy with Saint Euphrasia Pelletier; see Catta I, chaps. 7 and 8. He now re-enters the story as a member of the archbishop's staff in New Orleans. He became archbishop of New Orleans in 1870 and died in 1883.

25. Catta I: 943–44.

26. Ibid., 944, note 62.

27. Ibid., 944.

28. Ibid., 947.

29. Ibid., 948.

30. Ibid., 949.

31. Dec. 8, 1851.

12. MANY CHANGES AND TROUBLES

1. *Marianite Annals*, 46–47.

2. Ibid., 45.

3. Catta I: 954. It seems almost impossible that this letter and the one mentioned in the next paragraph could both be correctly dated.

4. Catta I: 964, note 24.

5. See chap. 7, above.

6. Catta I: 963.

7. Ibid., 964.

8. Ibid., 965.

9. Ibid., 966.

10. Lemarié, *De la Mayenne à l'Indiana*, 19.

11. He seems to have pre-dated Prime Minister Churchill in the coining of this expression.

12. Sorin to Moreau, Nov. 17, 1854.

13. For Rooney's and Guesdon's letters see box New Orleans, envelope Letters of Father Rooney and Father Guesdon. Originals in Indiana Province Archives.

14. Guesdon to Sorin, June 2, 1855.

13. AN ENTIRELY DIFFERENT STYLE

1. Moreau, *Circular Letters*, Oct. 25, 1855, I: 340.

2. Ibid., Nov. 15, 1855.

3. Sorin's letter to Moreau of Dec. 31, 1855, refers to Moreau's letters of Nov. 3 and 4, neither of which is extant. Sorin's letter is quoted by Moreau in his of May 25, 1856; *Circular Letters* I: 353.

4. Sister Immaculate Conception to Moreau, Nov. 28, 1855. All letters quoted in this chapter are in the New Orleans box; originals in Holy Cross general archives, Rome.

5. Rev. Gilbert Raymond to Archbishop Blanc, Nov. 27, 1855.

6. Idem.

7. Report of Saint Mary's council to Moreau, Dec. 29, 1855. Mother Ascension's report was submitted through the council to emphasize that it was official, not personal.

8. Ibid.

9. Report of the Brothers' council, box New Orleans, envelope Miscellaneous Documents.

10. *MMSD*, 161.

11. Sister Immaculate Conception to Moreau, Nov. 27, 1855.

12. Letter of Father Raymond to Moreau, Nov. 28, 1855.

13. Sisters' Council Report.

14. Raymond to Moreau, Nov. 28.

15. Sister Mary of the Passion to Moreau, Dec. 5.

16. Raymond to Archbishop Blanc, Feb. 2, 1856.

17. Raymond to Moreau, Nov. 28, 1855.

18. Raymond to Blanc, Feb. 2, 1856.

19. Raymond to Moreau, Nov. 28, 1855.

20. Raymond to Moreau, Dec. 13, 1855.

21. Sister Mary of the Passion to Moreau, Dec. 5, 1855.

22. Sister Immaculate Conception to Moreau, Nov. 27, 1855.

23. Sisters' Council Report.

24. Raymond to Moreau, Nov. 28, 1855.

25. Chronicles of the Sister Marianites of Holy Cross, New Orleans, 1855, 1. Trans. Sister M. Georgia (Costin), C.S.C. Hereafter NOC (New Orleans Chronicles).

26. The Rule of 1854 would have been in force in New Orleans in 1855. It provided for supper at 7, night prayer at 8:30, and added, "Ten

minutes after prayers, all the Sisters should be in bed and all the lights extinguished" (Rule XX, no. 172–74).

27. NOC, 2.

28. Sisters' Council Report.

14. THE HOUSE AT NEW YORK

1. *Marianite Annals*, 55.
2. Ibid., 165.
3. Ibid., 56.
4. Catta II: 258.
5. Ibid., 284.
6. Ibid., 288.
7. Ibid., 289.
8. *Annals*, 56.
9. Nowlan I: 84. This account is a very close paraphrase but not quite an exact copy of the account in *N.D. Chronicles*, 164–68 and 181–84.
10. Nowlan I: 85.
11. Ibid., 88.
12. Ibid., 87.
13. Ibid.
14. Ibid., 89.
15. Ibid.
16. Catta II: 286.
17. Nowlan I: 90.
18. Ibid., 91.
19. *N.D. Chronicles*, 183.
20. Nowlan I: 95.
21. *Annals*, 56.

15. WONDERFUL UNHEARD-OF EVENT

1. Moreau, *Circular Letters*, May 25, 1856, I: 347. Hereafter *CL*.
2. *CL*, Jan. 1, 1857, I: 381–82.
3. Catta II: 308.
4. *CL*, Sept. 25, 1857, II: 33–34.
5. Ibid.
6. Lilly III: 455.
7. Ibid., 456–57.
8. For those who may have forgotten, those were the days of fasting from midnight before Communion.
9. Lilly III: 459.

10. Ibid., 459–60.

11. *CL*, Sept. 25, 1857, II: 33–34.

12. *N.D. Chronicles*, 149.

13. Father Moreau had suffered several months of mental and spiritual distress during 1855.

14. Nowlan I: 144–45. This is a very close paraphrase but not an exact copy of the English translation of the *N.D. Chronicles*, 169–70.

15. Lilly III: 463–64.

16. Ibid., 464.

17. Ibid., 466.

18. Ibid., 468.

19. Ibid.

20. Ibid., 469.

21. *CL*, Sept. 25, 1857, II: 41–42.

16. THEY DO ALL THE GOVERNING

1. *MMSD*, 56.

2. *Règles et Constitutions à l'Usage des Soeurs de Notre-Dame-des-Sept-Douleurs du Mans* (Le Mans: Gallienne, Imprimeur-Libraire, 1847), 3. Mimeographed copy in box Constitutions, Collected Materials. Trans. Sister M. Georgia (Costin), C.S.C.

3. *Marianite Annals*, 70.

4. In "Bishop Luers and the Autonomy of the Sisters of the Holy Cross," *Fruits of the Tree* II: 12.

5. Bishop Luers to Bishop Martin J. Spalding, May 22, 1867.

6. *Fruits of the Tree* II: 20–21 and note 34.

7. In fact, Sister Arsene did return to France in order to enter the Trappistines after forty years of service in America. She was sixty years old and this was her form of retirement. She lived another twenty-one years and died in 1913.

8. Quoted in *Marianite Annals*, 73.

9. Ibid., 74.

10. The number of Sisters serving in schools and academies is not necessarily a measurement of the level of education in the community. In 1865 there were sixty-five Sisters assigned to Saint Mary's Academy, of whom only thirteen were teachers.

11. The Canadian records say quite specifically that she left Saint-Laurent Tuesday morning, May 29, 1860, with Sister Mary of St. Léocadie, capitulant. They also say that she spent a month at Saint Mary's of the Lake, but their reference for this is the Saint Mary's Chronicle by Sister Emerentiana. This Chronicle, in turn, says, "Mother Seven Dolors came on a visit to Notre Dame in the autumn of 1860," with the word

"autumn" crossed out and "spring" written in. If she came in the spring, she did nothing officially recorded — no council meetings or local chapters were held between Feb. 25 and July 5. The *Marianite Annals* mention her reluctance to go to Indiana and quote Father Moreau's letter of advice to her (Mar. 23, 1860) to "be very circumspect. . . . The chapter will regulate everything." They speak of her finding "the dispositions she had feared" of restlessness and occasionally "a disrespectful attitude toward the motherhouse." The Cattas' life of Mother Seven Dolors follows this scenario but adds a visit in November and December, citing Father Charles Moreau's "Report of the Regular Visitation, 1862–63." There is some support for this in the Saint Mary's council minutes. On Nov. 25 the council examined some novices according to a procedure "as directed by V. Rev. Mother General," and on Dec. 13 "Mother General, not finding Sister F. de Paul efficient to belong to the council not being able to read or write replaces her by Sister M. of the Circumcision." Neither of these entries proves that the mother general was present in person (and if so she did not sign the minutes), but they comprise more of a mention than she has in the spring.

12. *MMSD*, 201.

17. AUTONOMY WITHOUT SEPARATION

1. *Marianite Annals*, 70.
2. Ibid., 87.
3. *CL* II: 239.
4. Sorin, "Account of Visit of Father Charles Moreau," ms. p. 1, box Separation from France, 1862–1889: Some Correspondence (hereafter box Separation), envelope Separation Materials, 1862.
5. Ibid., 2.
6. Ibid.
7. Ibid.
8. Ibid., 3.
9. CM Aug. 3, 1862.
10. CM Sept. 12, 1862.
11. *Marianite Annals*, 93.
12. Basil Moreau to Sorin, Sept. 1, 1862. Catta II: 490.
13. Quoted in *MMSD*, 231. This is Father Charles' Report, p. 79, quoting Father Basil. No date is given for the report, but the Cattas say in ch. 15, note 11, that the Report was "drawn up from day to day." A letter arriving late, however, would have had to be added to the Report before it was submitted, probably after Charles had returned to France. We do not know just when this was, except that it was sometime after March, 1863.

18. GOOD AND BAD AND VERY BAD

1. Sept. 16, 1859, box: Separation; envelope: Mother M. Liguori (Chrétien) Letters. All of Mother Liguori's letters referred to in this chapter are from this collection.

2. Ibid.

3. Younger blood sister of Sister Ascension.

4. Mother Liguori to Sorin, Aug. 23, 1861.

5. Idem.

6. Idem, Sept. 16, 1861.

7. Idem, Sept. 17.

8. Idem, Oct. 15.

9. Idem, Oct. 19.

10. Idem, May 20, 1862.

11. Idem. Letter is dated Aug. 30, 1862, which would be after her meeting with Bishop Luers. Perhaps it is a mistake for July 30.

12. Mother Elizabeth probably to Mother Seven Dolors, Feb. 16, 1863, box Separation; envelope Letters of Mother M. Elizabeth (Lilly). All of Mother Elizabeth's letters referred to in this chapter are in this collection.

13. Idem, Oct. 13, 1862.

14. Idem, Nov. 1, 1862.

15. Idem, Dec. 14, 1862.

16. Box Separation; envelope Letters from Various Sisters.

17. This has been one of the best hidden documents in the history of the community. It does not appear in any of the collections of Father Basil Moreau's letters, and the Cattas apparently never saw it, for they do not mention it in their biographies, either of Father Moreau or of Mother Seven Dolors. But Sister Emerentiana copied the English version in her Chronicles (I, 143–45) and the original was found among the oversized letters of Father Moreau in the General Archives in Rome by the Reverend Jacques Grisé, C.S.C., general archivist. Unflattering as it is, the history of the Sisters of the Holy Cross would certainly be incomplete without it.

18. Nowlan I: 143.

19. Box Separation, envelope Letters from Various Sisters.

20. Box Separation, envelope Letters from the Sisters in Morris.

21. Idem. "[H]owever it shall be fixed I shall not stir out of the States, except that Obedience shall make it absolutely necessary." Sister Francis Assisium to Mother Liguori. Undated but internal evidence places it some months after Mother Liguori's departure, probably autumn of 1862 or winter of 1862–63.

22. Idem, undated.

23. Idem, Sister Francis Assisium to Father Charles Moreau. Undated; "Letter eighteen seventy-two" is written in French in the upper left corner of the original in a different hand and with different ink. If it is intended as a date it is ten years too late, as she speaks in the same letter of having seen the Bishop of Chicago "yesterday."

24. The present author is also a certified graphoanalyst, but it takes no expertise to see what there has been no attempt to hide.

19. OVERFLOWING WITH PATIENTS

1. Several years after the Civil War, Mother Augusta called for the reflections of all the Sisters who had taken part in it. The short quotations used in this chapter and the next are taken from these replies. Box, Civil War: Sisters' Services.

2. Samuel P. Lee was a cousin of Robert E. Lee, and the only Lee of Virginia to fight on the Union side. When asked why he did not fight for the South like all the other Lees, he replied, "When I find the word Virginia in my commission, I will join the Confederacy." Burton J. Hendrick, *The Lees of Virginia: Biography of a Family* (Boston: Little, Brown and Company, 1935), 430.

3. Quoted in Ellen Ryan Jolly, *Nuns of the Battlefield* (Providence, R.I.: Providence Visitor Press, 1927), 134.

4. Actually Sister Veronica's family name was Scholl and Sister Adele was Moran.

5. "History of the U.S. Navy Hospital Ship *Red Rover*," Navy Department: Office of the Chief of Naval Operations, Division of Naval History (OP O9B9), Ships' History Section, p. 7.

6. Ibid., 8.

7. Ibid., 9.

8. Ibid., 10.

9. Ibid., 11.

10. Ibid., 13.

20. A TASTE OF OUR HOSPITAL TEA

1. "History of the U.S. Navy Hospital Ship *Red Rover*," Navy Department: Office of the Chief of Naval Operations, Division of Naval History (OP 09B9), Ships' History Section, p. 3.

2. Nowlan I: 240. The account is credited here to Mother Angela; it is also found in typed form under Sister Paula's name.

3. Not further identified in any source.

4. George W. Anderson, S.J., "Bernardine Wiget, S.J., and the St. Aloysius Civil War Hospital in Washington, D.C.," *The Catholic Historical Review*, October 1990: 755.

5. "Antietam," *Encyclopedia of American History,* 1965 ed.

6. Box Civil War, envelope Father Charles Moreau's regulations for the Sisters in St. Aloysius Military Hospital, Washington, D.C., 1862.

7. Brosnahan, 260.

8. Second cousin. Mother Angela's father, John Gillespie, was first cousin to Ellen's mother, Maria Boyle Ewing. This made Minnie Sherman a second cousin once removed to Mother Angela.

9. Minnie's younger brother, who later became a Jesuit priest over the general's disapproval.

10. Noted Catholic artist, writer, and lecturer, friend of Mother Angela and occasional resident at Saint Mary's. In 1865 she became the first woman to receive Notre Dame's Laetare Medal. Her work "The Three Archangels and the Guardian Angels in Art" brought her a medallion from Pope Leo XIII.

21. CHANGE IS UNANIMOUSLY REQUESTED

1. *Marianite Annals,* 94.
2. Ibid., 95.
3. Catta II: 546.
4. Ibid., 98.
5. Ibid., 96.
6. Nowlan I: 289.
7. Bishop Bourget to Mother Seven Dolors, Feb. 22, 1865, box General Chapters 1861–1887 (Including French Minutes of Chapter of 1865).
8. Moreau to Mother Alphonsus Rodriguez, Feb. 24, 1865, box Separation; envelope Separation Materials, mostly in French, 1865.
9. Minutes of the Chapter of 1865, 14.
10. Ibid., 16.
11. Ibid., 18.
12. In 1880, when the Canadians were petitioning for autonomy, they asked to have the two-class system restored. Box Sisters of Holy Cross, Canada; envelope Separation of Canadian Sisters from French Motherhouse. Letter from Capitulants of the Provincial Chapter of the Sisters Marianites of Canada dated August 1880, to Bishop Charles Edward Fabre of Montreal, detailing their difficulties with the motherhouse. This petition is no. eight of twelve.
13. *MMSD,* 278.
14. Ibid., 278–79.

22. THE SECRET VOTE BEING TAKEN

1. Catta II: 536.
2. *Marianite Annals,* 105.

3. Ibid.

4. Ibid., 113.

5. Bishop Luers to Cardinal Barnabo, June 8, 1867. Box Separation, envelope Separation Materials, 1867.

6. Undated letter of Mother Mary of Egypt to Cardinal Barnabo. Context shows it was written after the chapter. Box Separation, envelope Separation Materials, 1867. Catta says Mother Mary of Egypt was "one of the oldest Sisters in the Congregation" (*MMSD*, 343). The *Marianite Annals* say she was born in 1827 (p. 251), which would make her forty the year of the chapter. She died in 1907.

7. Nowlan I: 310.

8. Chapter Book 1865–1871, 55.

9. Nowlan I: 313.

10. *Marianite Annals*, 116–18.

23. A PROVINCE YET NOT A PROVINCE

1. CM, Aug. 16, 1869.

2. CM, Aug. 9, 1869.

3. CM, Dec. 7, 1869.

4. Purcell to Sorin, Mar. 3, 1872. Archives of professed convent at Notre Dame.

5. Brosnahan, 303.

6. CM, Sept. 3, 1874.

7. CM, Sept. 26, 1870. "Decided . . . that Sister Léonie be received at St. Mary's but *not* in that event giving others to understand the same would be extended to them."

8. Eugene Nadeau, O.M.I. *Your Ways Make Known to Me: The Unforeseen Paths of Mother Léonie, Foundress of the Little Sisters of the Holy Family (1840–1912)*, trans. Emmett O'Grady and Alfred M. Burmon (Sherbrooke, Quebec: Editions Mont-Sainte-Famille, 1975).

9. Brosnahan, 302.

10. Brosnahan, 304.

11. Arthur J. Hope, C.S.C., *Notre Dame: One Hundred Years* (Notre Dame, Ind.: University of Notre Dame Press, 1943), 184.

12. Anna McAllister, *Flame in the Wilderness*, 313.

13. Ibid.

14. By actual count, we know of eleven, including all of Mother Liguori's group of 1862, who went to Canada. Of these eleven, at least four returned. We know of five Canadians who came to Indiana, one of whom was Mother Léonie. None from Indiana are known to have gone to France at this time. Sister Assumption (Riopelle) and Sister Nativity (Daily) were transferred to France as a matter of obedience long before the separation. Sister Assumption was dead before the separation occurred, and

Sister Nativity lived on in France to become first assistant to the superior general.

15. Sorin to Sister Ambrose (Corby), May 22, 1872, box Rev. Edward Sorin, C.S.C., Letters to Sisters, envelope Letters of Father Sorin to Sister M. Ambrose, Superior — Principally at St. Cecilia's Academy, Washington, D.C., 1868–1890.

24. PRICELESS SPIRIT

1. Constitutions of 1870, no. 4.
2. Ibid., no. 22.
3. *World Almanac and Book of Facts* (New York: 1988), 825.
4. *Superior Generals* is volume II of the *Centenary Chronicles of the Sisters of the Holy Cross* (Paterson, N.J.: Saint Anthony Guild Press, 1941). The contributors to this volume were some of the finest writers the congregation ever enjoyed but seem to have been allowed neither sufficient time nor proper access to documents to produce historically accurate work. As a result, many legendary, questionable, and simply incorrect accounts have been accepted as community history. This is possibly the most serious example.
5. *Superior Generals*, 84–85.
6. Ibid., 86.
7. Box Mother Augusta, folder Reminiscences of Sister Cyril.
8. *Superior Generals*, 83.
9. Ibid., 84.
10. Ibid., 85.
11. Local archives, professed convent, Notre Dame, 98.
12. McAllister, *Flame in the Wilderness*, 335.
13. Father Shortis served at St. Peter's parish in LaPorte in 1852, thirty-five years before the time in question. In the 1880s he was chaplain at Saint Mary's.
14. *Superior Generals*, 87.
15. Augusta to Dwenger, July 6, 1884, box: Mother Mary Augusta, envelope Correspondence with Most Reverend Joseph Dwenger, Bishop of Fort Wayne. All the correspondence on this matter is in this location.
16. Dwenger to Augusta, July 26, 1884.
17. *Superior Generals*, 87–88.
18. Ibid., 88.
19. The Most Rev. Richard Gilmour.
20. Sorin to Bishop Dufal, Mar. 6, 1887, box Mother M. Angela: Memorial Tributes, Photographs, *Flame in the Wilderness;* envelope, Memorial Tributes.
21. Idem.

22. Dwenger to Sorin, Aug. 1, 1888.
23. Minutes of Chapter of 1888, 7th Session, Aug. 14.
24. Nowlan II: 449.
25. Local archives, professed convent, Notre Dame, 107.
26. Hope, 254.
27. Ibid., 255.

WORKS CONSULTED

PUBLISHED WORKS

Annals of the Congregation of the Marianite Sisters of Holy Cross 1841–1941. Le Mans: 1947.

Brosnahan, Sister M. Eleanore, C.S.C. *On the King's Highway.* New York: D. Appleton and Company, 1931.

Brown, Sister Mary Borromeo, S.P. *History of the Sisters of Providence of Saint Mary-of-the-Woods.* New York: Benziger Brothers, 1949.

Catta, Canon Etienne, and Tony Catta. *Basil Anthony Mary Moreau.* Trans. Edward L. Heston, C.S.C. 2 vols. Milwaukee: Bruce Publishing Company, 1955.

Catta, Canon Etienne, and Tony Catta. *Mother Mary of the Seven Dolors and the Origins of the Marianites of Holy Cross (1818–1900).* Trans. Edward L. Heston, C.S.C. Milwaukee: Catholic Life Publications, Bruce Press, 1959.

Centenary Chronicles of the Sisters of the Holy Cross: vol. II, *Superior Generals.* Paterson, N.J.: St. Anthony Guild Press, 1941.

Connelly, Rev. James T., C.S.C. "Charism: Origins and History." In *Fruits of the Tree, Sesquicentennial Chronicles, Sisters of the Holy Cross*, ed. Sister M. Georgia (Costin), C.S.C., vol. I. Notre Dame: Sisters of the Holy Cross, 1991.

Connelly, Rev. James T., C.S.C., "Bishop Luers and the Sisters of the Holy Cross." In *Fruits of the Tree*, as above, vol. II.

Français, Rev. Gilbert, C.S.C. *Circular Letters.* Notre Dame: 1913.

Heffernan, Sister M. Rita, C.S.C. *A Story of Fifty Years.* Notre Dame: Ave Maria Press, 1891.

Hendrick, Burton J. *The Lees of Virginia: Biography of a Family.* Boston: Little, Brown and Company, 1935.

Hope, Rev. Arthur J., C.S.C. *Notre Dame: One Hundred Years.* Notre Dame: University Press, 1943.

Lemarié, Charles, C.S.C. *De la Mayenne à l'Indiana: Le Père Edouard Sorin (1814–1893).* Angers: Université Catholique de l'Ouest, 1978.

McAllister, Anna Shannon. *Flame in the Wilderness.* Paterson, N.J.: St. Anthony Guild Press, 1944.

McDougal, Sister M. Francesca, C.S.C. *Our Motherhouse:* vol. IV, *Centenary Chronicles of the Sisters of the Holy Cross.* Paterson, N.J.: St. Anthony Guild Press, 1941.

Moreau, Rev. Basil Anthony, C.S.C. *Circular Letters.* Trans. Edward L. Heston, C.S.C. (No publication data.)

Moreau, Rev. Charles, C.S.C. *Le Très Révérend Père Basile-Antoine Moreau, Prêtre du Mans, et Ses Oeuvres.* Paris: Firmin-Didot et Cie., 1900.

Nadeau, Rev. Eugene, O.M.I. *Your Ways Make Known to Me: The Unforeseen Paths of Mother Léonie, Foundress of the Little Sisters of the Holy Family (1840–1912).* Trans. Emmet O'Grady and Alfred M. Burmon. Sherbrooke, Quebec: Editions Mont-Sainte-Famille, 1975.

Règles et Constitutions à l'Usage des Soeurs de Notre-Dame-des-Sept-Douleurs du Mans. Le Mans: Gallienne, Imprimeur-Libraire, 1847.

Ryan, Ellen Jolly. *Nuns of the Battlefield.* Providence, R.I.: Providence Visitor Press, 1927.

Sorin, Rev. Edward F., C.S.C. *The Chronicles of Notre Dame du Lac.* Trans. John M. Toohey, C.S.C., ed. James T. Connelly, C.S.C. Notre Dame: University of Notre Dame Press, 1992.

UNPUBLISHED WORKS

Unless otherwise cited, all of these materials are in the Congregational archives of the Sisters of the Holy Cross, Saint Mary's, Notre Dame, Indiana.

Big Book of Accounts 1844–1904. Sisters of the Holy Cross, Notre Dame. Contains financial and historical material from years cited.

Chronicles of the Sisters Marianites of Holy Cross, New Orleans, 1855. Trans. Sister M. Georgia (Costin), C.S.C. Original in the archives of the Sisters Marianites of Holy Cross, New Orleans.

Exemplaire Primitif et Documents Relatifs à l'Approbation des Constitutions de la Congrégation des Soeurs Marianites de Sainte-Croix, 1862–1869. Archives of the Sisters Marianites of Holy Cross, La Solitude, Le Mans.

Gleeson, Sister Mary of the Compassion, C.S.C. Unpublished recollections.

"History of the U.S. Navy Hospital Ship *Red Rover,*" Navy Department: Office of the Chief of Naval Operations, Division of Naval History (OP 09B9), Ships' History Section.

Lilly, Sister Mary of St. Elizabeth, C.S.C. Unpublished recollections. 4 vols.

Nowlan, Sister M. Emerentiana, C.S.C. Unpublished Chronicles. 2 vols.

Pepin, Sister M. Euphrosine, C.S.C. Unpublished recollections.

Sisters of Providence. Book of Important Events I: 1840–1880. Sisters of Providence Archives, Saint Mary-of-the-Woods, Indiana.

Sorin, Rev. Edward F., C.S.C. Account of the Visit of Father Charles Moreau, 1862. Trans. Sister M. Georgia (Costin), C.S.C.

CONGREGATIONAL RECORDS

Council Minutes

These have been kept consecutively since Sept. 11, 1843. The last handwritten entry was made Oct. 8, 1953. Except for a few of the very early ones, they are signed by the presiding officer. The minutes of each administration are kept in the administrative offices during the immediately following administration and are then sent to the archives.

Chapter Books

The chapter is the legislative and electing body of the congregation. Until 1889 a chapter was held every year. From 1890 to 1979 a general chapter was held every six years. From 1933 to 1969 provincial chapters were held every three years between the general chapters; from 1969 to 1989 these were regional chapters. Since 1979 the general chapter has been held every five years.

Sisters' Apostolic Service Records

These are records for each Sister containing basic personal information and a record of the dates and places of all her assignments.

Local Archives

These are written in each house and sent annually to the congregational archives. They contain the story of the year, based on the school or fiscal year. Because of the multiple authorship, they vary considerably in detail and value, though all (more or less) follow specific guidelines.

Other Materials

Letters and other documents pertaining to certain places, persons, or topics are arranged in archives boxes in the congregational archives. Some materials are further sorted and placed in labeled envelopes within the boxes.

INDEX